T0301803

International Economics and Confusing Politics

International
Economics and
Confusing Politics

by

David Robertson

Formerly University of Melbourne, Australia

Edward Elgar
Cheltenham, UK • Northampton, MA, USA

Published by
Edward Elgar Publishing Limited
Glensanda House
Montpellier Parade
Cheltenham
Glos GL50 1UA
UK

Edward Elgar Publishing, Inc.
136 West Street
Suite 202
Northampton
Massachusetts 01060
USA

A catalogue record for this book
is available from the British Library

Library of Congress Cataloging-in-Publication Data
Robertson, David, 1935–
    International economics and confusing politics / by David Robertson.
        p. cm.
    Includes bibliographical references and index.
        1. International trade. 2. International economic relations. 3. Globalization.
    I. Title.

    HF1379.R63 2006
    337–dc22

                                                            2005057449

ISBN–13: 978 1 84376 503 5
ISBN–10: 1 84376 503 9

Typeset by Cambrian Typesetters, Camberley, Surrey
Printed and bound in Great Britain by MPG Books Ltd, Bodmin, Cornwall

Contents

List of acronyms

ACP	Africa, Caribbean, Pacific countries
AGC	anti-globalization coalition
ANZCER	Australia–New Zealand Closer Economic Relations (trade agreement)
APEC	Asia Pacific Economic Cooperation
ASEAN	Association of South-East Asian Nations
ATC	Agreement on Textiles and Clothing (Uruguay Round)
AU	Africa Union
BIAC	Business and Industry Advisory Committee (OECD)
CAFTA	Central American Free Trade Agreement
CAP	Common Agricultural Policy (EU)
CER	Agreement on Closer Economic Relations between Australia and New Zealand
CITES	Convention on International Trade in Engendered Species (of Wild Flora and Fauna)
CSR	corporate social responsibility (NGOs)
CU	customs union
DSU	Dispute Settlement Understanding (WTO)
EBA	'Everything But Arms' (EU agreement with ACP)
ECJ	European Court of Justice
ECOWAS	Economic Community of West African States
EEC	European Economic Community (1956–89)
EFTA	European Free Trade Association
EMU	European Monetary Union
EU	European Union
FCCC	Framework Convention on Climate Change
FIELD	Foundation for International Environmental Law and Development
FTAA	Free Trade Area of the Americas
GATS	General Agreement on Trade in Services (WTO)
GATT	General Agreement on Tariffs and Trade
GMO (GM)	genetically modified organism
GSP	Generalized System of Preferences (UNCTAD 1973)
HIPC	Highly Indebted Poor Countries
IBRD	International Bank for Reconstruction and Development

ICC	International Criminal Court
ICSID	International Centre for Settlement of Investment Disputes
ICT	information and communication technology
IDA	International Development Association
ILO	International Labour Organization
IMF	International Monetary Fund
IPCC	Intergovernmental Panel on Climate Change
ITO	International Trade Organization
LAFTA	Latin American Free Trade Association
LDC	least developed country
MAI	Multilateral Agreement on Investment (OECD)
MDGs	Millennium Development Goals (UN)
MERCOSUR	free trade agreement comprising Argentina, Brazil, Paraguay and Uruguay
MFA	Multi-Fibre Arrangement
MFN	most-favoured nation
MIGA	Multilateral Investment Guarantee Agency
MNE	multinational enterprise
NAFTA	North American Free Trade Agreement, comprising Canada, Mexico and United States
NEPAD	New Partnership for Africa's Development (AU)
NGO	non-governmental organization
NIEs	Newly Industrializing Economies
OECD	Organisation for Economic Co-operation and Development
OEEC	Organisation for European Economic Co-operation
Paris Club	Group of Ten meetings to re-schedule debt payment arrears
PPMs	production and processing methods (WTO)
PSE	Producer Subsidy Equivalent (OECD measure of agricultural protection), now called Producer Support Estimate
QRs	quantitative restrictions (quotas)
RTA	regional trade agreement
SADC	Southern African Development Community
SPS	Sanitary and Phyto-sanitary Agreement (WTO)
SRES	Special Report on Emissions Scenarios (IPCC)
SSA	Sub-Saharan Africa
TCF	textiles, clothing and footwear
TRIMs	trade-related investment measures (WTO)
TPRM	Trade Policy Review Mechanism (WTO)
TRIPs	trade-related intellectual property rights (WTO)
TUAC	Trade Union Advisory Committee (OECD)
UNCED	UN Conference on Environment and Development

UNCTAD	UN Conference on Trade and Development
UNDP	UN Development Programme
UNESCO	UN Educational, Scientific and Cultural Organization
UNGA	United Nations General Assembly
UNO	United Nations Organization
UNRISD	UN Research Institute for Social Development
VERs	voluntary export restraints
WIPO	World Intellectual Property Organization
WTO	World Trade Organization
WWF	World Wildlife Fund for Nature
World Bank	Collective title for group of agencies: IBRD, IFC, IDA, ICSID, MIGA

Preface

Humanity seems to have an insistent need for an impending disaster to give focus to life. Perhaps this characteristic evolved in the eras of struggle to survive and it became innate. Wherever it came from, that characteristic is now interfering in the process of spreading unprecedented prosperity around the globe. To verify this assertion, visit any reputable bookshop. In the non-fiction shelves you will find endless rows of books about impending or historic disasters, but very few expressing optimism about the future of humankind. Even scientists have joined the pessimists and regard predictions as inevitable and impossible to divert. In large measure, this is a consequence of the 'Fourth Estate', because as everyone knows, good news does not sell newspapers (or TV news and current affairs programmes).

In the first half of the twentieth century, there was much to be concerned about: two devastating World Wars, many revolutions and recurring civil strife, economic recessions, unemployment and poverty. After 1945, the Cold War was an overhanging threat. In the 1960s, scientists threatened the world with a new Ice Age to follow a nuclear conflict. Then, in 1989–90 it became apparent that the Communist Bloc was crumbling. We had reached 'The End of History and the Last Man' (Fukuyama, 1992).

Relieved of the threat from nuclear destruction, it did not take long to drag up a new phantom that threatens the world – GLOBALIZATION! Partly in response to favourable political events, including the collapse of communism and the enthusiasm created by the implementation of the Single European Act, the world economy began a long upswing, facilitated by deepening economic interdependence and new communications and transport technologies. Such optimism and enthusiasm could not be allowed. How could people live without a disaster against which to measure their concerns?

So pessimists looked back to resuscitate old disaster scenarios: damage to flora and fauna from industrial pollution (environmental damage), poverty in developing countries (underdevelopment), repressed minorities (human rights), redistribution of manufacturing industries (labour exploitation), air pollution (ozone depletion and climate warming), etc. These 'public' concerns were issues the disaster-hungry media wanted and they gave reasons why revolution should still be on the streets.

Moreover, the collapse of communism in Eastern European countries brought a new tool – 'civil society'. Citizens gathered together to pursue common interests when the command governments vanished. In Eastern Europe these groups were instrumental in establishing democratic government. This new form of political cooperation based on social activism appealed immediately to many groups with specific interests that survived on community lobbying. Hence, non-governmental organizations (NGOs) came together to react against perceived evils and injustices that beset humankind. They have become a new force in national and international politics.

It was not long before left-wing activists recognized the opportunities these NGOs provided as skirmishers to deploy against capitalism, under its new guise as 'globalization'. With dedicated propaganda machines to ensure media coverage, this 'anti-globalization coalition' of non-governmental organizations found a new and more comprehensive cause after communism had been demystified. Left-wing activists found camouflage by attracting cooperation from peaceful NGOs concerned to save rare species or to protect the poor and the weak.

The media scavengers spread the word about 'new threats'. Humankind was once more confronted by disasters of its own making. These new causes provide standards against which to assess misery. People could measure 'the costs' of their rising living standards, their growing comfort and their security – and be made to feel guilty!

This volume demonstrates that 'globalization' is still a distant dream. The present levels of economic interdependence have evolved over the 60 years since the Bretton Woods meetings established the post-1945 economic regime. It was not a sudden development. Rather it was a return to the gradually rising living standards experienced since the Industrial Revolution began in the mid-eighteenth century, which had been interrupted in the first half of the twentieth century. Even the post-1945 recovery has not been without its problems.

International political economy has a long history. Traditionally, national governments create the laws and policies that people live by, but international treaties and agreements, and the international agencies that administer them increasingly circumscribe national powers. Moreover, NGOs have introduced a new dimension into international relations. They take advantage of international cooperation to form coalitions with sympathetic governments and UN agency officials to promote acceptable resolutions to further their goals, on environmental, development or human rights issues. NGOs have become a third force at international meetings and negotiations. With so many international treaties and agreements now in place, governments' powers are being curtailed and the concept of 'global governance' is being promoted.

The balance of world affairs is changing, too. Old alliances are fracturing and new players are increasing their influence. The North Atlantic alliance is weakening as Europe, represented by the 25-nation EU, has entered into commercial rivalry with the US and is pursuing its social and environmental policies aggressively. The centralization of Europe's political and economic decisions in Brussels has increased Europeans' sympathy for 'international law'. Divergences in economic and social policies also increase differences across the North Atlantic. The multi-polarity of the world economy is increasing as industrialization spreads in East Asia, and more changes lie ahead.

The rest of the world falls into two principal groups, both regarded as developing regions. Latin American countries' development has progressed by fits and starts, aggravated by recurrent political instability. Sub-Saharan Africa (SSA) and West Asia have widespread poverty, which became the focus for special attention from OECD countries in 2005. In both cases the principal problem is bad government, which, combined with poverty, promotes terrorism and civil unrest.

These tensions affect international relations. The final two chapters of this volume examine the links between economic developments and the UN system. It is not too late to find economic reconciliation if governments return to the principles of free and open trade, and genuine market-determined exchange rates. Free trade policies in developed countries (including agriculture and labour-intensive manufactures) would remove any need for trade preferences to be granted to developing countries. Development responsibilities would then rest with developing countries to put their own economies in order.

The global system is facing major reviews following the High-Level Panel Report on the UN, released in January 2005, and the Millennium Development Report. Both these reports have economic content and they take account of influence of NGOs.

Any increase in global governance is unlikely to improve the quality of decision-making, because UN agencies and global meetings can only resolve differences by compromises. The answers rest with national governments with genuinely elected representatives. They have authority to represent their peoples, and they can be held responsible for decisions. If NGOs want to influence decisions they should deal with national governments. Governments have to retrieve their responsibilities (and their courage) and take charge of international negotiations. If an agreement cannot be reached, then so be it. Failure to agree is better than compromise agreements that obfuscate.

In preparing this assessment of economic institutions and their problems, I owe a vote of thanks to former colleagues, friends and students who stimulated my thoughts over several decades, without upsetting my optimism about the future. The 'dismal' science has never been idle!

I owe a special vote of thanks to several friends who have given their time to comment on my scribblings. Ken Heydon found time to read my draft and to explain some contradictions in my arguments. Wolfgang Kasper patiently commented on several sections of the draft. Two old sparring partners, Andy Stoeckel and Sandy Cuthbertson, and Nic Brown also gave me valuable assessments. I am grateful to them all, although they should not be thought responsible for any unacceptable thoughts or errors that remain, which are mine alone.

Two former colleagues have greatly assisted me in the production of this volume: Barbara Hulse, who patiently and precisely converted my scribbled pages into a readable text, and Denise Moule who energetically tracked down many vague references for me.

Finally, I dedicate this volume to Geraldine for her ceaseless support, inspiration and companionship for over 40 years. Above all, I admire her patience and understanding when I took to my study to write this volume, immediately after I had retired!

The remaining faults and blemishes, and all the opinions expressed in this volume are the responsibility of the author.

REFERENCE

Fukuyama (1992), *The End of History and the Last Man*, London: Hamish Hamilton.

1. International political economy

International economic interdependence and technological advances have dominated the world economy in the past half-century, guided by market forces, multilateral investment, labour and technological migration and inter-governmental cooperation. The foundations of this cooperation were laid at the end of World War II, and they were strong enough to withstand the Cold War, regional political disturbances and serious economic shocks. The record shows how the international organizations and rules established at the end of World War II gradually induced countries to liberalize international economic transactions, to re-establish competition and to deregulate capital and foreign exchange markets.

After 60 years, the Bretton Woods 'twins' – the International Monetary Fund (IMF) and the World Bank – are under pressure to change. Various international commissions, UN agencies, non-governmental organizations (NGOs), Third World governments, and now some OECD governments have proposed changes to their responsibilities, management structures and objectives.

The third and most sensitive element at the 1944 Bretton Woods conference was international trade. It was referred to in Article I of the IMF Articles of Agreement but, studiously, trade was not discussed until the two financial institutions were in place in 1946. Negotiations on the International Trade Organization (ITO) commenced in London later that year. They immediately ran into difficulties as the agenda of subjects to be covered increased. As frustrations grew, a subset of UN members established the General Agreement on Tariffs and Trade (GATT) in 1947. GATT membership increased gradually and the comprehensive World Trade Organization (WTO) was established in 1995. That in turn now faces serious difficulties in the Doha Round negotiations.

From small beginnings, these international economic organizations now have between 140 and 180 member countries. Participation of so many governments with such disparate interests makes reaching any new agreement in these institutions a daunting task.

The economic analysis of what needs to be done to make these organizations more effective, in dealing with new tasks being thrust towards them from many directions, raises many technical questions. However, amending their responsibilities, administrative structures and procedures will also require reconciling many different political perspectives. The governing boards of the IMF and the World Bank, and the WTO Council, are subject to many political influences. Conflicts of interest arise because governments judge policies, programmes and institutions by 'hoped for' results, whereas economic analysis is concerned with finding efficient means to achieve specific goals. Rather than trying to sell declared goals to the public, economists should think about the chain of events that will be set in motion by change, and how the world economy might look after two or three rounds of adjustment to a specific policy decision. Economists support liberal markets because they work to expand income, wealth and economic opportunities. The alternative approach, based on dirigisme, paternalism and protectionism, is more readily adapted to suit the interests of oligarchies. Both these approaches are evident in reviews of the Bretton Woods system (Sowell, 2004).

Political considerations have featured prominently in recent proposals to amend the powers of international economic organizations. In the campaign to establish economics as a science, prominent nineteenth-century writers such as Jevons and Marshall rejected the title 'political economy', because it was linked with political and social questions that detracted from the 'science of economics'. Robbins (1932) defined economics as 'the science that studies human behaviour as a relationship between ends and scarce means, which have alternative uses'. This definition became a guiding light for economics students over the next two generations. 'Political economy' was reserved for applied economics topics, such as monopoly, fiscal policy and planning, where political and social interests had to be allowed for.

Bhagwati (1990) has elaborated on political economy:

> The new theory of political economy is distinguished by its explicit consideration of political action by economic agents in the simultaneous determination of economic policy and economic phenomena. In practice, economic agents within an economy seek to influence policy to their advantage. It follows that the interaction of these different interests, the government and other interest groups (including NGOs), determine policy and economic outcomes. Unfortunately, the outcomes are heavily influenced by emotions and circumstances, so the economist's view of rational analysis faces an uphill task.

Some economists see this definition of political economy as a sell out to social justice, as interpreted by political activists and others. But the reverse is also true. If such political and social activists were encouraged to provide cost–benefit analyses, the opportunity costs of many civil society targets would be shown to be prohibitive; for example, banning new water reservoirs to protect and preserve insects or lizards; or legislating new national parks to protect forests, yet allowing feral animals to run free and failing to manage the forests against fire; etc. If active lobbyists were asked to establish the financial/economic (real cost) case for their interventions, decision-making would be both more open and more scientifically determined.

Evidently, international political economy is a hybrid of applied economics and social and political considerations. It has three components:

1.   How does economic change affect political decisions, and vice versa?
2.   What political conditions facilitate the development of a strong interdependent world economy?
3.   What effect does a strong world market economy have on national policies?

These combine positive economics and normative economics to establish what the position is, and what the outcome ought to be.

Liberal economists believe that the international division of labour, based on exploitation and development of comparative advantage, establishes efficiency in advancing international markets, and that relations between states improve as economic links increase. Nationalists, on the other hand, see trade as creating tensions between governments and interest groups, and believe that trade gains depend on sound political foundations. Any attempt to dominate a market will lead to political tensions. Hence, some commentators believe genuine economic interdependence requires a hegemonic power, such as the US after 1945 (or the UK in the nineteenth century). Evidently, US leadership was crucial to the establishment of the Bretton Woods system, just as the UK adherence to the gold standard had facilitated the spread of prosperity in the nineteenth century. This line of analysis suggests that political tensions over IMF and World Bank strategies in the 1990s may be attributed to the weakened position of the US dollar (Gilpin, 1987).

Structural changes in the world economy – such as the recent rapid economic growth in China, which is drawing in raw materials and capital equipment in exchange for low cost manufactured exports – affect other economies directly and indirectly, and that provokes political reactions. Efficient international markets and flexible domestic economies should manage these economic changes easily: imports and exports adjust as prices change and exchange rates rise or fall to maintain balanced trade. Unfortunately, some governments react protectively and adjust policies to meet narrow objectives (e.g., introducing anti-dumping duties or export subsidies, or easing monetary policy to maintain or increase domestic employment levels). Such political reactions interrupt or delay the international economic adjustment processes.

Such disturbances lead to the third element of political economy: how do changes in the world economy affect national policy? What are the consequences of change for economic development and economic welfare in other societies? It is a familiar criticism from developing countries' governments, frequently expressed by development NGOs, that the Bretton Woods system discriminates against the poor. The aim of these critics is to obtain easier access to funds for poor countries to support their economic development. In practice, however, the sources of developing countries' problems are more often to be found in domestic political shortcomings and inadequacies in social rules and organizations (Kasper, 2005). Undemocratic governments are not answerable to their peoples. Inherent nationalism in developing countries predisposes them to distrust international markets. Many leaders in former colonies believe they are still exploited by the trading system, particularly over commodity prices and export opportunities. All act as impediments to development.

On the other hand, some OECD governments suggest that aspects of IMF and World Bank operations have been made redundant by the restoration of free capital markets (Meltzer Report, 2000). In which case, why should these organizations act as intermediaries between borrowers and the capital market? This is an economic argument, which is strongly opposed by 'anti-globalization' groups and development NGOs. They object to the whole concept of international capitalism while calling for debt relief and grant aid for developing countries. Under these influences, it is no surprise that governments in many unsuccessful developing countries believe the financial system is biased against them and that their interests are neglected. On the other hand, successful emerging economies in Asia have little to say on these matters. Even after the 1997 financial crisis, they accept that financial policy is largely an internal problem.

UN agencies and development NGOs, supported by churches and social justice groups, favour debt forgiveness, increased financial aid and the introduction of formal bankruptcy for sovereign debtors. Accumulated debt is presented as a natural disaster that deserves charity or indemnity. However, governments that accept or raise loans must recognize that they are mortgaging some future income to repay capital and interest. Their failures to perform, for whatever reason, cause debt-servicing problems. In many cases the moneys are misappropriated or mis-spent, and never reach the poor they are meant to help. Either way, the loans are generally beyond recovery and they have to be written off (forgiven). Perversely, new lending usually follows debts that are written off, which quickly restores the debt level and enables unreformed policies to continue, and to become more entrenched. Highly Indebted Poor Countries (HIPCs), as defined by the World Bank, had over $30 billion forgiven in the 1990s. Yet their new borrowing substantially exceeded this. New borrowing was highest in the countries receiving most debt relief – which indicates how irresponsible the lenders can be (Easterly, 2004). Nevertheless, further forgiveness resulted from the G8 meeting in July

2005, where the 'Make poverty history' campaign received overwhelming media coverage.

INSTITUTIONAL ECONOMICS

Since Adam Smith, economists have argued that the first stage in economic development requires stable institutions (rules and organizations). Individual liberty to act in self-interest, associated with secure property rights and supported by the law of contract, is necessary to allow trade to occur. So an effective and honoured justice system must support the rights of individuals. For this to be enforced requires a legislature to draft and agree laws that provide a system of justice and enforcement. This system of national administration and policy implementation establishes a liberal framework in which companies, individuals and the organs of government can work harmoniously and with understanding (Bethell, 1998; Kasper and Streit, 1998). These 'institutions' – organizations and rules – facilitate economic progress, as long as governments do not intervene to destabilize the process with frequent changes in laws or taxes.

The rules (soft institutions) are absent from many developing countries, especially in Sub-Saharan Africa (SSA). In many of these countries, the tribe, village or family own the land and other property (wells, animals, etc.), which is a form of socialism (common ownership). Such regimes act as an impediment to enterprise by individuals, because they cannot have access to assets as collateral, so cannot control the means of production. The poor are poor because they lack assets, and they cannot obtain capital. Worse, in many developing countries governments impose severe restrictions and complicated requirements (licences, etc.) on persons seeking to establish a business, which discourage initiative. This results in time-consuming bureaucratic processes that also impede enterprise (De Soto, 2000). The fundamental reason 'trade' does not benefit such economies is that they are ill-equipped to take advantage of opportunities. The problems are home-made, not international. Doubtless, many governments in SSA know this, but effective politics is to find someone else to blame.

Until developing countries find ways to mobilize capital and to facilitate commerce, aid flows and trade opportunities mean very little. Hence, social 'institutions' – organizations and rules – must be developed to facilitate domestic trade and commerce. This is an issue that will reappear in many different forms in the later chapters.

International political economy has become the focus of popular discussions about economic development, led by NGOs and 'the compassionate society'. However, reference to international political economy is, in most instances, an excuse to evade discussion of shortcomings in national governments, their policies and their domestic organizations and rules. That is where analysis and development assistance should really begin.

GLOBALIZATION AND 'PUBLIC INTEREST' GROUPS

Increasing economic interdependence has been the driving force behind rising living standards and economic security in many countries around the globe, most recently spreading to Eastern Europe, China and India. However, the uneven spread of rising living standards has been exploited to generate hostility and envy. Groups concerned with social justice see inequalities in market competition, because under-development, poverty and disease continue.

The origin of the term 'globalization' to describe this integration process is obscure. Its acceptance, however, suited the many disgruntled environmentalists, communitarians, anarchists, development charities, labour unions and other public interest groups, because it provided a common cause against which they could combine. They can conceal their ideological differences and fall in behind the banner of 'anti-globalization'. Evidently, the violence and antisocial behaviour of many of these groups at demonstrations in Seattle, Washington, Melbourne, London, Genoa and other cities as the new millennium approached, belied any claim to represent civil society.

True to character, the French have articulated the reasons to oppose 'globalization' most clearly. The French have produced a loose coalition called 'Politics against Global Markets'. In a political system that champions 'being different', this was not difficult. This group unites nationalists, anti-liberalists, greens, communists and the extreme Right in French politics. This anti-globalization movement is led by ATTAC. This loose alliance of political opportunists strikes effectively and gathers its support from people with a grudge against international financiers and multinational enterprises (MNEs), and policy-makers that support liberalization. Even the name ATTAC arises from a misunderstanding. ATTAC stands for, Association for the Taxation of Financial Transactions for the Aid of Citizens, which is based on a misinterpretation of the Tobin Tax! (The Tobin Tax, named after the late Professor Tobin, was proposed in 1978 as a small tax to discourage cross-border capital speculation and to increase national autonomy over monetary policy. It has never been implemented.) ATTAC proposes to use the tax to penalize all international transactions. ATTAC's rationale is that 'deepening economic integration and interdependence creates cleavages, re-distributive conflicts, polarization and local resistance to the global order' (Ancelovici, 2002). This description of anti-globalization describes some of the frustrations that drive anti-globalization movements, and indicates the difficulties faced when using rational economic arguments.

More generally, the anti-globalization coalition (AGC) is a collective term for NGOs acting together. Although many NGOs make a valid contribution to society, such as industry associations, labour unions and voluntary groups (fire and rescue, scouts, etc.), the politically active NGOs are usually single-purpose, uncompromising groups intent on disruption as the way to get attention to their pet concerns, for protecting butterflies, anarchism, social reform, human rights or treatment of sheep. It is important to differentiate between the constructive agencies that contribute to good government or poverty alleviation, and the single-issue, self-indulgent NGOs that seek to present themselves as pseudo-democratic coalitions. As such, they seek to bypass political processes and claim that governments and registered political parties do not represent them. (Nonetheless, many NGOs are subsidized by sympathetic governments [and the European Commission] where they promote a common interest, such as 'green' policies.)

Arguments supported by activist NGOs have been known to dominate debates in international meetings. NGOs pursue an argument based on hoped-for outcomes without establishing a path to be followed, or considering the consequences of their actions. Persuasive advocates can swamp the economic case for examining second and third round effects arising from a decision. They argue for stringent regulations, which have serious consequences for some people, without any cost–benefit assessment being undertaken. Decisions over Brent Spar (Greenpeace, 1998), monarch butterflies (WWF, 1998) and many others have shown that NGOs are about getting the results they want, without negotiation, welfare analysis or objective assessments. Their power is exerted through the media and persuasive propaganda, and often, a cooperative bureaucracy.

Most NGOs follow collectivist strategies and identify globalization and capitalism as the causes of the world's problems. The costs of their actions are not taken into account. For example, some NGOs have advocated trade sanctions against countries refusing to sign the Kyoto Protocol on climate warming, the Cartagena Protocol on genetically modified organisms (GMOs) and the Basel Convention on hazardous chemicals. Yet economic analysis has exposed the impotence of these restraints on trade:

- Governments know that trade sanctions tend to be porous (Hufbauer and Schott, 1983) or lead to trade-reducing retaliation. Would such costs be justified for these weak, imprecise and incomplete agreements?
- Demands are being made for developing countries to receive new trade preferences in the Doha Round (Oxfam, 2002). At the same time, discriminatory regional trade agreements are spreading, which weakens the principle of non-discrimination. In this process, many developing countries already receive discriminatory access to OECD markets, but others do not.

- EU countries are the strongest advocates of environmental conservation, emphasizing the Kyoto Protocol, global timber agreements and GM embargoes. EU 'greens' are strong advocates of the precautionary principle.

Some new agreements with restricted memberships are being established to enhance the influence of and provide a platform for NGOs, such as the UN Global Compact (2000) (reported in United Nations, 2002). Several international reports by UN agencies and independent commissions have recommended that NGOs should be invited to attend meetings, as evidence of so-called 'participatory democracy'.

The propaganda and organized demonstrations of NGOs provide cover for political malcontents, anarchists and anti-capitalists. They are united by disenchantment with Western democracies based on economic liberalism and market forces. The failure of socialist systems and their appalling record on human rights and environmental damage do not seem to weaken the zeal for regulations and common ownership, even among environmentalists. These coalitions are possible because NGOs focus on specific causes, not cohesive doctrines.

Many OECD governments yield to demands from domestic lobby groups, or perhaps they share the same views. This encourages lobby groups elsewhere with expectations of similar success. Farmers in most OECD economies receive massive production and export subsidies, as well as import protection (New Zealand and Australia are notable exceptions). Some other industries are similarly indulged: steel industries receive anti-dumping protection, textiles, clothing and footwear (TCF) industries continue to enjoy high levels of assistance even when the Uruguay Round agreement on textiles and clothing became fully effective at the beginning of 2005. Tariffs on manufactured imports in OECD countries now average around 3 per cent. However, many governments readily grant trade remedies (contingency protection) when local import-competing firms complain about unfair foreign competition.

With these kinds of special treatment for OECD industries, it is not surprising that developing countries – supported by development NGOs – demand preferences for their exports to OECD economies ('Political economy applies on both sides of the trade argument' [Irwin, 2004].) Attacking OECD trade discrimination in agriculture and textiles, clothing and footwear (TCF) becomes a rallying point for developing countries in WTO negotiations. By presenting trade liberalization as opportunistic, the NGOs can also join forces with nationalists and protectionists against globalization.

Governments in poor and small developing countries do not see the shortcomings in their policies either, especially when it is easy to accuse OECD governments of discriminating against their exporters. NGOs exploit both sides of this argument. OECD governments are not living by their own liberal economic model by blocking low cost imports. Developing countries claim they are unable to export and they may not be able to re-allocate resources to new export industries without development grants and debt forgiveness. However, for such assistance to work requires the governments of the poorest countries to pursue social change and to improve public infrastructure, such as establishing laws on property rights and other key institutions. There are few signs that developing countries' governments are contemplating such changes. Even so, that is not a justification for OECD governments' protectionism.

MILLENNIUM DEVELOPMENT EFFORT

The confrontation that represents today's debate about development policy for backward economies has degenerated into a 'blame game'. Yet the issues are confused, with sympathy for the poorest (living on less than $2 per day, as defined by the World Bank) regarded as a simple question of donations in cash or kind. Income distribution in these countries is more unequal than in developed countries. The history of SSA countries' records many instances of leaders appropriating aid funds, either into their own overseas bank accounts or to purchase armaments. Even food aid has been confiscated, and sold or delivered to armies fighting a civil war, rather than given to the starving. And, only a fraction of medical equipment and drugs reaches the patients it is intended to help (for example, Uganda, 2005). Most SSA countries lack any kind of secure political system, while those in power are ruthless. Mallaby (2004) reports on the waste and mismanagement in Côte d'Ivoire. Bad governments and civil strife disrupt other countries in West Africa too (*The Economist* 23 July 2005).

Concern about poverty alleviation and income inequality is long-standing. Efforts over the past 50 years have brought little relief. Countries that decided their own free trade strategies and pursued strong domestic policies have achieved rapid economic development (Bhalla, 2002). Objective assessments of how effective development can be achieved in the least developed countries conclude that domestic reform of institutions and policies must be the first step. It is social reform that is required to allow ordinary people to take advantage of changes. Policy changes and availability of finance will enable new activities in the private sector. For over 40 years, African and Middle Eastern governments have pursued socialist strategies, with the worst results in terms of poverty and disease. Vast sums in aid have been wasted or misappropriated, and where changes have occurred, they suggest that constructive strategies are recent. Putting in place institutions (organizations and rules) for moving towards democracy will support freedom for the individual (Bauer, 1984).

The UN's Millennium Development Programme (2000) received much media attention in the lead up to the UN General Assembly in September 2005. It fits closely with the fashion for 'conspicuous compassion' (West, 2004). Put starkly, this UN programme proposes massive transfers of funds to SSA economies and other poor developing countries over the next decade, with almost no conditions or undertakings by the recipients – a cry reiterated by the African Union meeting in Libya as a preliminary to the G8 Leaders meeting in July 2005. The commitments seem to be directed mostly to increasing government services (including health and education), with little attention given to developing or strengthening private industries. Moreover, neither the UN nor donor governments seem to want to impose timetables or deadlines for achieving specified reforms. With large sums of tax-payers' funds at risk this appears foolish to a fault. The donor governments agreed in principle to the Millennium Development Goals in 2000, but they still have to make their aid commitments (Chapter 7).

Simultaneously, developing countries are running a strong programme for reforms to WTO agreements, especially for amendments to agreements reached in the Uruguay Round and for new preferences on access to OECD markets, while seeking to preserve existing access rights. The demands made by G90 and G20 groups of developing countries could offer mixed benefits. For example, if especially the US and the EU removed all subsidies on agricultural production, the effects on developing countries would be mixed. Removing subsidies would raise world market prices to the benefit of unsubsidized exporters, but net food importers among developing countries would have to pay more for food, only ameliorated where local producers could increase output in response to higher market prices. In the long run, however, reduced regulation means a more efficient market, with the prospect of more output and lower prices.

The logic of developing countries' trade positions is confused. If they are still committed to 1960s' import substitution strategies, they will increase imports of food, materials and capital equipment. But what will they do to raise their exports to pay for them? The key remains domestic structural adjustment, otherwise they will remain dependent on aid grants to pay for imports indefinitely. One alternative that is seldom mentioned would be to negotiate trade agreements with other developing countries. Where regional trade agreements have been negotiated among developing countries they have shown only limited benefits, and several have failed.

SUSTAINABLE DEVELOPMENT

This expression was first used in the Brundtland Report *Our Common Future*, produced by the UN World Commission on Environment and Development in 1983, This commission was chaired by Mrs Gro Harlem Brundtland, a former Prime Minister of Norway. It interpreted 'sustainable development' as 'economic growth that meets the needs of the present without compromising the ability of future generations to meet their own needs'. However, several qualifying statements supported this broad definition. It referred to

> limitations imposed by the present state of technology and social organization on environmental resources . . . technology and social organization can be both managed and improved . . . meeting the basic needs of all . . . sustainable development can only be pursued if population size and growth are in harmony with the changing productive potential of the ecosystem . . . [and] sustainable development must rest on political will. (Brundtland Report, 1987: pp. 8–9)

Sustainable development has become an excuse for all manner of restrictive behaviours since it was first conceived. Fortunately, some sensible economists were able to argue that voluntary cooperation via the market was more likely to achieve amelioration of damage to the environment and facilitate economic development in developing countries than heavy-handed government interventions (Pearce and Warford, 1993). Developing countries, including some of the largest, were highly critical of 'inter-generational equity' when the problems of their poverty were immediate. Their priorities are clean water, sewers for over-crowded cities and improved health and education services, not carbon emissions, climate warming and disposal of wastes.

The Brundtland Report generated bureaucratic activism: subsidies to NGOs, environmental movements and green NGOs swamped the media. Backed by scientists, they enjoyed the shift towards more government management and interventionism, while NGOs bypassed national governments to promote global agreements. The Earth Summit in Rio de Janeiro in 1992 gave some shape to the environmentalists' cause with the drawing up of Agenda 21 and the establishment of the UN Commission on Sustainable Development, to monitor environment developments. However, with 153 countries participating (and thousands of NGOs caucusing on the other side of the city), the different interests in environmental protection were exposed. Perhaps the main lesson from this extensive exercise was to highlight the wide differences among governments, and their distance from environmental groups.

The questions raised by the term 'sustainable development' are not considered by advocates who use this as a justification for curtailing present-day activities, in favour of future generations. The widely accepted definition in the Brundtland Report is a politician's statement. It does not consider a role for markets in determining sustainable growth, or a trade-off between economic growth and future needs. Beckerman (1996) has pointed out that 'need' is a subjective concept, which differs at different times, at different incomes and with different cultural backgrounds. Hence, it cannot be known in advance. Sustainable growth seems to be a joint product comprising growth over time and a stock of resources to meet future needs. This compares a flow of income (welfare) over time with a stock of resources to meet future needs. A fundamental economic paradox! But it also encourages the assumption that technology and resources are fixed (with due reference to Meadows et al., 1972), and that sustainable development is necessary for inter-generational equity. Because since 1820, each generation has enjoyed ever-higher living standards than those preceding it (with only short-term, occasional reversals), special concern for inter-generational equity requires justification (Beckerman, 2003).

Discourse about sustainable development tends to understate the role of technology, which plays a crucial role in economic development. It ignores also the role of changes in the 'soft technology' of institutional growth (property rights, etc.). New technologies, entering markets through production and consumption, rebutted the charge made by the Club of Rome (Meadows et al., 1972) that mineral stocks would run out in the 1980s. Why should technologies not resolve the problem of future needs just as effectively? Markets, via the price mechanism, generate many changes in supplies and demand, and in products and technologies, as long as institutions favour markets. These forces of change do not get such prompt responses when production is regulated by governments. Technologists must be separated from the conservationists, who seem to think economics conflicts with social justice. Do they really prefer social order to freedom?

Environmental activism has become more focussed since the Earth Summit (1992). Small groups agitate locally about insect and animal rights when land re-development is mooted, claiming to act to protect biodiversity. Many governments have taken up the protection of forests, fisheries and national heritage with alacrity, because it is good electioneering, especially in inner city electorates. It may be justified, but it should be assessed using thorough cost–benefit analysis. The crucial items in the international arena are climate change, genetic modification of crops, bacterial research and waste disposal. In all these, there are economic consequences that complicate the politics of the Kyoto Protocol, the Cartagena Protocol and the Basel Convention. Although the focus has been on governments that refuse to sign these agreements, many technical questions remain unanswered.

Environmental NGOs are becoming active in more focussed ways. They begin to understand that it is possible to have economic growth without wrecking the global environment. Some recognize that market solutions are possible if property rights are properly assigned and traded. Business and industry have given more attention to community concerns, with firms now subscribing to corporate social responsibilities. There are still issues and tensions, but hostilities caused by sustainable development propaganda are receding as both sides acknowledge that time and technology are important.

GLOBAL ORGANIZATIONS

Recent exchanges over the strategies, effectiveness and administration of the Bretton Woods organizations, the WTO and especially the UN and its agencies demonstrate that change is on the agenda. Even so, the direction of change is controversial. Some OECD governments would like to reduce the declining roles of the IMF and the World Bank further, and US Administration among others, would even amalgamate them. Some developing countries want to ease borrowing conditions and to increase their representation on governing boards. Least developed countries simply want debt forgiveness and more money as unconditional grant aid. Such revisions pose many difficulties, because the bureaucrats in these agencies have already indicated their interests.

The United Nations itself is under review. The UN Secretary General presented a comprehensive draft of reforms to the UN Summit meeting in September 2005. Fundamental reform of the 191-member UN will take time, and the proposals suggest that the UN Secretariat is making a bid for more power, despite its recent troubled history.

A new development in international organizations is the shedding of specialized tasks to groups of countries. For example, various kinds of financial surveillance have always been delegated to the Bank for International Settlements (BIS) (e.g., Basel II on capital regulations) and the Institute of International Finance (IIF), where commercial banks formulate strategies for dealing with serious debtors and implement rules akin to professional self-regulation. These agencies present their reports and recommendations to the World Bank, the IMF, the Paris Club, the IIF, debtor nations, etc.

On the other hand, arguments in favour of centralized (top-down) global governance is gaining support, especially from NGOs who regard such centralization of power as an opportunity for them to influence decisions, especially on environment and welfare issues. So far, however, there is little sign that the influence of national governments is in decline, except perhaps in Europe. Among developing countries, nationalism remains rampant, as shown in their responses to the UN Millennium Development Report (2005). Equally, OECD and emerging economies reveal nationalism in their pursuit of regional trade agreements and continuing protection of agriculture and labour-intensive industries of interest to developing countries. Even the members of the harmonized EU market are seeking to safeguard their national interests against new initiatives on market integration (e.g., trade in services).

In spite of fears about globalization, international integration has far to go. International rivalries continue.

THE TASK IN HAND

This introductory chapter has identified some of the critical issues confronting the international economy. The problems are determined by complex relationships between social, political, scientific and economic forces and above all, contradictions between economic analyses and power politics. At the centre of the relationships stand the existing international organizations, which some regard as out of date. Others support them, believing that to negotiate amended agreements and governing boards would jeopardize the whole structure of international cooperation. They believe the extant organizations are tried and tested, and it is within this known structure that changes should be made. Opening new negotiations within the UN, where support for 'participatory democracy' is growing, would be fraught with incompatibilities. The UN system is under conflicting pressures, with NGOs and international bureaucrats promoting an increasing role for 'global governance', while the growing importance of developing countries (China, India, Brazil) adds support for exercising national sovereignty.

In the IMF and the World Bank agencies, it is inconceivable that the lending economies would accept that the borrowers should have an equal or blocking vote. In the WTO, decisions are made by consensus in the WTO Council. Here the developing country governments already have a majority and can block decisions they do not like. One worrying aspect of the growing support for NGO participation is that (like most charities) they are not subject to reporting or accounting requirements, even at the national level.

One thing is clear: the international organizations (economic and other) are facing new problems and some changes are likely. The report of the UN High-Level Panel on Threats, Challenges and Changes, has proposed changes to the UN system. The Treaty of Rome (2002) has established the International Criminal Court. The Kyoto Protocol, Cartagena Protocol and other agreements (including the IMF and the World Bank) are on probation. Some countries have legitimate objections and refuse to sign some of these agreements, which lead some proactive member governments to threaten sanctions. Media propaganda has convinced many people that the UN creates and implements 'international law'. Already citizens threaten their own governments with international agreements when they believe governments flout so-called international law, regardless of domestic law. NGOs and parliamentary oppositions identify this international law lever as a threat, while the media repeats such arguments to confuse the public. The value of national sovereignty and independence is undermined. With national governments reluctant to clarify their different views and to confront the NGOs, uncertainty plays into the hands of anarchists and communitarians seeking to undermine economic interdependence. New steps towards political and judicial integration in the EU have exacerbated this disruption, enabling NGOs, with help from the European Commission, to promote the idea of global governance.

In what follows, the series of threats that face international integration will be treated in turn. Chapter 2 examines the state of the Bretton Woods twins and reviews some of the plans to amend these agencies. The next three chapters examine the basis for trade relations, the role of trade in economic development and the difficulties facing the Doha Round negotiations. With lack of progress in these WTO negotiations, many OECD countries and emerging economies' governments have negotiated regional trade agreements (RTAs) or are in the process of negotiating them with neighbouring countries. Chapter 6 reviews this new regionalism.

Chapter 7 reviews proposals to promote economic development in the world's poorest countries. This was triggered by the UN Millennium Development Council (2000) and was given new momentum by the UN Millennium Development Report (2005) and campaigns to increase aid from G8 countries. Despite some temporary enthusiasm, it is not clear what will happen.

Chapter 8 examines some of the environmental disasters predicted for the world. The concept of 'sustainable development' is bandied about readily and this will be examined. After so much pessimism about economic and political prospects, Chapter 9 asks whether the global system is under serious threat. Evidently, it is facing threats from many directions. The final chapter returns to the central theme. What do all the preceding assessments mean for the international political economy in coming years?

REFERENCES

Ancelovici, M. (2002), 'Organizing against globalization: the case of ATTAC in France', *Politics and Society*, **30**(3), 427–63.
Bauer, P.T. (1984), *Reality and Rhetoric*, London: Weidenfeld and Nicolson.
Beckerman, W. (1996), *Through Green-Coloured Glasses: Environmentalism Reconsidered*, Washington, DC: Cato Institute.
Beckerman, W. (2003), *A Poverty of Reason: Sustainable Development and Economic Growth*, Oakland, CA: The Independent Institute.
Bethell, T. (1998), *The Noblest Triumph*, New York: St Martin's Griffin.
Bhagwati, J.D. (1990), 'The theory of political economy, economic policy and foreign

investment', in M. Scott and D. Lal (eds), *Public Policy and Economic Development*, Oxford: Clarendon Press.

Bhalla, S.S. (2002), *Imagine There's No Country: Poverty, Inequality, and Growth in the Era of Globalization*, Washington, DC: Institute for International Economics.

Brundtland Report (1987), *Our Common Future*, Oxford: Oxford University Press.

De Soto, H. (2000), *The Mystery of Capital*, New York: Basic Books.

Easterly, W. (2004), *The Elusive Quest for Growth*, Cambridge, MA: MIT Press.

Gilpin, R. (1987), *The Political Economy of International Relations*, Princeton, NJ: Princeton University Press.

Hufbauer, G.C. and J.H. Schott (1983), *Economic Sanctions in Support of Foreign Policy Goals*, Washington, DC: Institute of International Economics.

Irwin, D.A. (2004), *Free Trade Under Fire*, 2nd edn, Princeton, NJ: Princeton University Press.

Kasper, W. (2005), *Economic Freedom and Development*, London: International Policy Network.

Kasper, W. and M.E. Streit (1998), *Institutional Economics*, Cheltenham, UK and Lyme, USA: Edward Elgar.

Mallaby, S. (2004), *The World's Banker*, New York, Penguin Press.

Meadows, D.H. et al. (Club of Rome Project) (1972), *The Limits to Growth*, London: Earth Island.

Meltzer Report (2000), Report of the International Financial Advisory Commission.

Organisation for Economic Co-operation and Development (OECD) (2005), *Trade and Structural Adjustment; Brochure for MCM 2005*, Paris: OECD Secretariat.

Oxfam (2002), *Rigged Rules and Double Standards: Making Trade Fair*, London: Oxfam International.

Pearce, D.W. and J.J. Warford (1993), *World Without End*, Oxford: Oxford University Press.

Robbins, L.C. (1932), *An Essay on the Nature and Significance of Economic Science*, London: Macmillan.

Sowell, T. (2004), *Applied Economics: Thinking Beyond Stage One*, New York: Basic Books.

United Nations (2002), *The Global Compact (1999): Report on Progress and Activities*.

United Nations (2005), Millennium Development report.

West, P. (2004), *Conspicuous Compassion*, Sydney: Centre for Independent Studies.

2. Internationalism: in the beginning…

In an open global economy, transborder transactions (trade and investment flows, transfers of technology and migration) depend on policies at home and in other countries. To establish reliable conditions for international transactions, inter-governmental agreements (treaties) are negotiated. Traditionally, these treaties were mainly bilateral, sometimes implemented by force of arms or colonization by major powers – Britain, France, Netherlands, Belgium, etc.

Since World War II, multilateral agreements have established rules for international behaviour. Many have been negotiated within the ambit of the United Nations. The most effective economic organizations, however, were agreed separately at Bretton Woods and in Geneva. This divorced day-to-day economic issues from political complications, and preserved post-war economic recovery and integration from the disturbances that strangled progress on political confrontations in the same period.

Even before the United States entered World War II, it sought an agreement with Britain on basic rights and new organizations to facilitate future international commercial and financial transactions in the Atlantic Charter 1941 (see Appendix 2.1). The Bretton Woods Agreement 1944 that established the IMF and the World Bank put the Atlantic Charter commitments into an ordered structure. The IMF Charter included a reference to trade liberalization in Article I, but the GATT, which established rules and consultative processes to promote international trade, was not drafted until 1947. A multilateral approach, agreed between UK representatives and the US State Department was put on hold, because it raised sensitivities with Congress that might have upset the Bretton Woods negotiations. Congress was protective towards its powers in the Reciprocal Trade Agreements Act (1934). The US Administration did not want to antagonize Congress when it had so many programmes of post-war reconstruction to get approved. In 1944, this tension and Churchill's unwillingness to sacrifice imperial preference excluded trade negotiations from the Bretton Woods' agenda (Enders, 2004). Nevertheless, a commitment was made 'to facilitate the expansion and balanced growth of international trade' (IMF Articles of Agreement, Article I (ii)).

International agreements add an important dimension to international relations, and particularly to economic transactions. This is often neglected, or regarded as mutable or re-negotiable by many with international ambitions.

The history of the past 60 years, however, shows it is very difficult and time-consuming to amend an international treaty once it is signed and ratified. Some major players have used their power on administrative councils to re-shape decisions, but each time they do this they lose goodwill and create tensions (e.g., US amendment to GATT to allow an exception for agriculture). More importantly, amendments become increasingly difficult as memberships expand. The IMF and World Bank boards (and the boards of the regional development banks) have limited membership, with some directors representing and reporting to a constituency of several countries. This way the boards are restricted to a manageable 25 members or so.

The GATT (now part of the WTO) operated differently. The GATT council, comprising all members, made decisions by consensus; one rejection of a proposal was sufficient to prevent its adoption (Jackson, 1990). This made amendments to the General Agreement difficult, so they were usually left to periodic negotiating rounds.

Detailed understanding of international agreements is crucial to any attempt to adapt them to new circumstances. NGOs are given to making exaggerated claims for specific reforms without any attention to the mechanics of existing organizations or their founding charters. Usually, they demand representation in international forums or access to committees. Ostensibly, they base their claims on participatory democracy, without acknowledging the inter-governmental character of the Bretton Woods institutions. Alternatively, NGOs demand more representation for developing countries, knowing that shortages of specialist skills in small countries will enable NGOs to take a strong advisory role (in their own interest). These self-appointed lobby groups want representation on international agencies to increase their influence on policy outcomes, to raise their media profiles and to facilitate their fundraising. However, their manner towards international agencies shows little understanding of their role. Nominally, at least, international agreements are 'owned' by member governments.

Most NGOs are tolerated by national governments as long as their demands do not contradict domestic policies overtly. Street marches and demonstrations for debt forgiveness or against capitalism or GM crops are not specifically against a government, and such events are soon forgotten. Such stand-offs apply to political parties in general, which tend not to challenge minority groups on sensitive issues (e.g., the 'greens') because it might cause them electoral damage. Some national governments, and the European Commission in particular (Rabkin, 1999), contribute money to major NGOs. This could be regarded as protection money.

When it comes to modifying existing international agreements or drafting new ones, however, national governments give minute attention to details, such as membership rights, decision processes, escape clauses and safeguards.

The histories of the Bretton Woods agreements, including the GATT/WTO, show how difficult and time-consuming it has been to amend or to extend agreements. As memberships increase, amendments and organizational changes become even more difficult.

IN THE BEGINNING . . .

The foundations for post-war economic prosperity were laid in the Atlantic Charter. This short document established a framework of principles on self-determination, independence, free trade and international economic stability. Such an agenda required a fundamentally new system of international agreements. The first stage was achieved at Bretton Woods in 1944, when fighting in Europe and the Pacific was at its height. The United Nations Organization was initiated in the following year.

With only minor amendments and extensions, the International Monetary Fund (IMF) and the International Bank for Reconstruction and Development (now the World Bank) – the Bretton Woods twins – have stood for 60 years. With the present complaints about their perceived inadequacies and shortcomings, and proposals to amend their articles to cover new responsibilities, this is a suitable time to review their effectiveness.

Gardner (1980) contributed a comprehensive and insightful study of post-World War II economic agreements. He described his original 1956 thesis as 'a study in international economic diplomacy'. It was both thorough and perceptive about the difficulties of negotiations between democratic nations and the constraints imposed on negotiators by national constitutions. The US negotiators at Bretton Woods were acutely sensitive to what the US Congress would accept and the strength of US economic nationalism in 1944. When revising his book 25 years later, these constraints had become instruments for others to use against the United States. Roles had been reversed. The pressures of economic adjustment were still on deficit countries, which then included the United States. Surplus countries accepted increasing quantities of gold and currency reserves. These changing fortunes allowed Gardner to expose how capricious economic fortunes can be, and the dangers of extrapolating from periods of good fortune.

As the end of World War II approached, the Allied governments were preoccupied with establishing the economic basis for a durable peace and trying to avoid the mistakes made at the 1919 Paris Peace Conference, aggravated further by the US withdrawal from international commitments in the 1920s (MacMillan, 2001). The US negotiators, led by the Treasury, sought to avoid international problems of exchange rate instability and trade protectionism that had plagued the 1920s and 1930s. The UK team, on the other hand, focussed on preventing high levels of unemployment and advocated adjustable exchange rates and access to trade controls to support domestic production. In addition, the British representatives wanted to retain imperial preference tariffs and the sterling area, that is, a reserve currency role. These goals conflicted with the US proposals for multilateralism and non-discrimination in trade and payments, not to mention the US anti-imperialist crusade.

In July 1944, when they met at Bretton Woods, the British, led by Lord Keynes, and the Americans, led by Harry Dexter White, had already held many meetings. The other 40 or so countries that attended the Bretton Woods conference were less prepared; many were represented by governments-in-exile. Attention focussed on the International Monetary Fund (IMF) and the outstanding differences between Keynes's Clearing Union, which would provide immediate access to financial resources for currencies under pressure, and White's US 'Stabilization Fund', which would allow limited 'drawing rights' to members in deficit to ease pressures on their currencies, according to predetermined quotas and under agreed conditions. The US Fund prevailed, which provided less liquidity to support faltering currencies than the British wanted (Skidelsky, 2000).

Eventually, the drawing rights in 'the Fund' became inadequate because post-war recovery and rising inflation far exceeded the expectations of 1944. The liquidity problem remained a weakness of the IMF as long as exchange rates were managed, with only occasional adjustments allowed to the IMF 'pegged' exchange rates. Surplus countries, of which the US was the only one for many years, were not required to appreciate their currencies. (IMF Article VII on scarce currencies was insisted on by Keynes but never invoked, though its negotiation occupied much time at the Bretton Woods meeting.) Hence, forcing deficit economies to restrict domestic activity to restore external balance imposed economic adjustment on countries drawing on the Fund.

This unbalanced mechanism was insisted on by the US delegation to avoid critical reactions from the Micawberish US Congress. In the post-war years, the US was in external surplus, which created the so-called dollar gap. However, the US did provide generous financing to deficit countries using the Marshall Aid programme, as well as 'ad hoc' short-term lending. These funds were meant to support exchange rate stability, balanced budgets and sound money. The success of the Marshall Aid programme was – and still is – resented by the communist parties in some Western European countries (e.g., France and Italy), because it prevented them from seizing government in the 1940s.

The IMF took centre stage at Bretton Woods because no participants wanted to return to the deflationary, unstable conditions of the 1930s. The strong economic recovery in the post-1945 Western world came as a pleasant surprise. Reconstruction in Western Europe was rapid, assisted by generous

US financial assistance and the catch-up process of adopting advanced US production processes, which accelerated growth further. In addition, the return of full-employment backed by social welfare programmes raised confidence in new economic growth. IMF liquidity was inadequate to meet the needs of rapid economic growth and some inflation, but the new loan arrangements and pooling of financial reserves kept the IMF system in place for 25 years. That was long enough for industrial economies to adapt to new-found prosperity.

When the US moved into external deficits in the 1960s, the Bretton Woods adjustment mechanism required cooperation from the new surplus countries, via formal lending arrangements (Group of Ten, the Basel Club). This diffused responsibility for international adjustment among several reserve-rich governments. Eventually, pressures on the US dollar became such that the IMF had to adopt flexible exchange rates in 1972. That this transition was achieved smoothly demonstrated the strength of support for the IMF.

The IMF has continued to promote international monetary cooperation, to safeguard financial stability and to provide short-term financing to members with external adjustment problems. Since 1980, this has been mostly to developing countries.

The focus on exchange rates and liquidity at Bretton Woods in 1944 left little time to consider the financing and functioning of the World Bank. The two charters approved at Bretton Woods, after some further negotiations on details, were presented for signature at a meeting in Savannah, Georgia in March 1946, and began to operate in 1947.

The World Bank began quietly, raising money on the US capital market to supplement the Marshall Plan to finance reconstruction in Europe. Bank members provided capital contributions to guarantee this borrowing, while borrowers paid a small margin above the borrowing cost. Nobody was sure how economic development would be financed, and there was no strong voice speaking for development at Bretton Woods. Loans were made to governments on commercial terms, for investment in public infrastructure (dams, railways, roads etc.). This worked with the backing of World Bank board members. Without the security offered by World Bank bonds, however, it is doubtful whether even the sums provided in the 1950s would have been forthcoming for investment. Everyone remembered the heavy defaults that had occurred in the 1930s. Gradually, lending shifted away from European reconstruction and more funds were raised for development in poor countries. The Bank also diversified into other forms of lending, combining Bank funds with private sector investment in developing countries, using a new subsidiary agency, the International Finance Corporation (IFC). In 1960, a 'soft loan' affiliate (International Development Association [IDA]) was established, based on members' contributions. IDA's interest-free, long-term loans were repayable over 50 years (with a ten-year grace period), but their continuation depended on periodic replenishments by IDA members. The significance of IDA has increased since the debt crises of the 1980s and the granting of debt forgiveness to insolvent states.

In the 1950s and 1960s, the World Bank's contribution to development assistance increased, and it inspired other development assistance, too. It became a model for regional development banks in Latin America, Africa and Asia. By the late 1960s, development lending had become accepted and one-quarter of all development assistance was disbursed by multilateral agencies; the remainder was provided as bilateral loans or grants by OECD governments through their development assistance programmes. The World Bank also provided training and offered advice and technical assistance. Aid recipients and their NGO sympathizers have always regarded development funding as inadequate.

Since the 1980s, NGOs and some aid donors have progressively imposed stringent conditions on development projects before financing can be approved. These conditions provide environment protection (forest preserva-tion, no flooding of farmed land, etc.), human rights concerns (including indigenous rights) and prohibitions on development of oil and raw material resources, unless health and education standards are attached. These new screens, along with assessments of projects by co-opted NGO committees, have increased the development banks' operating costs and often delay project approvals. This reveals the paradox of NGOs. They complain about too little development finance, yet at the same time they introduce strict conditions on approvals that slow the release of funds and increase implementation costs (Mallaby, 2004). The World Bank has become a gate-keeper for aid donors and debt relief schemes.

The World Bank (like the regional development banks) is struggling to meet more and more conditions imposed by development NGOs, which put them under popular and media pressures. The Bank's major shareholders and fund providers appear to be withdrawing from confrontations with these media-conscious NGOs. The board discusses general strategies and needs, but leaves the Bank staff to cope with lending approvals. The introduction of NGO screening committees does not seem to have evoked any public response from major shareholders. Like the IMF, the World Bank has sufficient flexibility to fulfil its role, but bad publicity generated by confrontations with NGOs and their media sympathizers are weakening the institution.

TRADE LIBERALIZATION

International trade reform was held over from the Bretton Woods negotiations. Priority had been given to establishing financial stability and full-employment.

By delaying the discussion of trade rules until hostilities had finished, the negotiations were doubly cursed.

First, many more independent nations wanted to participate in negotiations once hostilities had ceased. This increased the number of issues on the agenda, as well as the numbers participating in the negotiations. Second, the US Congress had returned to its traditional nationalist stance on economic matters, which meant that many protectionists in Congress had to be satisfied before any negotiations could begin. When the ITO negotiations became bogged down in 1947, the Truman Administration, with some close allies, drafted the General Agreement on Tariffs and Trade (GATT), using its powers under the 1945 Reciprocal Trade Agreements Act, which ran out in three years. The GATT text drew on the ITO chapter on commercial policy. Congress never approved the GATT but the agreement survived for many years as a provisional entity, despite its legal obscurity. GATT received permanent authorization only when the US Congress made a financial contribution to it in 1968 (20 years after the GATT began to operate).

This 'ghost' institution was more effective than the cluttered ITO draft would have allowed. The Havana Charter contained chapters on restrictive business practices, job protection, full employment and inter-governmental commodity agreements, among other things. It could have become another heavy-handed UN bureaucracy, which would have regulated trade rather than removed controls (Irwin, 1995). Instead, the contracting parties to the General Agreement established procedures to fulfil four basic tasks:

1. to negotiate trade liberalization among contracting parties;
2. to establish rules to cover trade relations;
3. to provide arrangements to resolve trade disputes; and
4. to collate records of tariff schedules applied by contracting parties.

These procedures introduced order to the complex trade policies that survived World War II. In addition, a process of tariff dismantling was implemented that reduced most tariffs by more than half by 1968. This tariff liberalization together with the removal of many quantitative import restrictions by the OEEC (Organisation for European Economic Co-operation), promoted rapid growth in trade. The creeping increases in non-tariff barriers to trade in agriculture and textiles, clothing and footwear (TCF), were always a problem and they became more restrictive, even as other protection declined. The GATT, with some amendments, remains in effect as one agreement within the World Trade Organization (WTO) 1994.

Like the Bretton Woods twins, however, the GATT did not take account of developing countries' interests. Initially, only 23 countries were party to the GATT, though they accounted for around 80 per cent of global trade in 1948.

There were 12 developing countries among the original contracting parties to the GATT (Brazil, Burma, Ceylon [Sri Lanka], Chile, Republic of China, Cuba, India, Lebanon, Pakistan, Southern Rhodesia, South Africa and Syria). By late in the 1950s, as their numbers increased, developing countries were expressing their dissatisfaction with the GATT.

Shortly afterwards, contracting parties agreed to add Part IV to the GATT, to provide 'special and differential treatment' for developing countries, and early in the 1970s, the Generalized System of Preferences (GSP) was established for developing countries. This began the fracturing of the GATT non-discrimination principle. Many OECD governments regarded this gesture as an excuse to introduce discriminatory restrictions on sensitive labour-intensive imports from developing countries.

INTERNATIONAL NEGOTIATIONS

Gardner (1980) points out that obtaining agreement at Bretton Woods among 44 participants was just as difficult as it is to get agreement on international matters today (see also Skidelsky, 2000). For example, the 145 countries at the WTO Ministerial Council meeting in Cancun in 2003 achieved very little after several years of preliminary discussions. Where agreements were reached they included 'conditionality' in order to get acceptance. In the WTO (GATT), escape clauses are extensive, even though everyone knows that they weaken the organization.

In his 1956 study, Gardner criticized three assumptions that were foundations of post-war diplomacy. First, he criticized the drafting of the international economic agreements while the war was still in progress, before political settings were known. However, once the difficulties surrounding the ITO Charter became apparent and the unity of the allies dissipated when hostilities finished, the wisdom of forcing agreement at Bretton Woods became clear.

Second, Gardner regarded universalism as risky when even cooperation on a bilateral or regional basis had been rare in the 1930s. Fortunately, experience showed that universal institutions held the system together during the turbulent post-war years, and during the inflationary and recessionary 1970s. Now many NGOs and political activists are calling for 'global governance' to establish uniform standards for human rights, environment standards and to reduce economic inequalities and injustices. At the same time, dissatisfaction with the WTO is leading to new regionalism. These new forces create tension in global markets and even the viability of existing global agreements must be uncertain.

Finally, post-war negotiators sought agreement in form (legalism), rather than agreement in substance. In other words, agreements were negotiated in detail, without complete meeting of minds, and without adequate procedures for adjustment to changing conditions. This was demonstrated in the failed ITO Charter, where catering for the wishes of all participants meant that agreements were overwhelmed by conditions and exceptions. Now NGOs, and others dissatisfied with the outcomes of national democratic processes, are supporting 'global governance' as an alternative process with which to threaten governments. Most of these international laws are not universally approved (e.g., Kyoto Protocol, International Criminal Court, Cartagena Protocol), and not enforceable against non-signatories. Legalism has attractions to dissenters, but ultimately it requires enforcement, like the use of trade sanctions to enforce WTO dispute settlement decisions. Often such sanctions impose costs on both parties and cause economic losses. Both parties to such disputes would suffer less if a negotiated solution could be found. NGOs do not respect such cost–benefit studies of their single-issue demands.

Despite the concerns expressed by Gardner, the records of the post-war international economic institutions stand up well. They were successful in fulfilling the tasks they were given and adapted to meet unforeseen circumstances. Now there are new threats to be faced and some far-reaching reforms are being considered. For example, the IMF was intended to fill liquidity gaps, but the widespread adoption of exchange rate flexibility has reduced the need to hold large reserves. However, external imbalances are still serious among developing countries, where domestic adjustments are difficult to achieve and financial support may be necessary for long periods. Such assistance falls between the responsibilities of the IMF and the World Bank, and temporary collaboration devised by the two institutions since the debt problems of the 1980s are under review.

Conditions attached to lending can be used as levers of political influence by large shareholders on the governing boards. The technocratic functions of the IMF are constrained by shortages of resources. In recent years, the IMF's principal function has been to help emerging economies with high debts. Part of the problem is that financial quotas and voting powers have not changed much since Bretton Woods, which leaves some large countries under-represented. At the same time, the board may not be sufficiently responsive to economic imbalances in small economies.

The World Bank's problems have changed as private capital flows to middle-income economies increased and left the Bank to deal with low-income, slow growth, less developed economies, mainly in Africa. It has sufficient resources for economic projects in these countries, but increasingly the Bank is asked to meet more and more non-economic conditions. Lobbying by NGOs has taken decision-making on loans away from the Bank's board and into the hands of screening committees. Rather than assessing potential loans as a trade-off, these new committees demand that all requirements be met before approval is given. This causes long delays and slows the flow of development assistance (Mallaby, 2004).

ADAPTING TO CHANGE

The Bretton Woods institutions and the GATT established the organizational structure and the rules for inter-government relations after World War II. The need for order to be established after the economic and financial chaos of the 1930s was undeniable and it was fortuitous that a small group of allied governments decided to establish that institutional framework when only a limited group of countries was available to participate. In particular, the US Administration was able to put together a team of officials and academics with great experience and commitment, who were aided and abetted by a similarly committed British team (Skidelsky, 2000). This provided the core of like-minded expert representatives. (Although the USSR, China and some Eastern Europeans attended the early meetings, they withdrew soon after hostilities ceased, and the Iron Curtain descended.) Some overseas colonies and Latin American governments were represented also at Bretton Woods and later sessions. These countries were preoccupied with domestic problems, but it is untrue to say that developing countries were not present at Bretton Woods, as some critics of the IMF and the World Bank now claim.

The make-up of the principal participants was one reason why development issues were not sponsored at Bretton Woods or in the GATT negotiations. Most former enemies were allowed to join these international economic institutions by 1950. However, Japan faced strong opposition when it sought to become a GATT contracting party. The subject was broached by the United States in 1949 but was strongly opposed by many of the original contracting parties, on the grounds of Japan's pre-war record of unfair competition and labour exploitation. Eventually, in September 1955, Japan was allowed to join the GATT, but many contracting parties continued to discriminate against imports from Japan for many years. As developing countries acceded to GATT, they faced similar problems with their low-cost, labour-intensive manufactures.

While neglect of development issues was understandable late in the 1940s, because of other anxieties and the quite different political regimes prevailing at that time, changes occurring in the following 50 years would be expected to have generated amendments to the Bretton Woods institutions, and to the GATT. Disparities about the economic development of nations and the growing inequalities within them deserved attention, particularly since the major post-war concerns of OECD governments about liquidity and economic adjustment had been largely resolved by the 1970s. Some minor changes were introduced into IMF and World Bank operations. However, the GATT membership showed little sympathy for developing countries' exporters.

IMF lending programmes now focus mainly on structural adjustment issues in middle-income (emerging) nations, following the adoption of flexible exchange rates by OECD countries over 30 years ago. Development strategies conforming to the so-called Washington consensus in the 1990s were gradually made more flexible in response to criticisms. Complaints that IMF staff were being heavy-handed in pursuing flexible exchange rates and rigid domestic stances on fiscal and monetary policy have exacerbated demands for changes.

The World Bank has concentrated on economic development, with gradual extension of its development financing beyond infrastructure investment into health and education projects, poverty reduction and entering into joint ventures with the private sector. However, progress has been slow because the World Bank board comprises mostly representatives from major developed countries, the providers of the basic capital. Nevertheless, 25 per cent of all aid to developing countries comes from the World Bank. Most of the remainder comes directly from national governments, and from regional development banks. Most OECD governments prefer to manage their own development assistance programmes (see Chapter 7).

International commerce through trade, migration, travel and investment promotes development through transfers of knowledge and understanding, and especially technology. The spread of economic development in the past 60 years shows what is possible. That many countries have progressed little indicates that much remains to be done inside these economies to make them responsive to financial assistance.

In the 60 years since Bretton Woods, many formerly poor countries have made rapid advances in living standards and social progress. The 'Tiger' economies of South-East Asia are now rich and stable states. The rewards of such efforts had been demonstrated by Japan. Others have followed this route. The two most dramatic take-offs in the past 20 years have been China and India. These countries account for approximately 40 per cent of the world's population and their progress is rapidly reducing the numbers living in absolute poverty (defined by the World Bank as living on less than $2 per day). These successes derive from stable domestic political, social and economic infrastructures and organizations, features that are absent in countries facing severe poverty in Sub-Saharan Africa and other small island and land-locked countries.

More effective international organizations can also play a role in reducing economic disparities between countries and inequalities within them. This applies not just to incomes or living standards. It includes responses to diseases, hunger, education, land reform, property rights, the rule of law and justice. These domestic institutions are essential for development to begin and for markets to work effectively.

In contrast, many 'marginalized' countries are run by corrupt oligarchies, dictators or the military – or indeed, exist in a state of permanent civil war. They are unlikely to even comprehend what is missing. Some outside assistance from the World Bank and the regional development banks can facilitate effective development, but most of the dysfunctional states are fiercely independent. They are eager to accept aid, but without conditions and on their own terms.

After 60 years it is time to re-examine the international economic organizations. Many NGOs demand more say in the functioning of the World Bank and the regional banks, but experience suggests this would be counter-productive. Development NGOs would like to see these banks – really funding agencies – contribute more to economic development, especially in Sub-Saharan Africa, both in terms of grants and technical assistance. These groups favour re-structuring both Bretton Woods institutions. Environment NGOs and human rights groups, however, impose conditions on aid proposals that both delay programmes and deny economic development in order to protect their minority interests (Mallaby, 2004). The development NGOs presumably accept globalization but would like to see it re-directed. Other groups however, are opposed to globalization, except perhaps by continuing aid to protect living standards, and their pet conservation schemes.

The serious contradictions among NGOs need to be examined and used to establish an accord that will assist international organizations to promote development. Only then can efforts be focussed on specific development issues, including inequalities. Economic growth is essential if poverty is to be relieved, but to achieve a satisfactory distribution of gains requires appropriate domestic social and economic policies.

One of the surprising features of economic development over the past 50 years has been the inability to forecast which of the former colonies and independent developing countries would be most successful. Initially, Latin American countries, such as Brazil, Argentina and Chile appeared to have advantages of self-government, mineral resources and fertile land, as well as traditional links with global capital markets. India and the Gold Coast (Ghana) had inherited effective government structures and export industries with their independence. Yet, the real stars of economic development have been small states with largely immigrant populations (Singapore, Hong Kong, Taiwan). In 1950, Korea was a very poor, former Japanese colony with few resources and an agrarian population. Large labour reserves, capital inflows and enterprise have driven its successful economic development. Strong economic growth comes from institutions and policies, as the 'take-off' in India, China and

Chile show. Such institutions facilitate market creation, increase efficiency (output/input ratios), improve security (reduce risk) and provide scope to expand public investment and services. On the other hand, centrally planned or heavily socialized economies (with under-developed market structures) have failed totally.

CHANGING NEEDS: IMF

The Bretton Woods negotiations were to resolve an emergency. The world economy needed order and stability, and monetary cooperation to prevent a return to the beggar-my-neighbour monetary and trade policies of the 1930s. The IMF was a success. There were only occasional monetary disturbances. The IMF was established to oversee international monetary cooperation, to facilitate expansion of international trade (using commercial credits, etc.), to monitor macroeconomic strategies (Article IV reviews) and to provide short-term financial support to meet temporary balance-of-payments difficulties with fixed exchange rates). These roles were managed effectively until the collapse of the fixed exchange rate regime early in the 1970s.

All currencies were pegged to the US dollar, which had a fixed gold value. So the system relied on the US dollar as numeraire and reserve currency. Uncertainties surfaced late in the 1960s when the US balance-of-payments deficit and increasing overseas holdings of US dollars undermined confidence in its convertibility. With capital mobility increasing as euro-currency markets expanded, under-valued currencies (the deutschmark and the yen) faced upward pressure in the markets. Political statements about currency parities added to speculation, because if not supported by appropriate domestic policies, credibility gaps developed. The IMF introduced Special Drawing Rights in 1968, to supplement gold and dollar reserves. This 'paper gold' was valued in terms of a portfolio of widely used currencies and issued and allocated according to IMF voting rights. In 1971, the US ceased converting dollars into gold, and the world shifted to flexible exchange rates. The IMF continued to supervise the payments system and to maintain surveillance and coordination among members. The transition to flexible exchange rates was painless and the need for IMF financial support receded as far as OECD economies were concerned.

The financial system now has three reserve currencies, and both fixed and flexible exchange rate regimes. International capital markets have expanded, with many players and many instruments. Although most OECD countries now operate flexible exchange rates, many emerging economies have fixed exchange rates against the US dollar, the euro, or a basket of traded currencies. These complicate economic management, as demonstrated by the East Asian financial crisis (1997–98), when currencies had fixed parities against the US dollar. This is still largely the case. However, the fixed parity for the renmimbi was adjusted slightly in July 2005, and then it was announced that the renmimbi would be allowed to float against an undisclosed basket of currencies. This is a welcome change and it remains to be seen how much the exchange rate varies against the other major currencies. In global terms, China's current account surplus is small. Its surplus with the US is largely offset by deficits with other countries.

Severe structural crises in some countries in Latin America and Africa require IMF financial assistance. The IMF has introduced new 'lender-of-last-resort' credit facilities to prevent crises. Such immediate access to funding without conditions, however, carries a moral hazard. Many non-OECD governments believe they have a right to IMF financial assistance, without accepting responsibility to correct the causes of disequilibrium. In the 1950s and 1960s, OECD governments seeking IMF support were shamed into corrective policies and prompt repayments. The new supplicants, however, seem to expect financial support without commitment (e.g., Argentina). Development NGOs and Western politicians, who argue for grants and unrequited transfers to Sub-Saharan Africa, encourage such claims. They seem not to understand the differences among IMF short-to-medium-term monetary support, development bank loans and grant aid.

The IMF has made some internal reforms, including establishing an international department to monitor capital markets and to obtain independent risk advice to use in policy reviews. Since IMF financial support influences private capital flows, there is interdependence here. New strict rules were established in 2003 to limit lending beyond regular access levels, to show that public sector funding was limited. IMF exposure to high-risk debtors (e.g., Argentina, Turkey, Brazil) indicates that credits should not be rolled over repeatedly.

The IMF's key role remains surveillance of macroeconomic policies and support for adjustment policies, according to Article IV. Any financial assistance should be short term. Rodrigo Rato, IMF Managing Director, has stated, 'the role of the IMF in low-income countries is defined by our core business of macroeconomic assistance. There is no poverty reduction without macroeconomic stability' (*Financial Times*, 27 July 2004). In this role the IMF must collaborate with the World Bank, which has its own adjustment assistance programmes. As globalization continues, research into the links between economic development and capital account liberalization needs intense research and analysis. The kind of instability that created the Asian financial crisis in 1997–98 has to be avoided, and this requires scrutiny of domestic financial regulations in emerging economies.

There is a tendency for many advocates of massive assistance to overcome poverty to call for financial support from all sources to be increased to SSA economies. The IMF is in danger of being drawn into the enthusiasm for financial transfers set down in the UN Millennium Development Programme, as part of poverty-reduction strategies. Its role should continue to be to facilitate current account adjustment, leaving aid agencies to provide long-term assistance. There is a danger that the differences between the functions of the Fund and the World Bank are fading.

Another danger is that the IMF becomes entangled in the fashion for wider representation regarded as an indicator of an organization's legitimacy. What is 'fair' representation for all members? The present allocation of voting rights depends on capital contributions to the Fund. Would anyone advocate a one-country one-vote system to decide IMF lending programmes? Surely, the stalemate in the United Nations General Assembly (UNGA) processes is not a model for good financial practice. So many SSA countries have unreliable political systems and dysfunctional governments, it would be naive to allow them more voting power in IMF decisions, at least until they can demonstrate competence and stability. (Even since the UN Millennium Development Report was released in January 2005, several well-regarded countries have fallen into disrepute.) Legitimacy should not be allowed to interfere with the effectiveness of economic agencies.

The international banking community seems satisfied with existing arrangements. They are familiar with risk assessment in the capital markets. Private bankers and investors in development financing will be assisted if the new Basel rules on banks' capital adequacy are implemented. Basel II will improve their risk management and increase supervision. The importance of bank supervision was painfully demonstrated in the 1997–98 Asian financial crisis.

The IMF is less practised in risk assessment than the banking sector, so it could be vulnerable to political appeals from desperate debtors. So a case can be (and has been) made for it to withdraw from its role as lender-of-last-resort (Meltzer Report, 2000).

CHANGING NEEDS: WORLD BANK

The World Bank is a group of agencies. The International Bank for Reconstruction and Development borrows on world capital markets at favourable interest rates, because of its strong capital market rating (backed by OECD governments). It lends to developing countries at rates they would not be able to achieve themselves on capital markets. IDA was established in 1960 to provide 'soft' loans and grants to least developed countries, drawing on periodic donations from OECD governments. Initially, most of these grants were for projects. As debt burdens increased and external imbalances worsened, however, more IDA money has been distributed as structural adjustment lending (often in conjunction with IMF stabilization programmes). The IFC was established in 1956 to lend on commercial terms and take minority equity positions to support private foreign investments in developing countries. In addition, the World Bank administers the Multilateral Investment Guarantee Agency (MIGA) and the International Centre for Settlement of Investment Disputes (ICSID).

The IBRD has made cumulative lending of almost $400 billion, with current new lending of around $11 billion per annum. IDA has become the strongest arm of the World Bank, because with debt forgiveness increasing, its interest-free, long-term credits and grants are increasingly in demand; $9 billion of new commitments were made in 2004, mostly to the poorest countries. The relaxation of World Bank conditions on loans and grants has been cautious, and the ineffectiveness of debt-forgiveness programmes in SSA countries suggests this is wise.

In its early days the Bank supported reconstruction in Europe after World War II. In the 1960s, as more countries became independent, development projects increased, mostly infrastructure projects (dams, roads, railways etc.). The catch was that World Bank money was lent at interest rates slightly above market rates, and it had to be repaid, albeit over long periods. These rates were far below what developing country governments would have to pay on capital markets. Even so, these interest rates exceeded developing countries growth rates, so the stock of debt kept rising. Under pressure from NGOs, the World Bank has redirected its funding away from capital infrastructure (dams, roads, etc.) and into government infrastructure, education, health, etc. The impact of NGO nagging and bad media coverage generated by NGO criticisms has worn down Bank activities to politically correct options (see Chapter 8).

The Bank's balance sheet is difficult to interpret. It has borrowed about $US100 billion, which is on loan to developing countries. How much is liable to become bad debt is unknown. With loans and IDA loans/grants 'blended' in some countries, the overall picture is difficult to read. It is assumed that G7 governments underwrite Bank loans, but this represents a hidden cost to taxpayers that is not declared. With capital markets working effectively – unlike in 1947 when the Bank began operating – why does the Bank need to lend to creditworthy borrowers? Rogoff (2004) argues that the Bank and the IFC should close down lending operations and leave financing to the capital market. Many experts concur in this (Meltzer Report, 2000).

The US Administration has suggested that all World Bank loans should be written off, with repaid funds to go to IDA, which provides 100 per cent grants to the poorest economies. Other donors worry about the reliability of future funding of IDA, especially from the US. Donations always depend on economic circumstances when donations are called. Politics could play a major role.

Just three weeks after a communiqué committed G8 countries to debt relief for least developed countries, World Bank officials have demanded that donors should provide more money (or future commitments) to ensure that money is not taken away from developing countries. The G8 proposed write-off of 100 per cent of debts owed by 27 HIPCs (Highly Indebted Poor Countries), but they have not guaranteed to compensate IDA for the repayments it will not receive. So far only $1.4 billion has been promised for three years.

The Bank has argued that it provides expert advice to developing countries, which could be lost if the Bank's lending function is closed. Its reduced income would make it necessary to charge market rates for services. Advice going to governments might deteriorate. After all, there are many emotionally committed but ill-informed NGOs willing to fill such gaps.

POST-BRETTON WOODS

After 60 years, a strong case can be made for reviewing the role of the Bretton Woods twins in the circumstances of the twenty-first century. They were created to overcome serious economic (and political) mismanagement in the 1930s and to overcome market failures anticipated in the post-war period. They were highly successful in filling gaps in capital markets and supporting exchange rate stability. Public institutions, once established, tend to take on a life of their own, and governments (who own them) are reluctant to re-visit their agendas, constitutions or programmes. That is natural because any review of public institutions arouses diversionary issues that excite strong reactions and complicate any revisions.

The patched-up Bretton Woods system has survived 30 years of recurring crises since the adjustable peg was suspended. Many commentators would argue that the problem facing the international system is over-enthusiasm for flexible exchange rates, although they have played a key role in the process of globalization. Yet the world financial markets are faced with a question that is reminiscent of the negotiations between Keynes and White, and their formidable colleagues, at Bretton Woods 60 years ago (Skidelsky, 2005). In the presence of a persistent external deficit, should deficit or surplus economies adjust?

Substantial economic disequilibrium has appeared with an asymmetric version of the fixed exchange rate linkage between East and South Asian currencies and the US dollar, and flexible exchange rates between the US dollar and other currencies. China and its Asian neighbours keep under-valued currencies to maintain their export surpluses by official purchasing of US government securities. This finances the US external deficit. The imbalances arise because of deficient domestic demand in these emerging Asian economies, which depend on export expansion to maintain growth and employment. Yet, there must be other motives for continually building reserves. One reason could be as a reaction to capital account difficulties in 1997–98, because they could be regarded as insurance against future deficit contingencies (Bird and Mandilaras, 2005).

The US has little manoeuvrability in its domestic policy as long as the Asian currencies remain stable against the dollar, and it is too early yet to assess how much the renmimbi will adjust under the new adjustable peg. Yet, the US external deficit is unsustainable. This reverses the US position in 1944. Now the US has the deficit and the surplus countries are relaxed about adding to their reserves. Keynes had argued at Bretton Woods that economic adjustment should be made by both debtor and creditor economies. The Americans insisted on the orthodox doctrine that it was the responsibility of deficit countries to 'put their house in order'. Hence, the IMF provided access to adjustment finance on condition that suitable correction was made. (The only concession to Keynes in the IMF articles was to include the scarce currency clause [Article VII], which has never been invoked.) Now the US has the deficit and the creditors are happy to finance it, but will not adjust their policies or vary their exchange rate.

With markets the driving force of globalization, and flexible exchange rates the rule in OECD economies, monetary assistance to deficit economies should not be necessary. The IMF system worked because the US financed post-war recovery in Europe and Japan from its reserves. In the 1960s, Japan and Germany financed US external deficits by relaxing capital controls. Such adjustments are not evident in the fixed exchange rate between the US and the emerging Asian economies, including China. Their under-valued currencies are maintained to sustain their export-led growth. The US has little manoeuvrability in its domestic policy because deflationary policies (in the private or public sectors) will not reduce the competitiveness of Asian exports in the US market. Yet the US deficit is unsustainable. Eventually, foreign investors will lose confidence in the US dollar and a sharp depreciation will bring serious disruption to foreign exchange markets. The problems will spread well beyond the G8. But any help will come at a high political price in terms of US political freedom, and in terms of global political balance. European politicians seem to be waiting for that day, though the economic damage from a stronger euro will be a chastening experience for the electorate.

This flaw in the international monetary system could bring down the whole structure, because the US and Chinese economies are driving global growth. Several of Europe's large economies are stagnating, with substantial public sector imbalances, slow growth and high levels of unemployment. The key question is what kind of international financial system can be established to restore an effective adjustment mechanism? One obstacle to that is the Asian preference for fixed exchange rates, which impedes financial adjustment.

Another question is whether two financial agencies are still necessary? The IMF and the World Bank were designed to overcome the failures in international financial markets experienced in the 1930s. Since debt crises struck in the 1980s, efforts by both agencies to ease economic adjustments in developing countries have created an overlap in their activities. Moreover, some of the functions prescribed 60 years ago are no longer relevant after the revival of private capital markets and strong growth in private investment flows. If as suggested above, lending by both agencies is phased out, they could be combined without any loss in effectiveness. Administrative costs would be reduced and duplication avoided, while technical advice could continue to developing countries. The financial arm of the World Bank would have to continue while outstanding loans mature and are repaid. Some technical adjustments may be necessary as some debt forgiveness for least developed countries is accommodated. In financial terms, the single institution would continue to monitor macroeconomic developments (IMF) and would become the source for development grants, presently administered by IDA and the IMF. Technical advice would continue as long as it is needed.

The case for these radical changes was made in the report of the Commission established by the US Congress in 1998 at the International Financial Institution. This body was chaired by Allen Meltzer and was directed to consider the activities of the major international financial organizations, the Bretton Woods agencies, the three regional development banks and the BIS (Meltzer Report, 2000). A new call for serious review of the IMF was made by the governor of the Bank of England in February 2006.

Another Bretton Woods conference is unlikely. There are too many conflicting interests to be reconciled to believe that effective and enforceable agreements would be reached. Moreover, political tensions are high and international agencies have their own agendas. The most likely response to the problems mentioned above will be to discuss them at the annual Fund/Bank meetings, or to convene ad hoc meetings on specific subjects.

APPENDIX 2.1

The Atlantic Charter

On 14 August 1941, President Roosevelt and Prime Minister Churchill at the conclusion of their mid-ocean conference, made the following joint declaration of 'certain common principles in the national policies of their respective countries on which they base their hopes for a better future for the world':

First, their countries seek no aggrandizement, territorial or other;

Second, they desire to see no territorial changes that do not accord with the freely expressed wishes of the people concerned;

Third, they respect the right of all peoples to choose the form of government under which they will live; and they wish to see sovereign rights and self government restored to those who have been forcibly deprived of them;

Fourth, they will endeavor, with due respect for their existing obligations, to further the enjoyment by all States, great or small, victor or vanquished, of access, on equal terms, to the trade and to the raw materials of the world which are needed for their economic prosperity;

Fifth, they desire to bring about the fullest collaboration between all nations in the economic field with the object of securing, for all, improved labor standards, economic advancement and social security;

Sixth, after the final destruction of the Nazi tyranny, they hope to see established a peace which will afford to all nations the means of dwelling in safety within their own boundaries, and which will afford assurance that all the men in all the lands may live out their lives in freedom from fear and want;

Seventh, such a peace should enable all men to traverse the high seas and oceans without hindrance;

Eighth, they believe that all of the nations of the world, for realistic as well as spiritual reasons, must come to the abandonment of the use of force. Since no future peace can be maintained if land, sea or air armaments continue to be employed by nations which threaten, or may threaten, aggression outside of their frontiers, they believe, pending the establishment of a wider and permanent system of general security, that the disarmament of such nations is essential. They will likewise aid and encourage all other practicable measures which will lighten for peace-loving peoples the crushing burden of armaments.

Franklin D. Roosevelt
Winston Churchill

(Brinkley and Facey-Crowther, 1994)

REFERENCES

Bird, G. and A. Mandilaras (2005), 'Reserve accumulation in Asia', *World Economics*, **6**(1), 85–99.

Brinkely, D. and D.R. Facey-Crowther (1994), *The Atlantic Charter*, New York: St Martin's Press.

Enders, A. (2004), 'Reciprocity in GATT (1947): from 1942 to the Kennedy Round' in R.E. Baldwin and L.A. Winters (eds), *Challenges to Globalization: Analyzing the Economics*, Chicago: University of Chicago Press.

Gardner, R. (1980), *Sterling-Dollar Diplomacy in Current Perspective*, New York: Columbia University Press.

Irwin, D.A. (1995), 'The GATT in historical perspective', *American Economic Review* **85**(2), 323–8.

Jackson, J. (1990), *The World Trading System*, Cambridge, MA and London: MIT Press.

MacMillan, M. (2001), *Peacemakers*, London: John Murray.

Mallaby, S. (2004), *The World's Banker*, New York: Penguin Press.

Meltzer Report (2000), report of the International Financial Advisory Commission.

Rabkin, J. (1999), 'Morgen die Welt: Green imperialism', *IPA Review*, **5**(13) (September), 8–10.

Rogoff, K. (2004), 'The Sisters at 60', *The Economist*, 24 July.

Skidelsky, R. (2000), *John Maynard Keynes: Vol. 3, Fighting for Britain 1937–46*, London: Macmillan, chs. 12–13.

Skidelsky, R. (2005), 'Keynes, globalisation and the Bretton Woods institutions in the light of changing ideas about markets', *World Economics*, **6**(1), Jan–Mar, 15–30.

3. Trade relations

WHY FREE TRADE?

Free trade is an important component of economic liberty. The economic case for free trade follows from the benefits that arise from competition in domestic markets, for goods, services and factors of production. That is, private profit-seeking leads to efficient resource allocation. This is founded on the long-standing principle of comparative advantage. If each person specializes in activities that offer the best returns, then exchanges some of this output for goods and services from others also specializing, this provides gains from exchange for all (Bhagwati, 1988).

So why should governments interfere at national borders to limit imports or, via tariffs and other taxes, raise the prices of imports? These interventions disturb relative prices facing individuals as consumers and producers. Increases in trade protection reduce economic prosperity at home and in the country or countries supplying its imports. In this way, countries as well as individuals make the most of their resources (and efforts) when they concentrate on producing what they do well compared with other occupations. It pays even to import goods (and services) that can be produced at home if the real cost in terms of resources expended is lower. That is, if the resources used to produce the exports to pay for imports are fewer than required to produce import substitutes at home. This maximizes the quantities of goods and services available at home (real income) from a given quantum of resources (labour, equipment, power, raw materials, etc.).

International trade occurs and countries derive benefits from it, because their different resource endowments create comparative advantages in the production of different goods (or services). That is, they have different comparative costs of production. These cost differences result from variations in the availability and quality of production inputs. The result of trade between countries (allowing for transport costs and any trade barriers) tends to equalize prices of goods and services in different countries, to encourage specialization in production according to comparative advantage, and to bring prices of factors of production in trading countries closer. The gains from trade depend on relevant conditions. However, border barriers to trade (tariffs, quotas, etc.) reduce gains from trade, and therefore real incomes (except in exceptional circumstances). (For a history of free trade and its struggles, see Irwin, 1996.)

Free trade is not necessarily a prescription for economic prosperity. It is only part of the story. Much depends on the national institutions, domestic regulations and economic policies, as well as political and social circumstances that exist in trading countries. The rule of law, protection of property rights and individual freedoms, with a democratically elected government, are required to allow markets to provide appropriate incentives for profitable commerce (Kasper and Streit, 1998). Moreover, effective markets are necessary to facilitate economic adjustment to change (OECD, 2005).

The arguments for free trade are strong. Liberal trade and investment policies promote income (output) growth by allowing individuals and businesses to engage in specialization and exchange – that is, to use their innate and acquired resources to the full. Freedom of exchange through domestic and international trade lowers prices, widens the range of goods and services available, diversifies risks, allows resources to earn highest returns and reduces the cost of capital. Liberalization promotes competition, raises productivity and encourages the use of best-practice production methods. International prices provide signals to encourage a country's resource-owners and consumers to adapt to shifts in comparative advantage.

Restricting trade causes economic losses, which affect some residents more than others. It is inequitable. Yet, democratic governments maintain protectionist policies, and invent new ones. This leads into the controversial area of political economy. In practice, each government pursues its own agenda, which includes retaining office by winning periodic elections. A government pursues policies to that end by acting as a clearing house for ideas and proposals from many agents pursuing economic, commercial, social and political self-interests. They seek to influence policy-making to their own advantage. Lobby groups participate in policy formulation, as is evident in agricultural policies, protection of clothing and textiles industries, and subsidies for high-tech industries in OECD countries. While such lobbying consumes real resources, it offers high returns for success, even though it reduces total economic output.

Trade policy is essentially about income distribution, with protected industries gaining at the expense of unprotected industries. For example, an import tariff raises the price of imports and the prices of domestic import substitutes. Expenditure is transferred towards these items and away from other goods and services (depending on demand elasticities); domestic resources are diverted to increase production of import-competing goods. This raises resource costs to all domestic producers, including the costs of efficient export industries. Hence, a tariff is a tax on exports (Clements and Sjaastad, 1984).

Trade policy is about domestic resource owners competing over income distribution. One consequence is to cause reactions in other countries, which can lead to increasing protection, inefficiencies and unemployment, and a downward spiral in economic fortunes, as occurred in the 1930s.

These are the two forces acting on trade policy. First, the general welfare gains from trade, if domestic and foreign barriers to free trade are reduced. Second, private returns from achieving government interventions that redistribute income towards protected industries, even if the result is a net loss of welfare for the community at large. The balance between these forces shifts over time and depends on governments' shifting interests.

MULTILATERAL TRADE LIBERALIZATION

At the Bretton Woods conference (1944), it was understood that the financial institutions would be supported by an agreement to liberalize trade, as foreshadowed in the Atlantic Charter. The subject of an International Trade Organization (ITO) was raised at the first meeting of UNESCO in February 1946, just before the IMF and the World Bank were formally approved. The first preparatory meeting was held in London in October 1946, and the fourth and final meeting to complete the ITO Charter was held in Havana in 1948. By the third meeting in Geneva in 1947, the ITO Charter had become so complex, with every UN member trying to protect its interests, that the US pressed ahead with a limited group of countries prepared to negotiate a multilateral agreement for mutual reductions of tariffs, based on the draft commercial chapter of the ITO. This GATT alternative, which was based on the familiar US reciprocal tariff-cutting technique, made ratification of the ITO Charter unlikely.

The ITO proposal was typical of so many subsequent UN initiatives. It attempted to allow for everyone's interests, which resulted in no agreement at all. The negotiations expanded to include many non-trade issues, including full-employment, investment, restrictive business practices, commodity market arrangements and economic development. In consequence, the Havana Charter had so many exceptions that it had little value. Everything was so qualified that they represented only best-endeavours rather than real commitments. The Havana Charter represented 'a victory for the forces, which placed complete freedom of national action to pursue full-employment above requirements of international cooperation for a free, multilateral trading system' (Curzon, 1965: p. 31). Facing strong opposition from Congress, the US Administration did not present the ITO Charter for ratification. Without US support, other countries also dropped the Charter. As early as 1948, the cooperative ambience at Bretton Woods had been replaced with real politics.

Once again, US negotiators had extracted an important and effective multilateral agency from a talkfest and laid the foundation for international trade liberalization. Left out at Bretton Woods because the Roosevelt Administration did not want to jeopardize that meeting, with imports representing less than 5 per cent of GDP and with Congress focussing elsewhere, it was the State Department's initiative to open trade negotiations in Geneva. At this stage, trade was regarded as a foreign policy matter in the United States. This changed as US industries began to face competition from the European and Japanese economies as they recovered, and US producers sought protection using their representatives in Congress. Then US trade once more became a domestic political issue (Krueger, 1995).

The General Agreement on Tariffs and Trade (GATT) was hurriedly drawn up in 1947 in order that negotiating powers granted to the US Administration by Congress in 1945 would be used before they expired. The GATT drew on the commercial chapter of the ITO Charter. The principles of non-discrimination, reciprocal tariff reductions and tariff bindings were the instruments adopted to reduce protection. In addition, commitments were made to remove quantitative restraints on trade in GATT Article XI, except for agriculture (Curzon, 1965: ch. VI).

Driven by the US Administration's commitment to Reciprocal Trade Agreement legislation, five rounds of tariff negotiations occurred between 1947 and 1961. Removal of import quotas among European members was mostly achieved within the Organisation for European Co-operation (OEEC), one of the committees established to administer Marshall Aid in Europe.

By 1961, the European Economic Community (EEC) was in place and its linear 10 per cent tariff cuts had begun. The US Administration's response was the Trade Expansion Act 1962, which proposed a new round of GATT trade negotiations with a broad agenda to cover industrial and agricultural products, intended to minimize EEC discrimination against US exports. The EEC countries were working to establish a new agricultural regime as well as being occupied with the early stages of establishing their customs union. Hence, though negotiations proceeded well and large reductions in industrial tariffs were achieved, the EEC resisted the US efforts to negotiate on agricultural protection. ('To the Community the main result of the Kennedy Round in the agricultural field has been that it greatly helped to define its own common policy' reported by Preeg, 1970.) Other Western European countries (mostly in EFTA) followed the EEC lead. An opportunity for global liberalization of agriculture was lost. Once the Common Agricultural Policy (CAP) was established and protection rents distributed, the opposition to a liberal agricultural regime became entrenched on both sides of the Atlantic.

The Kennedy Round negotiations (1963–67) were further complicated by developing countries' demands for trade preferences at the United Nations Conference on Trade and Development (UNCTAD) in 1964, which diverted attention to negotiate GATT Part IV and granted 'differential and more favourable treatment' to developing countries. Reciprocity was not expected from less developed countries in the Kennedy Round, while efforts were made to reduce barriers to their exports.

The GATT has always been an inter-government agreement. The Final Act of the Uruguay Round negotiations for the first time made the WTO agreements (including GATT, 1994) an international treaty. The GATT was an agreement administered by consensus among governments. Its powers did not reach out to commercial relations between individuals, or corporations. It was possible, therefore, for commercial companies to agree to restrictive practices that were not covered by GATT rules. For example, 'voluntary' export restraints between companies (a producer in, say, Malaysia and an American retailer) were not subject to GATT rules, unless a government made a complaint under GATT Articles. The Uruguay Round brought such private sector accords within the WTO disciplines; trade-related investment measures (TRIMs) and trade-related aspects of intellectual property rights (TRIPs) were attempts to bring anti-competitive practices within WTO agreements.

GATT RULES

The text of the General Agreement was technically complex, but its operation was based on four principles:

1. Non-discrimination was defined by the most-favoured nation (MFN) obligation in Article I. Only two exceptions were allowed: the provisions for customs unions and free trade areas (GATT Article XXIV), and pre-existing trade preferences (such as British Commonwealth preferences) were frozen but allowed to continue, subject to negotiation. Consistent with MFN, national treatment was accorded to all imports once they entered a country (GATT Article III).
2. Tariffs were the only permitted protection. All import quotas were to be eliminated. Exceptions applied in circumstances of temporary balance-of-payments difficulties (GATT Article XII) and as part of programmes and policies of economic development (GATT Article XVIII). In addition, protection for agriculture was allowed under limited circumstances using GATT Article XI. When the US was allowed a waiver for dairy produce in 1955, agriculture became a deep-rooted problem in all trade negotiations. Part IV added to GATT in 1965 allowed 'special and differential' treatment for developing countries. Commencing in 1973, further exceptions were provided as part of the Multi-Fibre Arrangement (MFA) aimed at preventing market disruption in textiles and clothing.

3. Consultation between contracting parties, provided in GATT Article XXIII, was intended to overcome potential trade problems and to settle trade disputes.
4. Negotiations were convened periodically (Article XXVIII *bis*) to reduce trade barriers on a reciprocal, non-discriminatory basis among 'contracting parties'.

The GATT negotiating process was criticized because it lacked balance. Reciprocal tariff negotiations began with 'offers and requests' from principal suppliers (exporters). This gave the initiative to the major trading countries and effectively granted them the influence to exclude negotiations in sectors where they wished to maintain protection (e.g., agriculture, materials processing). Moreover, it was mercantilist to balance tariff concessions granted and received. Fortunately, because concessions were multilateralized, forecasting precise costs and benefits of tariff reductions was impossible. The GATT founders were sensitive to the turbulent and competitive protectionism of the 1930s, when any suggestion of tariff dismantling had aroused fears that unemployment and external disequilibrium would result. Reciprocity, on the other hand, allowed participating governments to focus on potential increases in exports (regarded as employment increasing) that would be generated by other countries' liberalization, which sidestepped the impact on their own import-competing industries.

Tariff negotiations began in 1947 and they were repeated periodically thereafter (see Table 3.1). In the early years, US negotiators provided concessions on tariffs against mainly promises of future reductions from other countries. Tariff bindings (covered by GATT Article II) were important guarantees that negotiated reductions would not be nullified subsequently. So tariff bindings were accepted as concessions. In the period after 1945, most imports were regulated by quotas or by foreign exchange controls, except in the United States. These controls were relaxed gradually in Western Europe using the OEEC, which had been established to administer Marshall Aid and to facilitate intra-European trade.

The GATT tariff negotiations were based on 'first-difference' reciprocity. That is, mutual and balanced concessions in tariff negotiations among contracting parties. This refers to reciprocity at the margin. That is, changes in trade restrictiveness: a 5 per cent cut in a 7 per cent bound tariff is worth more than 5 per cent on a 10 per cent tariff (given similar demand elasticities for the two imported goods). This was the principal technique for trade liberalization in eight rounds of GATT negotiations. (Since the Kennedy Round, more complicated formulae have been tried to give more equity to liberalization, but negotiating a formula takes time, and many exceptions have to be balanced. The negotiating formula for tariff reductions in the Doha Round is still being negotiated.)

Table 3.1   GATT negotiating rounds

Round	Dates	Number of Countries	Average Tariff Cut
Geneva	1947	23	–
Annecy	1949	13	–
Torquay	1950	38	–
Geneva	1956	26	–
Dillon	1960–61	26	–
Kennedy	1963–67	62	35%
Tokyo	1973–79	102	34%
Uruguay	1986–94	123	30%

Source: WTO Secretariat, Geneva.

'Full reciprocity', on the other hand, implies balance in total market access and the overall tariff applied by trading partners. The terms 'reciprocity' and 'free trade' raise uncertainties when economic dominance is undermined by rapid progress in industrializing economies that are granted import-substituting protection and/or preferential access to OECD economies. Full reciprocity poses a threat to the open trading system, because it denies the flexibility of trade-offs between sectors that is politically necessary in negotiating reductions in trade barriers. One interpretation of full reciprocity is even more restrictive when it allows for bilateral trade balancing (Bhagwati and Irwin, 1987).

Most liberalization negotiated in the GATT has related to trade in industrial products. By 1960, tariff reductions in the GATT, plus quota relaxations within the OEEC, had promoted strong trade growth. However, this liberalization also exposed sectors where restrictions remained significant: agriculture, materials processing and labour-intensive manufactures, especially textiles, clothing and footwear. These sensitive areas were of major interest to developing countries, whose membership in GATT was growing. The Haberler Report (1958) and the UNCTAD (1964) raised the profile of developing countries' interests in international trade negotiations (see Chapter 4).

By 1960, the GATT 'club' had become an efficient problem-solving agency on trade matters. The curses of trade in the 1930s, beggar-my-neighbour policies and bilateralism, had been scourged. Political frictions among developed contracting parties were largely avoided, though developing countries were beginning to use their numbers in the UN agencies to press for preferential treatment. More progress had been made in liberalization than anyone had anticipated in 1947. But with most industrial tariffs at low levels, the easy stage was over.

Regional economic integration, according to GATT Article XXIV, occupied Western European governments (EEC and EFTA) even before the end of World War II. Since 1990, however, many more countries have become interested in RTAs using GATT Article XXIV. Slow progress in Uruguay Round negotiations was blamed at first, but the number of RTAs notified to the WTO has continued to increase since 1995. RTAs put an emphasis on reciprocity at the expense of multilateralism. They can also be selective about the sectors covered (e.g., excluding agriculture), while harmonizing rules in areas where GATT/WTO has not been able to negotiate, such as investment, competition, government procurement and environment standards. Lack of progress with Doha Round preparations has undoubtedly played a role too. The effect has been to divert attention from multilateral negotiations towards bilateralism, which had caused the trade collapse in the 1930s. The economic and political balance may be shifting (see Chapter 6).

The GATT principles were simple and created few controversies. But the GATT Part II (Articles III to XXIII) specified qualifications and escape clauses that have become the battlefield for trade negotiations since 1970s.

PROVISIONAL APPLICATION

The difficult and almost clandestine beginnings of the GATT created legal and institutional problems when the ITO was not implemented in 1948. For the GATT to succeed, it had to be adopted by mid-1948, when the 1945 trade negotiating powers granted by the US Congress expired. This was achieved by inclusion of the 'Protocol of Provisional Application', which allowed provisional accession on or after 1 January 1948. This protocol was intended to be provisional because it was anticipated that the ITO Charter would be adopted by the end of that year. However, several of the original 23 GATT members could not adopt the GATT without approval from their legislatures, or they required such approval for specific clauses in GATT Part II. To overcome these impediments to rapid implementation of the agreed tariff reductions and the principles in GATT Parts I and III, the Protocol of Provisional Application called for implementation of GATT Part II 'to the fullest extent not inconsistent with existing legislation'. This qualification allowed contracting parties to 'grandfather' rights for any existing legislation, even if it was inconsistent with obligations under GATT Part II. This allowed contracting parties to authorize membership without seeking to amend existing legislation on sensitive subjects, such as import quotas, subsidies, anti-dumping legislation and customs administration (Jackson, 1990). These were crucial aspects of the GATT and many of these issues remain unresolved even now.

The reasons for the Protocol of Provisional Application were accepted in anticipation of the ITO taking effect. The GATT was meant to be a temporary document. Because the ITO was stillborn, the Protocol of Provisional Application remained in the GATT. Governments that joined GATT after 1948 also adopted provisional application that allowed them to ignore important commitments in GATT Part II. Despite attempts to introduce definitive application of the GATT, contracting parties were unwilling to sacrifice protection for domestic policies. Attempts to strengthen commitments on anti-dumping, subsidies, etc. in the Kennedy and Tokyo Rounds only managed to establish 'voluntary' codes of behaviour, which protected grandfathering for all members who did not sign the codes.

The Protocol of Provisional Application was removed before GATT (1994) was included in the Uruguay Round Final Act. It would have been inconsistent with the single-undertaking commitment to the Uruguay Agreements. However, the habit of grandfathering dies hard. Assessments of regional trade agreements (RTAs), reviewed according to GATT Article XXIV, have been blocked by members of existing regional trade agreements, who argue that existing RTAs should be grandfathered and, therefore not subject to review. It is reported that most of the 250-plus RTAs that have been notified to the GATT/WTO do not meet the conditions set out in GATT Article XXIV (see Chapter 6).

TIGHTENING THE RULES

The Kennedy Round (1963–67) represented a departure from the first five rounds of GATT negotiations. The US Trade Expansion Act (1962) provided for a 50 per cent across-the-board tariff cut to replace the traditional product-by-product approach in the Reciprocal Trade Agreements Act (1934). The proposal was to reduce tariffs and non-tariff barriers, with minimum exceptions. The target tariffs were to be 10 per cent for manufacture, 5 per cent for semi-processed goods and zero tariffs on raw materials. This was a response to the discrimination anticipated as the Treaty of Rome tariff-dismantling among EEC members was implemented (scheduled for 1960–68). Unfortunately, the simple mechanism proposed by the United States was blocked by demands for exceptions for some sectors, and in particular, the EEC proposal to exempt agriculture. The US authorities were equally to blame because their tariffs had little impact on agricultural trade, where non-tariff barriers dominated. Because the EEC countries' tariffs were converging on a common external tariff by 1968, the average of member countries' individual tariffs, there would be fewer peaks in EEC tariffs than in US tariffs. The EEC countries, therefore, proposed some harmonization of tariffs by introducing a reducing scale of tariff cuts on lower tariffs. This would affect the degree of reciprocity received by many Third Countries (countries that are not members of the EC), which complicated negotiations even further. Ultimately, compromises were achieved by negotiating in industry groups (chemicals, steel, textiles, etc.). Even so, the across-the-board approach was complicated by the concept of reciprocity embedded in GATT folklore.

Leading agricultural exporters, other than the United States, were excused from negotiations, because with agriculture excluded, reciprocity could not be achieved for those countries. Similarly, developing countries were exempted under GATT Part IV, adopted in 1965. Only 16 countries (including the six EEC members) participated in the Kennedy Round, with another 32 countries negotiating on a reciprocal basis.

The Tokyo Round of GATT trade negotiation (1973–79) took place in turbulent economic times. Non-discrimination had been compromised by the long-standing exclusion of agriculture from GATT negotiations, the acceptance of UNCTAD's Generalized System of Preferences (GSP) (1971) and by the Multi-Fibre Arrangement (MFA) (1973), which managed bilateral trade in textiles and clothing. In addition, the global oil crisis undermined economic confidence. Resort to legal and illegal import quotas, and duty impositions using GATT escape clauses for anti-dumping and subsidy countervailing, increased as the 1970s progressed. This weakening of GATT principles represented a shift towards a more managed approach to trade policy, requiring continuous negotiations to deal with problems. Contingent protection, defined as permission to introduce trade policies to offset an injury according to existing escape clauses, became a key issue in the Tokyo Round. These non-tariff measures were discussed extensively during the Kennedy Round negotiations, but with little progress. The Anti-dumping Code (1967), drawn up at US insistence, ran into constitutional and legal problems even in the United States. The resultant publicity attracted interest in anti-dumping from other countries too.

Non-tariff barriers had increased after the Kennedy Round and, for the first time, they were addressed extensively in the Tokyo Round negotiations. At the same time, it was assumed that the linear-cut approach to tariffs adopted in the Kennedy Round would be followed again. However, true to form, the EEC argued for graduated reductions as a step towards tariff harmonization, because, it was claimed, EEC external tariffs on industrial goods were generally lower than other OECD countries. (This mercantilist approach focussing on full reciprocity showed no recognition of gains from unilateral liberalization.) This debate tended to divert attention from crucial non-tariff barriers, while raising problems about traditional reciprocity. The difference between first-difference reciprocity, which focussed on tariff reductions, and absolute tariffs levels (i.e., degrees of protection) became crucial. This meant that re-defining products could allow differentiation in tariff levels. Another bureaucratic impediment to trade was created.

Attempts to enforce the GATT prohibition on import quotas (GATT Article XI) ran up against the exemptions for agriculture in European countries and the United States. Despite 27 countries signing an agreement on import licensing, the matter became another problem left over to a working committee when the Tokyo Round finished. A catalogue of 800 non-tariff barriers compiled by the GATT Secretariat seemed to discourage negotiators. As the deadline for a final agreement approached, some new accords were reached on non-tariff barriers, which widened the coverage of the GATT. Their legal status, however, was not clear. These were stand-alone agreements. Some were codes; others were statements of objectives. They applied only to signatories and were only enforceable by joint action. In other words, they were optional. It was this 'take it or leave it' attitude at the end of the Tokyo Round that led to a hiatus in liberalization. This shambles of commitments and offers meant that it was essential to seek 'a single undertaking' in future negotiations, with only limited exceptions.

The Tokyo Round exposed the costs of emphasizing reciprocity in GATT negotiations. The economic case for unilateral liberalization, amply demonstrated by many medium-size economies (e.g., Australia, New Zealand and Chile), is lost on the major players. The EU and US negotiators preserve small nuisance tariffs as 'bargaining coin' regardless of inconvenience to traders. This problem is being exposed in RTAs where rules of origin are important.

ESCAPE CLAUSES

All international agreements contain 'escape clauses'. These are essential because governments have to protect their freedom to act in unanticipated circumstances. Such action may require derogation from commitments in an agreement. Such occurrences are best covered by specific rules in an agreement to appease other signatories and to preserve the agreement. There are two types of escape clauses in most international economic treaties.

1. An exceptions clause provides for signatories to be released in advance from obligations in defined circumstances. Examples are GATT Article XXIV for customs unions and free trade areas, and the provision of differential and more favourable treatment for developing countries under GATT Article XVIII and Part IV.
2. A contingency provision is a temporary action to meet unforeseen circumstances under prescribed conditions. Specific GATT articles cover obvious national interests, such as state security, quarantine, and so forth.

- GATT Article XIX provides for suspension, withdrawal or modification of a negotiated tariff concession if a domestic industry is threatened by disruptive import competition. Any defensive measures introduced have to be applied in a non-discriminatory manner and not before consultations with foreign suppliers, who may seek compensation or take retaliatory action.

- GATT Article VI relates to dumping, defined as the sale of products for export at a price below normal value, which usually means below the price in the home market. If dumping can be demonstrated to cause, or to threaten, material injury to competing domestic industries, anti-dumping duties are permitted. The interpretation of this Article rests with the authorities in the importing country and there is wide scope to use calculations of dumping margins to declare unfair competition. The Anti-dumping Code agreed during the Kennedy Round proved to be ineffective, but the renegotiation in the Tokyo Round was hardly more effective in constraining access to GATT Article VI – 27 contracting parties signed the 1979 Anti-dumping Code.

- GATT Article XVI in the 1947 text referred only to export subsidies, which, because of concerns about trade imbalances, were regarded as reprehensible. Other domestic or production subsidies, however, were complex and less certain. When disputes arose, direct confrontation between governments had to follow. The subsidy and countervailing tariff rules were gradually clarified and strengthened late in the 1950s. Countervailing actions became more common as tariffs declined, and the US, followed by other contracting parties, strengthened countervailing actions. Eventually, negotiations commenced in the Tokyo Round to establish a code on subsidies and countervailing duties, which was concluded in 1979. This Subsidies Code included domestic subsidies as well as export subsidies.

The complexity of Article XIX safeguards, and the inappropriate complexity of the instruments it permitted, caused contracting parties to seek alternatives (Robertson, 1992). A non-discriminatory import quota affecting all suppliers is not an efficient method of gaining temporary protection for a domestic industry against an injury from a specific source. So governments turned to less onerous trade remedies available in other contingency provisions – anti-dumping or countervailing duties. In addition, other discriminatory (targeted) trade restrictions were introduced that were not specifically proscribed by GATT articles. 'Voluntary' export restraints (VERs) became the new scourge of developing economies' export sectors.

VERs were bilateral agreements extracted from competitive overseas producers supplying a market, either imposed by importing governments or by large retailers in OECD markets. They were implemented either by exporters or their governments, with the rent component in agreed prices divided between the parties. These grey-area measures were not covered in GATT provisions. For example, quantitative import restrictions were not GATT-consistent, except in specific conditions (e.g., Articles XI, XII, XVIII or XIX). However, VERs agreed by both sides did not come to light unless one party objected. If both parties believed VERs offered advantages, they survived outside GATT rules. If a non-participant objected, they could be bribed to desist, but more often the objector would make a private approach or a general objection to grey-area measures.

Strong political pressures to tighten escape clauses in the GATT began in the 1960s. In general, temporary derogations from obligations in unforeseen circumstances increased governments' confidence that they were covered against unforeseen calamities. In practice, a distinction should be drawn between exceptions and escape clauses in an agreement, but this was often difficult. Another exception was GATT Part IV, which provided differential and more favourable treatment for developing countries. On the other hand, contingency measures in GATT Articles VI, XVI and XIX were safeguard provisions to deal with unforeseen developments. Because definitions, conditions and remedies in these GATT articles were ill-defined, non-tariff barriers evolved to provide protection against competition, as economic growth slowed in the 1970s and 1980s, leading to rising inflation and recession.

The Kennedy Round and Tokyo Round negotiations lasted much longer than any of the earlier rounds, mainly because serious efforts were made to tackle the burgeoning non-tariff barriers. In both negotiations, substantial reductions were made to industrial tariffs (see Table 3.1). However, yet again, no progress was made to reduce agricultural protection or rising protection against low-cost manufactured exports from developing countries. In both instances, the negotiating problems related to non-tariff barriers. Even where separate agreements were reached to clarify or extend GATT articles, they were applied only by a limited number of signatories. Non-tariff barriers and excluded sectors, particularly agriculture and TCF, have become the outstanding weakness in the multilateral trading system.

Since the conclusion of the Tokyo Round – 25 years ago! – GATT Article I has been under concerted attack as new (and long-standing) developing country contracting parties have sought trade preferences, in contradiction of the fundamental principle of the agreement. The benefits of GATT membership are supposed to derive from the removal of import barriers by each member to remove domestic distortions caused in production and consumption. This liberalization improves efficiency across the economy. Preferential access to OECD economies yields little when the industrial tariffs of these countries are close to zero (average applied industrial tariffs in OECD were estimated at less than 3 per cent after the Uruguay Round [Martin and Winters, 1995]). In areas where non-tariff barriers remain significant – agricultural and TCF markets – general preferences for all developing countries would yield little, even if limited to least developed countries. Unfortunately, even well-meaning development NGOs (see Oxfam 2002) are wedded to the myth that trade preferences bring substantial benefits to developing country exporters. If developing countries granted preferences to each other there would be better prospects, but persistence of the import-substitution strategy for developing countries makes such self-help policies unlikely.

AGRICULTURE IS DIFFERENT

When the GATT was drafted in 1947, special attention was given to protecting US domestic agricultural policies in Article XI. The US Congress was sensitive to the interests of the farm states. Nevertheless, the US Administration soon violated the provisions of the article, when restrictions were placed on dairy imports without domestic restraints on dairy production, as required by Article XI. In 1955, therefore, the United States was granted a waiver that was so general that agriculture was effectively exempt from GATT rules (Dam, 1970: ch. 15). This was a blow to the GATT that has since been exploited by all agricultural protectionists, and has become the major problem in GATT negotiating rounds.

One of the arguments made for developing countries to receive preferences is that many OECD countries retain high levels of protection in activities where developing countries hold comparative and competitive advantages. Two examples are agriculture and TCF industries. However, in a second-best world, where preferences (distortions) already exist, there is no certainty that introducing more preferences would bring any improvement (gain) for developing countries (Lipsey and Lancaster, 1956). In the realm of trade negotiations, any additional complications are likely to disrupt procedures and delay agreements. Certainly, the best solution to present discrimination against developing countries would be to liberalize all trade in agricultural products and to remove the many non-tariff barriers and domestic supports that distort production and trade in agriculture.

'It would be difficult to conclude that the GATT's record in temperate agricultural commodities is other than one of failure' (Dam, 1970). Even 35 years later, there is no reason to change that verdict. Effective protection in agriculture was higher than any other sector then and it has hardly fallen since. The acclaimed progress in the Uruguay Round came to nought. Tariffication was the process adopted to overcome quantitative restrictions, but many of the replacement supports introduced have proved to be just as restrictive as previous regimes. 'The overall level of support for agriculture as represented by the PSE [Producer Support Estimate] for OECD countries has fallen slightly between 1986 and 2003. . . . In 2003, over 30 per cent of gross returns to farmers in OECD countries came from transfers from consumers and taxpayers' (Stoeckel and Reeves, 2005). As on many earlier occasions, disputes over agricultural policies poisoned negotiations at the WTO ministerial meeting in Cancun in September 2003.

The GATT outlawed non-tariff protection, yet the most important trade negotiations affecting agriculture have always violated this requirement, and new imposts or subsidies are introduced without apology. The Uruguay Round Agreement on Agriculture, which several times threatened to stall the negotiations, included the following commitments:

- to establish a basis for initiating a process of reform in agriculture;
- to establish a fair and market-oriented agricultural trading system and reform process . . . [with] commitments on support and protection, through the establishment . . . of effective GATT rules and disciplines;
- a long-term objective is to provide for substantial progressive reductions in agricultural support and protection sustained over an agreed period;
- committed to achieving specific binding commitments in . . .: market access, domestic support, export competition, and . . . an agreement on sanitary and phyto-sanitary issues; and
- developed country members would take into account the particular needs and conditions of developing countries. (WTO, 1994)

These commitments were built into a last-minute accord between the EU and the United States. This has some irony because the two largest agricultural exporters have highly distorted trade and production regimes for agriculture. The details of the commitments have little relevance today because the major players have increased production subsidies and export subsidies (OECD, 2003). In addition, the EU has specific barriers against GM crops and hormone-treated beef. There has been little sign of willingness to liberalize, though both have provided import preferences to associated countries – for example, EU preferences to ACP countries and US preferences for CAFTA.

On tropical agriculture, many restrictions and taxes remain in place, even though such imports seldom compete with OECD produce. Processing industries in EU countries also receive high effective rates of protection (e.g., processing nuts, coffee, etc.). Administrative and quarantine regulations are used as arbitrary impediments to tropical imports, even under import preferences (Otsuki, Wilson and Sewadeh, 2001).

Quarantine regulations have been used in many OECD countries to impede trade. The Sanitary and Phyto-sanitary Agreement (SPS) included in the

Uruguay Round agreement allows governments to act against imports if they create a health risk to human, animal or plant life. The aim of this agreement is to ensure that the effects on trade of SPS actions are kept to a minimum. In particular, any measures introduced should be based on scientific evidence. Some high-profile disputes have arisen (e.g., US–EU beef hormone case), but definitive scientific findings take time and resources, and an error in risk assessment can result in an industry or species being wiped out.

It is difficult to explain or understand the evolution of agricultural protectionism over the past 50 years. Food shortages in the 1940s promoted concern for food safety in Europe, but that was long ago and massive agricultural surpluses have blown out subsidy costs since the 1950s. In the US, the voting power of the agricultural states has caused politicians to be sensitive to farmers' demands. None of this makes economic or financial sense when it comes to the massive transfers created between consumers/tax-payers and the farming/landowner classes. Self-sufficiency might have played a role in the early days of the GATT, when agricultural employment in several European countries was 5–7 per cent of the workforce. As time passed, however, mechanization and labour drift to urban jobs have reduced these numbers. With strong price supports, however, landowners have accessed large rents and returns on property. Thus, a strong vested interest, with political influence, entered the argument in favour of protected agriculture and promoted public support for agriculture. Once the European countries established the Common Agricultural Policy (CAP) in 1962, which combined the French price supports with Germany's high prices, the game was up. The aims of the CAP (Treaty of Rome, 1957: Article 39) were:

- to increase agricultural productivity;
- to ensure a 'fair' standard of living for agricultural workers;
- to stabilize markets and guarantee regular supplies; and
- to maintain reasonable prices to consumers.

The first three aims were met along with self-sufficiency in temperate agriculture output. EU farm support prices are higher than world prices, however, and consumers pay for self-sufficiency in prices and taxes, and have done for over 40 years. The guaranteed prices paid for produce have been a constant stimulus to over-production, leading to rising stocks (dairy products, cereals, sugar, etc.) and high storage costs. This led to dumping on world markets, supported by export subsidies (diplomatically referred to as restitution payments), which undercut traditional agricultural exporters such as Brazil, Thailand, Australia and Canada.

Despite repeated efforts to contain CAP outlays, little has really changed, as the EU Council repeatedly finds excuses to treat agriculture differently from other industries. The latest excuses include 'multi-functionality' (which incorporates environmental issues, care for the countryside, recreational access, etc.), anti-GM crusades and the precautionary principle.

The other major offender on agricultural over-protection is the United States, where the farm states carry great weight in elections, and generally in the Congress. Deficiency payments are used to supplement farm incomes, which protects them from competition. In addition, the US has an Export Enhancement Program providing subsidies to wheat exporters, restrictions on meat imports, and support schemes for cotton, peanuts, rice, etc., the latter particularly affect developing countries' exporters. Agricultural protectionism became embedded in US trade policy after 1947, and US governments must bear the blame for its spread because they gave the lead for others to follow.

The US and the EU countries are not alone in pursuing agricultural protection. Several small European countries provide even more generous support and protection for agriculture than the EU: Switzerland, Norway and Iceland. In addition, Japan and Korea have nationalistic programmes for rice. The traditional emotions over 'working the soil' still have far-reaching consequences for agricultural protection and attract support from the community at large. Public support in Europe for 'multi-functionality' with its metaphysical attractions is extraordinary. According to the OECD definition, multi-functionality refers to service externalities associated with agricultural production – that is, it relates to joint products or public goods, such that markets function poorly or are non-existent. The marketing of multi-functionality by European politicians and the green parties demonstrates the power of the media to confuse people with propaganda and non-monetary values (see Chapter 8).

FROM GATT INTERIM TO WORLD TRADE ORGANIZATION

Since the Kennedy Round negotiations began in 1963 the leading players in the GATT have attempted to extend this government-to-government agreement into a genuine international organization to manage international trade relations. It was evident in 1963 that most of the easy dismantling of trade barriers had been achieved and further liberalization posed unfamiliar problems. In addition, some developing countries were showing an interest in the GATT after the progress made at UNCTAD in 1964. They had been suspicious about the GATT as 'a rich man's club' when the ITO Havana Charter was not implemented. The economic progress achieved by 1964 attracted their attention and the adoption of GATT Part IV with special and differential treatment for developing countries provided new opportunities.

In terms of what had gone before, the Kennedy Round (1963–67) results were substantial: average industrial tariffs were reduced by 35 per cent, with across-the-board negotiations in many sectors; some discussion of agricultural trade took place for the first time, and a review of anti-dumping actions (which touched on other contingency protection) led to an Anti-dumping Code. At the end of the Kennedy Round the average tariff on OECD industrial products was 7.7 per cent.

The Tokyo Round negotiations opened in quite inauspicious international economic circumstances, with exchange rate uncertainty, rising inflation, an oil crisis and developing countries pursuing a new international economic order to promote economic development. In these circumstances, the Tokyo Round completed in 1979 was also an apparent success: average industrial tariff reductions were over 30 per cent, with average tariffs reduced to 4.7 per cent. Once again, despite extensive discussions, nothing was achieved on agricultural trade. Further progress was made on particular non-tariff measures: a Customs Valuation Code (Article VII); a revision of the Anti-dumping Code (Article VI); a Code on Subsidies and Countervailing Duties (Articles VI, XVI and XXIII). These codes applied only to signatories and did not become part of the GATT text. An important step, however, was the Decision on Differential and More Favourable Treatment and Reciprocity and Fuller Participation of Developing Countries, which replaced the Enabling Clause to allow continuation of trade preferences in favour of developing countries. Several new non-tariff issues were raised in the Tokyo Round negotiations, but the texts of the codes contained contradictions and obfuscations that left scope for abuses, even among the limited number of signatories. No agreement could be reached on safeguards. It was decided that discussions should continue, but no progress was made.

By granting differential and more favourable treatment to developing countries, the GATT contracting parties allowed new members to ignore the fundamental rules of the institution. In turn, the OECD countries regarded this as an excuse to take their own liberties with the rules. GATT disciplines were weakened by extending preferences under the guise of regional trade agreements (Article XXIV), by abusing 'unfair' trade remedies (safeguards and escape clauses), adopting new quantitative restrictions (VERs), etc. This was a high price to pay for attracting new contracting parties, especially when they were excused any commitments and when developing countries' benefits from the GSP were small. The GATT system was under siege throughout the 1970s and 1980s.

The new forms of protection adopted in the 1970s followed from the failure of trade-adjustment mechanisms in OECD economies. Shifts in comparative advantage required economies to reallocate resources. This occurred through product markets and factor markets over time. Incomes were redistributed and political pressures against change were created. As low cost manufactures from developing countries increased their penetration of OECD markets, and global inflation and recession spread, the rate of economic adjustment was inadequate and new protectionism became an easy response. This meant supporting domestic industries at the expense of foreign exporters – the latter having no votes in the importing countries!

The economic difficulties of the 1970s spilt over into the international debt crisis and deflationary policies in the 1980s. An attempt to open a new round of trade negotiations in 1982 failed. There was little enthusiasm among contracting parties, especially because agriculture was not included. It was not until September 1986 that the new round was initiated.

After the Punta del Este meeting of GATT ministers in September 1986 set down objectives for the negotiations:

- to halt and reverse protectionism and to remove distortions to trade;
- to preserve the basic principles and to further the objectives of the GATT; and
- to develop a more open, viable and durable multilateral trading system to promote growth and development.

The agenda comprised all the unfinished business from the Tokyo and Kennedy Rounds: improving safeguards and escape clauses and making dispute settlement procedures more effective; re-incorporating agriculture and textiles and clothing into the negotiations; liberalizing trade in services; links between trade and investment issues, competition policy and the environment; and strengthening intellectual property protection.

For the first time, many developing countries participated in these GATT negotiations. They helped to formulate new rules for the multilateral trading system and made important market access offers in the process of tariff bargaining for trade in manufactures, as well as in services and agriculture. When the negotiating agenda was drawn up at Punte del Este, GATT had 80 contracting parties. When the Final Act was signed in Marrakesh, the WTO had over 100 members. Now WTO membership is approaching 150 states.

Yet, the most far-reaching change was not on the Uruguay Round agenda. It evolved as the complex negotiations progressed over seven years. It became clear that the interim GATT, with its Protocol of Provisional Application, was not strong enough to manage the complex of commitments that would come out of the negotiations. The Marrakesh Declaration contained the Final Act of the negotiations with 30 legal agreements and a large number of supplementary decisions and declarations, including the revised General Agreement on Tariffs and Trade 1994 (GATT Secretariat, 1994).

These complex agreements, decisions and declarations were subject to a single-undertaking by signatories. This was a much stronger commitment than in earlier GATT negotiations, where extending or clarifying Articles was achieved using codes, which applied only to their signatories, not all contracting parties. (Annex 4 to the Marrakesh Agreement was an exception to the single-undertaking; it contained four plurilateral agreements, only one of which is still current.)

The Uruguay Round negotiations were quite different in scope and commitment from earlier rounds. The agreements were more comprehensive and included programmes for agriculture and TCF. Special measures were introduced to encourage developing countries to participate. Some agreements link trade to domestic economic policies, such as competition policy, investment rules and service sectors. There were high hopes for the WTO. Perhaps that enthusiasm was overdone and expectations were too high. Of the four WTO ministerial council meetings to consider a new round of trade negotiations (1999 Seattle, 2001 Doha, 2003 Cancun, 2005 Hong Kong) only the Doha meeting, in the shadow of the 9/11 terrorist attack on the New York Trade Center, made any progress. The scope of the negotiating agenda and the dominant numbers of developing countries participating make agreement difficult to achieve. Moreover, the high profile of the WTO makes it a target for NGOs and other malcontents, who seek to turn the negotiating agenda into a catalogue of complaints about everything.

REFERENCES

Bhagwati, J. (1988), *Protectionism*, Cambridge, MA: MIT Press.
Bhagwati, J. and D.A. Irwin (1987), 'The return of the reciprocitarians; US trade policy today', *The World Economy*, **10**(2), 109–30.
Clements, K.W. and L.A. Sjaastad (1984), 'How protection taxes exporters', Trade Policy Research Centre Thames essay no. 39, London.
Curzon, G. (1965) *Multilateral Commercial Policy*, London: Michael Joseph.
Dam, K.W. (1970), *The GATT: Law and International Economic Organization*, Chicago: University of Chicago Press.
GATT Secretariat (1994), *The Results of the Uruguay Round of Multilateral Trade Negotiations: The Legal Texts*.
Haberler Report (1958), 'Trends in international trade', report by panel of experts to the GATT Secretariat, Geneva.
Irwin, D. A. (1996), *Against the Tide*, Princeton, NJ: Princeton University Press.
Jackson, J. (1990), *The World Trading System*, Cambridge, MA and London: MIT Press.
Kasper, W. and M.E. Streit (1998), *Institutional Economics*, Cheltenham, UK and Lyme, USA: Edward Elgar.
Krueger, A.O. (1995), *American Trade Policy: A Tragedy in the Making*, Washington, DC: American Enterprise Institute.
Lipsey, R. and K. Lancaster (1956), 'The general theory of "second best" ', *Review of Economic Studies*, **24**, 11–32.

Martin, W. and A. Winters (1995), *The Uruguay Round: Widening and Deepening the World Trading System*, Washington, DC: World Bank.

OECD (2003), *Agricultural Policies in OECD Countries*, Paris: OECD Secretariat.

OECD (2005), *Trade and Structural Adjustment*, MCM brochure.

Otsuki, T., J.S. Wilson and M. Sewadeh (2001), 'Measuring the effect of food safety on African exports to Europe', Ch. 15 in K. Anderson, C. McRae and D. Wilson (eds), *The Economics of Quarantine and the SPS Agreement*, Adelaide: Centre for International Economic Studies.

Oxfam (2002), *Rigged Rules and Double Standards, Making Trade Fair*, London: Oxfam International.

Preeg, E.H. (1970), *Traders and Diplomats*, Washington, DC: The Brookings Institution.

Robertson, D. (1992), 'GATT rules for emergency protection', TPRC Thames essay no 57, London: Harvester Wheatsheaf.

Stoeckel, A. and G. Reeves (2005), *Agricultural Trade Policy Made Easy*, Canberra: CIE and RIRDC.

Treaty Establishing the European Economic Community (Treaty of Rome) (1957), March, London: HMSO (1967).

UNCTAD (1964), Final Act, New York: United Nations.

4. Trade and development

Social and economic development was not afforded much attention during the post-World War II discussions to establish international economic institutions. This may be regarded as a disgrace by today's politically correct generation, which finds it difficult to understand that priorities and standards have changed over time. Fortunately, institutions have adapted to circumstances over time and steps have been taken to promote economic development. Even so, development issues remain much more complex and more difficult to resolve than most development lobbyists, and many governments, seem willing to admit. The solution is not simply to provide economic assistance to poor countries – financial aid (or debt forgiveness), unrequited supplies of food and medical supplies, trade preferences for developing countries' exports or to allow their protection against imports to be raised, etc. These measures are not only temporary; some impede economic development.

Blaming OECD governments or populations for not doing more may be politically satisfying for development lobbies and human rights' groups, but limited resources still have to be allocated among competing demands. The most significant obstacles to economic development in the poorest countries are found in their weak domestic organization, their inadequate government services and their political corruption. Yet many of these governments refuse outside assistance (other than money) and claim that national sovereignty must be protected. It is easier to blame OECD trade policies, inadequate financial aid, undemocratic processes in international agencies, exploitative multinational corporations or inadequate foreign investment, whatever is the fashionable excuse at the time. NGOs give little attention to shortcomings in developing countries' policies.

The economics of development has been a popular area of economic research for the past 50 years, but it has been complicated by its interfaces with social development and political prejudice. Recently, the economics of development has become entangled with globalization issues, such as social justice, human rights and environmental protection. Most NGOs and many UN officials regard market integration as an impediment to economic development (UNDP, 1999).

ECONOMICS OF DEVELOPMENT

Economic growth has always been at the centre of economics. Even before Adam Smith's *Wealth of Nations,* the mercantilists focussed on increasing the national wealth as a source of tax revenue and as a means of strengthening military power. With the acceptance of neo-classical economics as the nineteenth century progressed, international trade became regarded as 'the engine of growth' for the countries of new settlement (described as 'the periphery' by Nurkse, 1962). Economic growth depends primarily on domestic resources and enterprise, but trade provides an extension to growth by converting domestic resources into imports of scarce goods and services, indirectly and on more favourable terms than domestic exchange provides. The Brundtland Report (1987; see Chapter 1 above) proposed 'sustainable development' as the politically correct term, which has complicated the politics of economic development.)

The process of development to raise living standards in poor countries did not become a focus of economic research until after 1945. As colonies achieved or were granted independence, it became clear that converting a traditional subsistence-based, agrarian system into a modern economy with growing income per capita required more than the stimulus of international trade. Indian independence activists tried to raise this issue in the 1930s, but at that time Western economics were preoccupied with their own economic problems. As self-government spread among former colonies, however, it became evident that independence alone was not a solution.

In the early post-war years, development economics focussed on structural inflexibility and trade pessimism, both inherited from the 1930s. The only way to achieve change from a traditional agriculture (or resources) -based economy was for newly independent governments to plan change; in particular to plan investment that would employ reserves of surplus labour. The problem was how to mobilize savings in poor countries, where taxation was difficult. The alternative was development aid. In addition, convinced export pessimism meant import-substitution had to be the target for investment. Above all, the assumption was that planned investment would be more productive than market-determined investment to improve living standards. Industrialization became the indicator of development.

Unexpectedly, expanding international trade became the driving force of economic development in the 1950s and 1960s. Trade pessimism was inappropriate. Commodity prices fluctuated but were not depressed as had been anticipated. Other assumptions in the 'structural' model that prevailed in the 1950s were equally inappropriate. Agriculture dominates many developing countries' economies even now and this was even more true 50 years ago. Farm output is flexible. Crops can be changed quickly – for example, if opportunities arise for cash crops or new techniques make higher yields possible. (It takes longer if tree crops are involved because they take time to mature.) Moreover, poor people are more mobile than those on higher incomes. They are untrammelled by possessions or capital assets (Little, 1982). Migration within and between developing countries has been recognized for a long time – labour migration was important to economic development in the nineteenth century.

Since most developing countries' governments showed little sensitivity towards welfare of their peoples, and they were preoccupied with industrialization or their own ambitions, many of these opportunities were missed in the 1950s and 1960s. Farmers were taxed and discriminated against in efforts to spread industrialization. Little scope was left for market-based development as industrialization and grand projects were pursued to enhance the image of governments. Yet, fundamental changes to social and political structures are necessary before national markets can evolve. Social change to establish property rights and individual freedoms, and decisions to promote political stability and effective government administration are necessary. It requires the transition of traditional social systems to allow mobility of resources, especially labour and capital, to promote productive efficiency. Time has shown that this transition is not easily achieved. Many traditional social structures are difficult to adapt and they absorb scarce resources that are required for economic transformation.

It was widely accepted that industrialization was the route to independence and nationhood. Faith in the neo-classical market economy had weakened everywhere after the turbulent economic experience of the 1930s and the disruption of World War II. After wartime mobilization and planning, direct government control was regarded as necessary to alleviate poverty, to redistribute assets and to regulate returns to different types of labour and capital, using price and wage controls. The composition of production and imports had to be directed to meet basic needs. The ascendency of Keynesian macroeconomic analysis as part of wartime planning put the analytical emphasis on aggregates, such as savings, the external trade balance and programmed outputs from major sectors, such as heavy industry and agriculture. The focal point of the new economics of development was the activity level, rather than relative prices of goods, services and factors of production. The emphasis on aggregates and programming overcame any suggestion of liberal trade regimes that depended on the price mechanism.

Gathering the information to design effective public policies required experience and appropriate resources. It soon became apparent that the risk of bureaucratic failure was no less than the risk of market failure. The best that could be hoped for in either case was a second-best solution (Lipsey and Lancaster, 1956). The enthusiasm for the success of Soviet planning, which had allowed Russia to rearm to defeat Germany in 1943–45, meant such theoretical criticism went unsaid. It remains as difficult today to persuade many people that government failures can be more dangerous than market failures.

Market failure is blamed on imperfect information and incomplete markets, which introduces a new role for government, to facilitate efficient markets. Stiglitz argues that for markets to flourish, governments must be deeply involved in creating the conditions necessary for markets to thrive (Snowdon, 2001). Similarly, Rodrik (2000b) argues that successful development requires markets underpinned by solid public institutions. While this is true, the fundamental problems in many developing economies are corrupt governments and ineffective public institutions. Correcting these failings is difficult because many of these governments reject any external interference in domestic affairs. In these circumstances, it seems unwise to reject market forces, while encouraging ineffective governments to take control. It becomes an exercise in 'nth best'.

Traditionally, economic growth was regarded as an outcome of prices determined in competitive markets, which generated trade among economies according to comparative advantage. This neo-classical model of economic behaviour was rejected because changes in relative prices were regarded as ineffective drivers of development. Instead, development economics focussed on growth and planning to raise income levels. The price mechanism was rejected because low incomes in developing countries allowed little flexibility to substitute between expenditures in response to price changes, and because fixed input proportions precluded substitution in production processes. These 'inelastic' conditions relegated market responses and made output the focus of policy. If the distribution of output/income was not deemed to be socially desirable within economic plans, government intervention was expected to achieve a desirable pattern.

This casual dismissal of neo-classical economic theory was justified by experiences during the 1930s' recession, scarcities during World War II and acceptance of simple-minded Keynesian macroeconomics. These experiences cast long shadows over global economic prospects in 1945. In the 1930s, new forms of trade protection were devised: quantitative import restrictions, bilateral trade agreements and foreign exchange rationing. All these were less easily overcome than traditional tariffs, which could be handled with competitive prices. These restrictions and declining economic activity reduced world trade volumes and commodity prices collapsed in the 1930s. These experiences caused post-war pessimism about export prospects for developing economies and cast doubts on traditional gains from trade arguments. Instead, developing countries' governments turned towards import-substitution strategies, using trade controls, licensing, etc.

Development was equated with planned industrialization. Governments put their faith in bureaucrats and their planning skills, though they, too, had to work within standard economic models. Many developing economies rejected an economic future dependent on primary commodity exports, where prices fluctuated according to global output levels. Any slowdown in economic growth in developed economies promised falling commodity prices, even before a cyclical decline. Equally, new investments in crops or mineral exploitation that increased supplies on the commodities markets would also result in falling prices, and even falling incomes. Developing countries' representatives argued that their terms of trade were in secular decline because uncoordinated production of primary commodities created over-supply, while for technical reasons demand would rise more slowly than world output. In addition, technical progress produced synthetic substitutes for many primary commodities, as well as reducing their content in manufactures. Because the income-elasticity of demand for commodities was low, the share of total expenditure spent on primary commodities declined over time. Technical progress in temperate agricultural production in developed countries increased their productivity, while protectionist policies reduced Third Countries' access.

These arguments were summarized in the argument that developing countries' terms of trade were in long-term decline. This had been true in the depressed 1930s, but empirical evidence in the post-1945 world economy showed a succession of short-term price fluctuations in primary commodity prices, with no clear long-term trend (Haberler Report, 1958). Even so, this argument was used to substantiate the case for a new trade policy for developing countries (Prebisch, 1964). It was employed to propose transfers from OECD economies to developing countries' governments, to compensate for deterioration in the terms of trade of primary commodity exporters, and as an argument to introduce international commodity agreements to stabilize prices. (Empirical evidence for this terms of trade decline was based on commodity price estimates drawn from British trade data from the nineteenth century.)

The second component of the new trade strategy was to increase developing countries' export earnings from their industrialization programmes. Because most developing countries have small domestic markets, manufactured exports are essential to achieve efficient levels of output. Large domestic markets and exports to open industrial markets, largely Britain, had fostered import-substitution development strategies by Germany and the United States in the nineteenth century (Irwin, 1996). In the 1960s, circumstances were different. Industrialization in Latin America in particular, occurred in watertight compartments, which were not focussed on export possibilities. That produced a policy bias of increasing protectionism in small, high cost domestic markets (Johnson, 1967). It was claimed then, as it is today, that the solution would be to reduce trade barriers against developing countries' exports to OECD economies – that is, to provide preferential access for developing countries' exports. A second proposal was for developing countries to form regional preferential agreements (see Chapter 6). Forty years later the Latin American regional trade agreements are still struggling.

Both the proposal to stabilize primary commodity prices on global markets and the recommendation of unilateral preferences for the manufactured exports from developing countries required compromising OECD trade policies to favour developing countries.

The Prebisch proposals on development embodied in the UNCTAD recommendations to facilitate economic development concentrated on altering the trading system to promote developing countries' interests. The first step in the post-1945 development economics had been to reject competitive markets and the benefits of international trade in favour of economic planning. Import-substitution strategies were adopted, which amounted to the transfer of resources from domestic consumers (required to pay tariff-inflated prices) to the new import-competing producers, with any trade deficit to be financed with external financial assistance to keep the economy afloat. When domestic markets proved to be too small to achieve efficient levels of production, preferential access to OECD markets was demanded to take up extra capacity. This implied transfers of resources from consumers and producers in developed economies to inefficient producers in developing economies. For this contrived system to work, the infant industries chosen in the first instance had to be healthy enough to survive, which required them to represent comparative advantage of those countries. If they did not, then the whole structure of assistance and income transfers would be wasted. It is a fundamental flaw in many arguments for development that existing planned industries, chosen by officials without reference to market efficiency, can succeed by being granted preferential trade access. Since they exist only because of protection from competition, is that likely?

If finance of development-created trade deficits was not forthcoming, only two alternatives remained. The first was to shift production into labour-intensive manufacturers where export prospects were good. This approach was behind the extraordinary success of the East Asian Tigers, which began in the 1960s. By specializing to exploit their comparative advantage in industries using low cost and abundant labour, they achieved strong income growth. The focus on exports imposed discipline on export industries and provided discipline elsewhere in the economy. With astute investment of surpluses (tax revenues) in education and infrastructure and careful manipulation of exchange rates, these economies achieved spectacular growth and rapid progress up the technology ladder (World Bank, 1993).

The second was to find financial aid to allow continuous trade deficits as essential capital equipment, manufactured inputs, raw materials and food for the industrialization process were imported. Long-term development aid needed to be supplemented with compensatory finance to meet fluctuating current account imbalances. Because of growing difficulties servicing the burden of debt as it accumulated, this additional financial assistance called for grants, as well as consolidation of outstanding debt and unpaid debt-servicing from time to time.

The thrust of the UNCTAD programme was essentially a massive transfer of resources to developing countries, with minimum conditions. Newly achieved independence had to be protected at all costs, which required financial support from developed countries. The sensitivity of most developing countries' governments to outside advice provides protection to powerful domestic elites in many of the worst-performing economies.

TRADE POLICY AND DEVELOPMENT

In 1947, when the GATT was being drawn up, the major players were concerned to protect their interests while restoring stability to the international trading system. The United States' interest was a non-discriminatory trading system consistent with its Reciprocal Trade Agreements Act, with no special treatment for developing countries. Many Western European countries had colonial links and they wished to protect their trade preferences and other interests. Independent developing countries had revealed their interests in the ITO negotiations by arguing for real resource transfers to assist their development, infant industry protection plus trade preferences in developed countries' markets, and exemptions from trade rules and reciprocity. The intention was to promote administrative protection against market forces for their development, including commodity cartels. All these requirements had been written into the ITO Charter.

Since financial assistance to developing countries was not practicable in the immediate post-war years, with so much to be done in post-war devastation, it was accepted that something had to be done within the trading system to accommodate developing countries' interests. The GATT included provisions to allow infant industry protection (Article XVIII) and balance-of-payments exceptions (Article XII). Stronger demands for tariff preferences and quantitative import restrictions were not acceptable to the US Administration, which was beholden to Congress. However, political pressures had already weakened the General Agreement. The principles combined mercantilism and reciprocity in the process of liberalization. Reluctance to reduce tariffs and to encourage imports was overcome by reciprocal reductions by trade partners (tariff bargaining) and the principle of most-favoured nation treatment (MFN). The idea of balancing tariff reductions denied the theory of comparative advantage, but it provided a political argument to satisfy domestic objectors.

This framework created an opening to exempt developing countries from the tariff bargaining process, while granting them MFN treatment. At each GATT negotiating round, developing countries gained progressively easier access to developed economies as tariffs were reduced and developing countries were not required to reciprocate. (New signatories to the GATT could choose to be classified as a developing country member, subject to MFN tariffs without any reciprocity.) Unfortunately, this discriminatory treatment induced some major players to raise trade barriers on agriculture and labour-intensive manufactures, the sectors where developing countries had comparative advantages. There is no evidence that this was retaliation, but OECD economies, too, were subjected to domestic demands for protection. This was referred to as 'a mutually disadvantageous stand-off' (Hudec, 1987).

Initially, the developing countries were concerned only with what they could get from developed countries, not with how GATT could help them to achieve their own economic development. When developing countries began to collaborate over their own trade policies, their attention turned to special and differential treatment, non-reciprocity and preferential access to OECD markets. The first target they achieved, with adoption of the UNCTAD proposal for a Generalized Scheme of Preferences in 1973. The OECD governments could not agree on a unified list of imports that should be subject to preferences. So each OECD government prepared a schedule of import preferences (GSP). The legal basis for GSP treatment was formalized when the GATT Enabling Clause was included in the final act of the Tokyo Round (1973–79).

This concession providing special and differential treatment to developing countries, however, was achieved at a price. Many OECD countries were under pressure at home to increase protection of industries facing increasing competition from cheap imports, in particular, textiles, clothing and footwear (TCF). Unwilling to apply non-discriminatory safeguards (GATT Article XIX), which would have disrupted trade relations with OECD partners, they adopted 'voluntary' export restraints (VERs) against the disrupting exporters located in developing economies. These export restraints were not legal under the GATT, but because they were negotiated between an exporter and an importer, and did not involve governments, there was no case for complaint to the GATT. In fact, exporters (or their governments) received a 'rent component' in the price received (Robertson, 1992). This practice of picking off competitive suppliers from developing economies was evidently discriminatory and demands for review of the GATT safeguards clause was met in the Uruguay Round.

In the years leading up to the Uruguay Round negotiations, discrimination had become the hallmark of the trading system. Questions were raised about the commitment of OECD governments to the rules-based system. Developing countries had little obligation to GATT for their trade policies. They received discrimination in their favour for market access, but at the price of discrimination against their main exports in OECD markets. The rules were honoured more in the breach than in the reality. The US authorities had accepted this as the price of a universal system, while most Europeans favoured equivocation rather than tight discipline to facilitate their ubiquitous systems of trade preferences.

Once Part IV had been incorporated into the GATT in 1964, developing countries became wedded to non-reciprocity. They were not expected to make commitments that were incompatible with their policies on economic development. Non-reciprocity had been described and politically justified (Hudec, 1987).

From the perspective of developing countries, special and differential treatment prevents them from enjoying the gains from trade liberalization, because the major benefits from liberal trade come from imports. Hence, unilateral liberalization provides an optimum strategy. Given external trade opportunities, specialization in production according to comparative advantage and trading with other countries, increases the total of goods available for consumption (and investment). The assumptions behind this are that the prices are not distorted by monopoly power in any market and external trade is not subject to border interference. Many studies have shown that most of the gains from trade liberalization to an economy come from reductions in its own import barriers (Bhagwati, 1988; Krugman, 1993). This lesson seems to be lost on many developing countries' governments and on development NGOs. They base their case for trade assistance on preferential access to OECD markets for developing countries' exports, while their protection against imports remains high. Oxfam claims 'import liberalisation in developing countries has often intensified poverty and inequality' (Oxfam, 2002: p. 10). Such outcomes result from bad government, inadequate domestic competition and unreasonable faith in the import-substitution model for development. Even casual observation of the success of emerging economies shows the approach of the Trade Justice movement is doomed to fail.

Granting a trade preference to a developing country changes trade and production of the economy receiving the preference, the country granting the preference and Third Countries. The preferences lead to trade diversion in favour of the preference-receiving developing country, with higher cost imports replacing non-preferred suppliers. The preferences benefit consumers in the protected market, because these imports are cheaper than the high cost protected domestic production they displace. Efficient Third Country suppliers also lose market share to the preferred supplier. The best outcome would be multilateral non-discriminatory trade liberalization, because all countries would gain. Trade preferences distract all countries from the efficiency of free trade (Stoeckel and Borrell, 2001).

Trade preferences are misleading. They combine developing countries' import-substitution strategies with trade preferences in OECD countries. This is evident in the EU's 'Everything But Arms' (EBA) initiative, which extends unrequited duty-free and quota-free preferences to 'least' developed countries. This approach grants new export opportunities to 48 least developed ACP countries, at the expense of non-preferred suppliers. Any reductions in EU protection from multilateral negotiations, however, would reduce the preferences and allow more competitive exporters to displace suppliers using the EBA scheme in EU markets. The countries covered by the EBA initiative are already complaining about the consequences if the EU reduces its protection in the Doha Round. This brings the recipients of EBA preferences and other developing countries, especially G20, into conflict in negotiations to reduce OECD countries' protection according to the Doha Development Agenda. It contradicts the development NGOs' pursuit of trade preferences as the instrument to promote developing countries' trade and development.

The emerging economies of East Asia have shown that unilateral liberalization and acceptance of reciprocity in terms of domestic policies is more effective and it has brought rapid economic growth (Krueger, 1990). Developing countries were forced to take on more commitments in the Uruguay Round by virtue of the single undertaking, which required acceptance of the entire package. New obligations included new market access agreements on agriculture and new rules on technical barriers to trade, and the agreement on services. This development encouraged 'emerging economies' in Asia and Latin America (G20) to seek new opportunities rather than differential and more favourable treatment from GATT/WTO rules.

Least developed countries, especially in SSA, are still seeking special and differential treatment, encouraged by development NGOs, which still argue that globalization and OECD policies have worsened poverty in developing countries. (It would be interesting to see the evidence to support this claim.) This argument is familiar in the NGO community because of the widespread belief that the global economy has a fixed size. Hence, the more taken by developed economies, the less remains for developing countries. Yet, economics teaches that more efficient allocations of scarce economic resources (which can be augmented by open trade), the larger the overall size of the global economy, including the share available to developing countries. NGOs seem preoccupied with the gap between rich and poor, which they blame on developed countries' policies, when in fact they should be concerned about policies to raise growth in developing countries' economies, which depends on domestic economic policies (Hart and Dymond, 2003).

The validity of this advice has been demonstrated by the different growth performances that developing countries have achieved in the past 50 years. Sustained growth in some East Asian economies, now being emulated in India and China, and recovery in several SSA countries, such as Zambia and Angola, indicate that economies have power over their own destinies. The GATT/WTO system provides assurance that developing countries face a relatively open trading system, and leaves them to seek their own development. The lack of growth in trade between developed and developing economies has less to do with remaining OECD protection than developing countries' inability to produce exports because of their own high levels of protection; 'a tariff is a tax on exports' (Clements and Sjaastad, 1984). A post-Uruguay Round study by Finger and Winters (1998) showed there is a strong correlation between openness and economic performance. Applied tariff rates for OECD countries averaged 2.6 per cent, while in low and middle income countries it was 13.3 per cent (bound rates were roughly twice these levels).

The Uruguay Round agreements on contingency protection (safeguards, countervailing duties and anti-dumping) reduced access to most trade remedies, except under specific conditions. However, a new problem is on the horizon with the rapid growth in China's exports and the completion of the transition phase of the agreement on textiles and clothing at the beginning of 2005. Both the US and EU authorities introduced new forms of protection (safeguards) early in 2005. The Chinese authorities had already taken steps to re-regulate TCF exports. One interesting development is that retailers in the US and the EU are strongly opposed to new restrictions on imports from China because their managements had already taken account of the completion of the ATC in their planning. Competition among developing countries' suppliers to OECD markets will cause adjustments, while it should benefit consumers in OECD countries.

After more than 40 years, trade policy remains one of the main areas of controversy in the development debate. The import-substitution strategy has faded with time, because of the high-profile successes of export-led growth in Asia and the fall from grace of economic planning. Nevertheless, demands for preferential access to OECD markets for developing countries' exports of labour-intensive manufactures and agricultural produce have intensified. On the other hand, OECD governments face yet more lobbying to protect domestic jobs from globalization, which includes low cost labour services used in call centres and computer programming. Trade policy is at the centre of the anti-globalization attacks by NGOs and on the development agendas of UN agencies. Both these and developing countries' governments participating in the preliminary negotiations for the Doha Development Round of WTO negotiations seem to be unaware that economic gains accrue to countries from their own trade liberalization (see above). After 20 years of import-substitution policies, comprehensive research completed in the 1970s demonstrated the chaos that existed in developing countries' trade policies (Krueger, 1980).

A major lesson of the past 50 years is that although developing countries have faced the same external trade circumstances, individually they have had quite different development experiences. This suggests that differences among countries are important, and for small economies (which means most developing countries) their own trade policies are crucial to their economic performance.

In the 1960s, the second-best aspects of policy choice, which had encouraged bureaucratic licence, were rationalized to show that trade protection was always well down the list of policy alternatives (Bhagwati and Ramaswami, 1963; Johnson, 1965). This analysis also undermined the infant-industry argument for protection. Predictably, the focus of attention shifted to preferential access to OECD markets for developing countries, made effective in GATT Part IV (1965) and UNCTAD's GSP (1973). The rewards from these strategies were not impressive (Baldwin and Murray, 1977; Langhammer and Sapir, 1987). The access to OECD economies has remained restricted even now for most exports of interest to developing countries. In addition, the differential and more favourable treatment of developing countries in GATT Part IV released them from the disciplines prescribed on import policies for contracting parties. For some reason, the benefits of trade liberalization and committed participation were regarded as costs to developing countries, despite the long-standing acceptance that free trade is beneficial. Waiving reciprocity seemed a simple and cheap way to draw developing countries into the GATT. However, as explained above, it contributed to undermining the multilateral system.

Casual observation of the media shows that trade policy continues to be an issue in the development debate. A bad trade policy can disrupt development, even if good policies are in place on education, health, infrastructure and macroeconomic management. Moreover, an interventionist trade policy encourages governments and officials to exploit rent-seeking in other areas of policy (Krueger, 1980). Getting trade policy right is a key step towards achieving steady growth and development. Unfortunately, developing countries have adopted a stance in the Doha Round that focusses on removing remaining OECD protection on agriculture and labour-intensive manufacturing, especially textiles and clothing. This brings G20 and G90 into direct conflict with domestic lobbies in OECD countries, which means that reductions in agricultural protection are likely to be small. Even so, food-importing developing countries unable to raise domestic food production will suffer because world food prices will rise as agricultural subsidies are reduced (Panagariya, 2003).

On the other hand, developing countries refuse to consider liberalizing their own protection, where experience shows that major efficiency gains may be achieved. Waiting for OECD economies to provide efficiency gains is an aggressive stance, but the poor need economic gains not 'victory' over OECD governments.

UNCTAD's CONTRIBUTION

The Secretariat established in 1964, after UNCTAD I, became the centre for developing country lobbyists. It became identified with a sympathetic view of trade intervention and criticism of market solutions. Any trade concession provided to developing countries was applauded, regardless of the consequences. One of the most detailed assessments of trade impediments was UNCTAD's compilation and categorizing of non-tariff barriers against developing countries' exports. This data-intensive research has been valuable but really adds little to the broad body of analysis of development problems. Greater focus on development problems in specific backward economies would be more constructive, but criticizing members of the developing countries' club was frowned on. Recent independent research has shown the frailties of domestic institutions and identified leadership in developing economies as crucial (Rodrik, 2000a; Meier and Stiglitz, 2001; Stiglitz, 1998).

Political elites in developing countries do not necessarily favour economic development and enfranchising the poor. Governments in poor countries receiving World Bank funding, especially in Africa, seldom improve the lot of their poor (Easterly, 2001). Yet the flows of resources continue on humanitarian grounds, regardless of government failures. So-called adjustment loans are run down, with no relief for the poor. Politically correct pressures in donor countries ensure that development funding continues, even though the target groups remain poor and debts outstanding rise – until it becomes time to forgive them. By sustaining the argument that slow development in poor countries is caused by OECD countries' inappropriate trade policies, UNCTAD is part of this cycle of transfers, which feeds corruption by elite groups behind the defence of self-government.

Another target of UNCTAD research has been transnational corporations, which have been the villains of the whole UN system for the past 30 years. In the 1970s, the output on this subject was one-sidedly consistent with government control of all economic development in developing countries. Even as access to funds on open capital markets increased, the need for foreign direct investment diminished in the view of UNCTAD staff. The outcome of excessive borrowing by governments and public enterprises in developing countries, of course, was the debt crisis of the 1980s. In the 1990s, as scepticism about the role of governments took hold, and faith in markets was restored, the benefits of the foreign direct investment packages were recognized grudgingly. Technology, management, access to overseas markets and labour training became accepted as valuable contributions to the development process.

Notwithstanding continuing criticisms of MNEs, many developing countries' governments now offer incentives to attract foreign direct investment. To ensure that benefits accrue to the host economy, they impose conditions to promote the use of national resources: local content rules, to reduce imported inputs and to ensure that local ancillary industries and labour are employed. Export performance requirements and trade balancing conditions are also applied to minimize foreign exchange costs.

When the Uruguay Round negotiations began in 1986, the United States proposed that investment measures that distort trade and affect foreign investment flows should be made subject to GATT Article I (non-discrimination) and GATT Article III (national treatment). While these proposals received some support, they were not looked on favourably by developing countries, which regarded investment matters as outside the GATT's mandate. Ultimately, these negotiations took place only on the narrowly defined subject of trade-related investment measures (TRIMs). Much more significant incentives and requirements, such as tax concessions, technology transfers, remittance restrictions, local equity rules, etc. remain available to most governments. In many ways, assessing the economic effects of foreign direct investment in developing countries is more complex than assessing the effects of import-substitution versus free trade. Many conflicting policy instruments apply to an investment and the manner in which these affect the economy differ from transactions at the border. Foreign investment rules remain on the international agenda. The EU and Japan agreed to remove them from the Doha Round agenda in the chaos of the final session at Cancun in September 2003, but they are still being pursued in working groups. The EU is reported to be considering introducing some of these conditions in its extended trade agreements (ETAs) with ACP countries.

An open trading regime has been strongly linked with development and growth (Bhagwati, 2004; Dollar and Kraay, 2004), but Rodriguez and Rodrik (2000) dispute this. They reject that trade liberalization is linked to economic growth and argue that 'import-substitution policies worked until the 1970s' borrowing orgy by developing countries'. This contradicts the work by Bhagwati and Krueger (1973). Instead, Rodrik (2000b) argues that so-called export-led growth in South-East Asia was probably investment-led. In other words, the importance of export growth was that it financed imports of capital equipment. Other recent studies have linked growth to technological innovation acquired from openness (Romer, 1993). The general conclusion seems to be that development policy should focus on domestic institutions and economic management. This is evident in the poor record of Sub-Saharan Africa.

At UNCTAD (2004), the secretariat showed a major change in direction. In his opening address, Rubens Ricupero (Secretary-General) urged developing countries to focus on 'the supply-side of their economies', to emphasize export development and to adopt policies to attract foreign direct investment. To cement the new approach, the conference in Sao Paulo adopted a new policy document that allowed work to continue on consensus-building, technical assistance and policy analysis, but with more emphasis on institutional reform. Evidently, this small change in direction displeased some of the development NGOs, which are still fighting old battles, such as depressed commodity prices and trade preferences for least developed countries.

Mr Ricupero was upbeat about the contributions that emerging economies were making to global economic activity. He described this as a new economic configuration where import demand in emerging economies (China, India, South-East Asia) is driving OECD growth. This structural evolution arouses apprehensions in some OECD countries concerned about job losses. Mr Ricupero also argued that improved market access for products from developing countries should be sought in the Doha Round negotiations and regional and bilateral agreements (*Financial Times*, 15 June 2004). Secondly, production capacities in emerging economies should be strengthened by increasing foreign direct investment inflows, incorporating capital and technology transfers. This approach was consistent with recommendations by the World Bank that action to reduce corruption was necessary to improve investment opportunities and to promote growth and poverty reduction (World Bank, 2005b).

The change in direction of UNCTAD's work shows realism and acknowledges the strong contributions that China and India are making to global economic recovery. It shows that new approaches to economic development are effective. Sticking with the problems of the 1970s does not offer solutions when the world economy has moved on.

GENERALIZATION MASKS REALITIES

When delving into the economics of development it simplifies the discussion to use a two-world framework. Differences among living standards in developing countries are much wider than between their average and the clustered group of developed (OECD) economies. Many developing countries are small islands or landlocked nations, while others are extremely large (China, India, Brazil, Nigeria). Other differences arise from systems of government: central planning stifles enterprise, but once controls are relaxed, rapid development becomes possible (e.g., China, India). Civil unrest and inter-tribal fighting often relate to history, though they are indicative of weak government, lack of proprietary rules and absence of social laws. This is the curse of Africa, but similar conflicts are present in Latin America and Asia.

Development problems vary among countries even on the same continent, but there are also some similarities worthy of note. Some Latin American countries had featured among the periphery economies in the nineteenth-century international economy, though they were outside the influence of colonial powers. For example, Argentina was a major grain and meat exporter to Europe and attracted both investment and migrants from Europe. Brazil enjoyed similar development based on agricultural and mineral exports. Some smaller states also exported minerals and Venezuela became a major oil supplier in the 1930s. The Latin American Free Trade Association (LAFTA) was established in 1960, soon after the EEC came into operation, which indicated the region's focus on trade-based development. Although plagued by political uncertainties, several of these economies have enjoyed intermittent periods of strong growth. Unfortunately, heavy overseas borrowing brought periodic debt crises and economic downturns (in the 1980s and late in the 1990s). LAFTA is now divided into two trade blocks – MERCOSUR and the Andean Community, but both continue to have tensions between members. Negotiations for a free trade area between MERCOSUR and the EU foundered early in 2005.

The US proposal for a Free Trade Area of the Americas (FTAA) has divided both MERCOSUR and Andean members. If US negotiators offer separate agreements to the willing, it will weaken the collective bargaining position (e.g., Chile already has an FTA with the US). Evidently, economic links with NAFTA countries should benefit and stabilize Latin American economies.

The most serious poverty is found in Sub-Saharan Africa (SSA), where UN estimates show that almost 50 per cent of the population survives on less than $1 per day, a proportion that increased in the 1990s. A similar proportion for South Asia in 1990 declined to around 35 per cent in 2001, as two of the largest poor economies grew strongly after opening their economies to competition. The UNDP *Human Development Report* 2003 criticized OECD countries for following the wrong development strategies in the 1990s, because their aid conditions required macroeconomic stability and better government and domestic institutions. The UNDP argued that social services and social infrastructure should have been the focus. But this facile response, consistent with UN and development NGOs' patent remedy, ignores the fact that 20 years earlier development banks' lending for social infrastructures (roads, drainage, dams etc.), was regarded as inappropriate when lending for health and education services were needed. It is evident that increased financial flows without appropriate government and technical expertise achieves little. The saga of development disasters in Africa and collapses of law and order show that some demonstration of viable institutions and orderly government must be a precondition – or at least should accompany – increases in financial aid. At the time of writing, at least a dozen well-endowed SSA countries are being destroyed by civil wars and civil unrest, so that even refugees cannot be helped. Often humanitarian aid is misdirected and provides succour to one warlord or another (e.g., Ethiopia in the 1980s). Easterley (2001) shows that debt forgiveness has been taking place since UNCTAD 1979, yet the debt continues to rise.

Something more fundamental is required from developing countries' govern-ments than pleas for help, supported by media celebrities and NGOs pointing to aid targets or trade liberalization as the answer, without establishing pre-conditions for success. The East Asian economies and now China and India have demonstrated the benefits of self-help.

Many former colonies in SSA achieved independence in favourable circumstances, yet disintegrated. Ghana, granted independence in 1957, chose central planning and single-party rule, which led to political confrontations, military takeovers and economic collapse. Massive infrastructure develop-ments went unused. Now, 40 years later and with IMF and World Bank assis-tance, order has been restored and prospects improved. Living standards are low (45 per cent of Ghana's population survives on less than $1 per day) and education is limited (only 13 per cent of Muslim women are literate and almost half of Muslim girls never attend school). GNP per capita is below the aver-age for SSA (*Financial Times*, 25 November 2004). This story has been repeated in Uganda, Tanzania and other former colonies in Africa.

SSA countries have 33 of the 54 countries covered in the Heavily Indebted Poor Countries (HIPC) initiative managed by the World Bank. By forgiving debt outstanding, this programme seeks to halve poverty levels by 2015. In July 2003, African finance ministers met with G8 leaders to review the HIPC's initiative and proposed a further increase in aid. African leaders sought more debt relief to bring their statistics into line with the UN Millennium Development Goals (see Chapter 7). Under the HIPC initiative, debt relief is awarded in return for the implementation of poverty reduction and govern-ment reforms. Under the new scheme, SSA countries are seeking more aid and investment flows in exchange for improved government. The latter would be assessed by voluntary review of a country's government and economic poli-cies by its neighbours (NEPAD). However, the Executive Secretary of ECOWAS (Economic Community of West African States) expressed the view that, 'Until we bring African crises under control, our efforts on infrastructure development, on economic development and on integrating our economies will come to nought.' Evidently, an effective system for assessing government effectiveness is required, but SSA governments are especially sensitive to outside interference.

Average tariffs in SSA are extremely high, so liberalization offers welfare gains. SSA merchandise exports were 5 per cent of world trade in 1980, but only 2 per cent in 2003. Many of the SSA economies are vulnerable to fluctu-ations in commodity prices: Ghana depends on exports of cocoa, timber and gold; Mali and Senegal depend on cotton exports; Nigeria depends on oil. These countries lack taxation systems and administrative powers to ensure productive returns from financial aid. The EU and US authorities, and other OECD governments, could contribute to SSA development by removing import protection and production subsidies from their agricultural sectors, especially on cotton and sugar, but the major obstacles to economic development are to be found at home.

Africa's poor economic performance when much of the world has enjoyed benefits of economic integration and growth, at least for periods in the past 50 years, derives from common weaknesses across the whole continent that arise from bad government and inadequate institutions. Development NGOs and activists place the blame for SSA backwardness on OECD governments, their trade protectionism and globalization. Yet the uniformly poor performance in SSA must have a common source; real GDP per head did not grow in the period 1965–90, and there was little improvement in the 1990s (World Bank, 2005a).

Research has shown that the extent of ethnic fragmentation can explain differences between countries' public policies. Easterly and Levine (1997) show that low education levels, political instability, inadequate financial systems, high government deficits and weak institutions have been identified as reasons for economic decline. These failings have been associated with ethnic fragmentation, which leads to confrontations and rivalries that prevent improvements in institutional structures and cooperation; different groups regard changes as welfare-reducing. Rent-seeking behaviour prevents the development of public goods, such as education (low school attendance by girls from Muslim families), banks and credit institutions, property rights and effective legal systems. Yet respect for sovereignty does not allow HIPC donors to comment on the corruption of many SSA governments or their disregard for the poor and the sick. While OECD governments deserve some blame for trade protectionism, especially in agriculture and TCF, the major problems rest with SSA governments because they have not developed adequate institutions to support sustained and robust economic growth. Government services are limited, property rights are scarcely acknowledged by the authorities and organization is limited. It is wrong to believe that development is only about trade and money.

The record of developing countries' trade growth since 1990 provides reasons for optimism, however. WTO statistics show that developing countries' total trade increased at 9 per cent per annum in the decade 1990–2000, compared with 6.5 per cent for OECD economies. Least developed countries' exports increased at 7 per cent per annum in that period.

World trade stagnated in 2001–02, but recovered strongly in 2003–04. Exports from South and East Asia recovered. Latin America, Central and Eastern Europe increased exports twice as fast as the OECD economies. *The Economist* (16 October 2004) reported that emerging economies are growing twice as fast as OECD economies. China and the US are growing and drawing in imports, particularly raw materials. Debt-servicing costs have declined, with low interest rates in OECD economies, while commodity prices are buoyant.

All this good news for emerging economies is driven off the media front pages by the NGOs promoting 'Make poverty history'. Poverty in Africa is disturbing and shameful, but it is a distinctly different question from those of other developing economies – the emerging economies. Its source is much deeper in the social, cultural, political and institutional history of SSA countries.

DOMESTIC REFORM

While economic development is promoted by trade opportunities, the main constituent of growth must come from within an economy. Benefits from trade preferences in overseas markets will stimulate growth in the export sector, but that is only a small part of developing economies. The real source of development comes from internal reform, even if change is stimulated by financial aid and export opportunities. Only structural adjustment can sustain exports, domestic savings, local services, etc. Whatever OECD countries do – reduce agricultural protection and supports; provide trade preferences; facilitate market development, etc. – producers can only benefit if they have the capacity to sustain supplies at competitive prices. Competition from other developing countries will be strong. The market is likely to be restricted because it is unlikely that OECD governments will allow the whole market to be dominated by foreign suppliers. So, agricultural trade is not just a question of costs. Reliability, quality (including quarantine standards, varieties, technologies) and links to wholesalers, etc., are key considerations for suppliers to OECD economies.

These considerations feed back into support services: transport reliability, quality controls, packaging and wholesale services. These depend on reliable public services (education and health services, government administration, construction of buildings and service back-up, etc.). Eventually this comes down to reliable institutions, both organizations and rules, and maintenance of law and order. These requirements are not available immediately. Hence, domestic reform precedes benefits from trade liberalization. Financial aid is a single act, even though the benefits should be enjoyed over time. Trade is a flow with a time dimension. One disruption in that flow and an opportunity can be lost forever.

The development process is not just a matter of increasing the share of manufacturing in GDP or employment, or the other simple indicators presented as development targets in the 1960s. Economic development depends on transforming society by establishing private property rights, the rule of law and organizations to support enterprise in the community. Not all countries have developed initially by exporting. In unorganized economies, substantial productivity improvements are possible by overcoming domestic inefficiencies. Wolfgang Kasper (2006) admirably describes the means of achieving such domestic changes. He explains that economic progress, otherwise known as growth, depends on the finding and testing of knowledge and information by enterprising and confident people, prepared to experiment with that knowledge. To do that the individual needs to feel secure about property rights, financial contracts and support from a stable judicial system. The quality of institutions and the coordination of rules are crucial for sustained development. Financial aid and trade opportunities can only help long-term development if the basic institutions are in place to encourage enterprise and risk-taking. Otherwise financial flows and trade opportunities will wither and fail.

Poverty relief and economic and social development are quite different. The former may be necessary in the short term to overcome bad harvests or the aftermath of a natural or man-made disaster. Development, however, is about transforming a society. The OECD countries should open their markets to more imports of agricultural produce and labour-intensive manufactures, but that still requires cost-effective production. Unless economic development is based on sound domestic institutions and constructive policies, this could be a once only advance. Too many commentators look at the international dimensions of development, focussing on international trade and capital flows (Hunter-Wade, 2002), without considering the domestic transformations necessary to provide a foundation for development in the long term. This foundation can only come from 'bottom up' integration based on sound institutions.

Proposals to increase aid grants and debt forgiveness for developing countries, and the prospects for trade liberalization to assist the poorest countries will be examined in the following chapters. It is wrong to think that all countries that declare themselves to be developing economies are in the same predicament. Recent experience in China and India, added to the history of the Asian Tigers in the 1960s, shows just how quickly development can progress. Equally, the Latin American economies are quite different from countries in SSA and Western Asia. But it is the latter regions where poverty is worsening and prospects are bleak, and where the OECD governments and the UN have proposed remedial action.

For five years, since the failure of the WTO ministerial meeting in Seattle in 1999, developing countries have been looking to the WTO Doha Round negotiations for an indication of OECD countries' commitment to open trade opportunities. The next chapter will examine the prospects for the Doha Development Agenda.

REFERENCES

Baldwin, R.E. and T. Murray (1977), 'MFN tariff reductions and LDC benefits under GSP', *The Economic Journal*, **87**, 30–46.

Bhagwati, J.D. (1988), *Protectionism*, Cambridge, MA: MIT Press.

Bhagwati, J.D. (2004), *In Defence of Globalization*, Oxford: Oxford University Press.

Bhagwati, J.D. and A.O. Krueger (1973), 'Exchange control, liberalization, and economic development', *American Economic Review*, **62**(2), 419–27.

Bhagwati, J.D. and V.K. Ramaswami (1963), 'Domestic distortions, tariff and the theory of optimum subsidy', *Journal of Political Economy*, **72**, 44–50.

Clements, K.W. and L.A. Sjaastad (1984), *How Protection Taxes Exporters*, Trade Policy Research Centre Thames essay no. 39, London.

Dollar, D. and A. Kraay (2004), 'Trade growth and poverty', *Economic Journal*, **114**(Feb), 22–49.

Easterly, W. (2001), *The Elusive Quest for Growth*, Cambridge, MA: MIT Press.

Easterly, W. and R. Levine (1997), 'Africa's growth tragedy: policies and ethnic divisions', *Quarterly Journal of Economics*, November.

Finger, J.M. and L.A. Winters (1998), 'What can the WTO do for developing countries?', in A.O. Krueger (ed.), *The WTO as an International Organization*, Chicago: University of Chicago Press.

Haberler Report (1958), 'Trends in international trade', report of panel of experts to GATT Secretariat, Geneva.

Hart, M. and W. Dymond (2003), 'Special and differential treatment and the Doha "Development" Round', *Journal of World Trade*, **37**(2), 395–415.

Hudec, R.E. (1987), *Developing Countries in the GATT Legal System*, Trade Policy Research Centre Thames essay no. 50, London.

Hunter-Wade, R. (2002), 'Globalisation, poverty and income distribution: does the liberal argument hold?', in *Globalisation, Living Standards and Inequality*, Canberra: Reserve Bank of Australia/Australian Treasury.

Irwin, D.A. (1996), *Against The Tide*, Princeton, NJ: Princeton University Press.

Johnson, H.G. (1965), 'Optimal trade intervention in the presence of domestic distortions', in Baldwin *et al.* (eds), *Trade Growth and the Balance of Payments: Essays in Honour of Gottfried Haberler*, Chicago: Rand McNally and Co.

Johnson, H.G. (1967), *Economic Policies Towards Less Developed Countries*, London: Brookings Institution, Allen and Unwin.

Kasper, W. (2006), *Economic Freedom and Development: An Essay About Property Rights, Competition and Prosperity*, London: International Policy Network, Eureka Project.

Krueger, A.O. (1980), 'Trade policy as an input to development', *American Economic Review*, **70**(2), 288–92.

Krueger, A.O. (1990), 'Asian trade and growth lessons', *American Economic Review*, **80**(3), 1–22.

Krugman, P. (1993), 'What do undergrads need to know about trade?', *American Economic Review*, **83**(2), 23–6.

Langhammer, R.J. and A. Sapir (1987), *The Impact of Generalized Tariff Preferences*, Trade Policy Research Centre Thames essay no. 49, London.

Lipsey, R.G. and K. Lancaster (1956), 'The general theory of "second best" ', *Review of Economic Studies*, **24**, 11–32.

Little, I.M.D. (1982), *Economic Development: Theory, Policy, and International Relations*, New York: Basic Books.

Meier, G. and J. Stiglitz (eds) (2001), *Frontiers of Development Economics: The Future in Perspective*, Oxford: Oxford University Press.

Nurkse, R. (1962), *Patterns of Trade and Development*, Wicksell Lectures, 1959; Oxford: Basil Blackwell.

Oxfam (2002), *Rigged Rules and Double Standards: Make Trade Fair*, Oxfam International.

Panagariya, A. (2004), 'International trade: think again', *Foreign Policy*, **139**, 20–28.

Prebisch, R. (1964), *Towards a New Trade Policy for Development*, New York: United Nations.

Robertson, D. (1992), *GATT Rules for Emergency Protection*, Trade Policy Research Centre Thames essay no. 57, London.

Rodriguez, F. and D. Rodrik (2000), 'Trade policy and economic growth: A skeptic's guide to cross-national evidence', *NBER Macroeconomic Journal*.

Rodrik, D. (2000a), 'How far will international economic integration go?', *Journal of Economic Perspectives*, Winter.

Rodrik, D. (2000b), 'Institutions for high quality growth: what are they and how to acquire them', *Studies in International Development*, Fall.

Romer, P.M. (1993), 'Ideas gaps and object gaps in economic development', *Journal of Monetary Economics*, December.

Snowdon, B. (2001), 'Redefining the role of the state', interview with J. Stiglitz, *World Economics*, **2**(3), 45–85.

Stiglitz. J. (1998), 'Towards a new paradigm for development: strategies, policies and processes', Prebisch Lecture, UNCTAD, October.

Stoeckel, A. and B. Borrell (2001), *Preferential Trade and Developing Countries*, Canberra: CIE-RIRDC.

UNDP (1999), *Human Development Report*, New York: United Nations.

UNDP (2003), *Human Development Report*, New York: United Nations.

World Bank (1993), *The East Asian Miracle* (World Bank Research Report).

World Bank (2005a), *Annual Report*.

World Bank (2005b), *World Development Report: A Better Investment Climate for Everyone*.

5. The WTO and the Doha Round

The General Council of the new World Trade Organization (WTO) held its inaugural meeting in Geneva at the end of January 1995. Through a framework of committees, the WTO administers the new global trade rules agreed in the Final Act of the Uruguay Round and adopted as a single undertaking by over 100 trade ministers at Marrakesh in April 1994. In addition, the WTO supervises the implementation of scheduled tariff reductions and liberalization of various non-tariff restrictions agreed in those negotiations.

Agreements annexed to the Uruguay Round Final Act set down comprehensive rules for trade in goods (including agriculture), trade in services, trade-related aspects of intellectual property rights and trade-related investment policies. An important development from the Uruguay Round is the integrated system of dispute settlement procedures covering all the WTO agreements.

The WTO is a more far-reaching and deeper organization than the GATT (1947), which was amended and incorporated into the WTO as GATT (1994):

* The WTO is an inter-governmental organization, like GATT (1947).
* All WTO decisions and rules are collective decisions based on consensus in the WTO Council (or in its various committees).
* The WTO Secretariat has no power of its own, though it advises on interpretations of agreements and provides information for committees, when invited.

It needs to be asserted that the WTO is an inter-governmental institution. Since 1994, many NGOs have tried to claim that the WTO has powers that make it an arm of global government. This fabrication is designed to provide NGOs with an international instrument to promote labour standards, social justice demands and environmental agendas. In recent years, the WTO Secretariat has opened unofficial dialogues with NGOs to deflect complaints of non-transparency and to explain the function of the Council within the WTO constitution.

The Uruguay Round negotiations produced extensive reform of the world trading system that raised hopes of restoring export-led growth to the global economy. Long overdue amendments and extensions to the GATT rules were made and incorporated into the WTO. In addition, new disciplines were introduced to give wider coverage of transactions and deeper commitments by member countries. For the first time, comprehensive agreements were reached on trade in agriculture and trade in textiles and clothing, and a new agreement was drawn up for trade in services (GATS). New disciplines were introduced to cover quarantine regulations (SPS), technical barriers to trade (industrial standards) and trade-related investment measures (TRIMs). A controversial agreement was incorporated to strengthen protection of trade-related aspects of intellectual property rights (TRIPs). Management of WTO activities was enhanced by a commitment to regular ministerial council meetings.

Trade review processes were strengthened by two new agreements: a Dispute Settlement Understanding (DSU), which established procedures for settling trade disputes among members, and a Trade Policy Review Mechanism (TPRM) requiring WTO staff to report periodically on member countries' trade policies. It has been suggested that the TPRM should be used to provide an independent, economy-wide assessment of the costs and benefits of an economy's trade policy stance. Over time such analyses would help to change public attitudes to trade policies (Stoeckel, 2004). In practice, the TPRM assessments are strongly influenced by meetings with national officials, and government representatives have the last word when reports are presented to the WTO Council. The DSU is examined in detail below.

The GATT was slightly amended and embodied in the WTO as GATT (1994). It retains the same form and is based on the same three fundamental principles: non-discrimination based on MFN and national treatment (Articles I and III), reciprocal tariff negotiations and transparency (notified tariff schedules and tariff bindings) (see Chapter 3).

Reciprocity and transparency have mutated with time. The first-difference reciprocity used in GATT negotiations referred to roughly equal value reductions in tariffs. Now full reciprocity is sought, meaning equal treatment – the same tariff applied to an identified product by all contracting parties (Bhagwati and Irwin, 1987). The shift towards full reciprocity is consistent with the adoption of regional trade agreements (see Chapter 6).

Because the Uruguay Round Final Act was regarded as a single undertaking, all signatories were committed to all its decisions and agreements. Where agreement could not be achieved among all the participants, vexatious issues were set aside in decisions for the WTO General Council to consider. For example, separate committees were set up to consider trade and environment and trade and development. At the first WTO ministerial meeting in Singapore in December 1996, working groups on trade and investment, and trade and competition policy were added. That meeting also decided that member governments would not use labour standards for protectionist purposes and that the comparative advantage of developing countries in labour-intensive production should be safeguarded.

These trade-linked issues proved to be a burden for the under-resourced WTO Secretariat, because they have been used to attack the WTO and its agreements. Many NGOs regard trade as an evil of capitalism. Something that could be sacrificed for environment protection, political principles or some perception of the greater good. Recalcitrant WTO members also pursue their political interests in the trade-linked committees and working groups. The tensions these frictions can create became apparent in the disruption of the Seattle and Cancun ministerial meetings. At Seattle, the Clinton Administration gave ill-judged support to US labour unions' demands that US labour standards should be applied to imports, and that this condition should be included in the WTO agreements. At the same time, the EU's myopia on agricultural protection and its commitment to environmental protection added to tensions on the streets and in the negotiating rooms.

The record of the GATT/WTO system speaks for itself. The volume of world output has increased strongly over the past 60 years, while world exports have increased more than twice as fast as output (WTO Annual Reports [various]). Trade liberalization promotes specialization and raises productivity. Reduced uncertainty and stable, multilateral trade rules have provided the foundation for this unprecedented economic progress.

GATT REFORMS CREATE THE WTO

At the completion of the Tokyo Round (1973–79) many issues were left unresolved, but it was not until 1986 that contracting parties meeting at Punta del Este were able to agree on an agenda for a new round of trade negotiations. The world economy in 1986 was quite different from that of 1973, when the Tokyo Round began. Several newly industrializing economies (NIEs) in Asia were established as middle-income countries. The North–South divide had become blurred. New issues had risen to prominence: investment rules, intellectual property, trade in services. Yet long-standing problems of protection still required attention in agriculture and textiles and clothing. Moreover, serious questions about trade rules and dispute settlement procedures remained after the Tokyo Round, which had increased the number of trade disputes. Developing countries appealed for special attention to be given to their export interests in temperate and tropical agriculture and labour-intensive manufacturing, especially textiles and clothing, and raw materials' processing. They proposed that these matters should be dealt with before the new issues of trade in services and investment rules were considered. The selective negotiations in earlier GATT trade liberalization were controversial. There was widespread concern that trade rules and escape clauses should be tightened and applied consistently.

After several false starts, the agenda for the eighth round of GATT negotiations was agreed at Punte del Este in September 1986. The agenda was long and complicated, to meet the requirements of all 80 contracting parties. (Anyone disillusioned about the failure to begin serious negotiations in the Doha Round should read about the preliminaries that preceded the Uruguay Round [Croome, 1995; Preeg, 1995]). The negotiations were not concluded until December 1993, and the Final Act was not signed until April 1994.

It was no surprise that the final step was a deal between the US and EU on agriculture. These two dominatingly large agricultural exporters have heavily protected domestic markets. Agricultural negotiations held up progress throughout the Round (including the crisis when the Latin American delegations walked out of discussions on agriculture at the ministerial meeting in Brussels in December 1990), so the final agricultural package received wide acclaim as a breakthrough. After 50 years of failing to make any impression on agricultural protection because of escape clauses, exceptions and derogations from GATT obligations, even minimal concessions were welcomed. The past decade, however, has shown that little was really achieved in 1993.

The Uruguay Round agricultural deal between US and EU negotiators comprised commitments to eliminate subsidies, to allow export competition and to reduce domestic support schemes. The re-incorporation of agriculture into the GATT system was regarded as a major step forward. Experience was to show that much remained to be done. Agricultural price supports, export subsidies and non-tariff barriers have continued to impede trade.

Market access was to be achieved by converting all import barriers (import quotas, variable levies, etc.) on agricultural trade to tariff equivalents (so-called tariffication). These tariffs were to be reduced by 36 per cent over six years commencing in 1995. As part of the single undertaking, developing countries committed to make reductions of 24 per cent over ten years. Least developed countries were not required to reduce protection. Some complicated safeguards were included to deal with cases of hardship. Agricultural subsidies were to be permitted only in exceptional circumstances, but they remain a contentious issue in the Doha Round preliminaries.

There is little evidence that access to OECD agricultural markets has increased since 1995. Most small, non-EU European countries, plus Japan and Korea, still have very high levels of border protection. US and EU agricultural supports have been rising in response to domestic lobbying since 1998, after falling slightly in 1996–98 (OECD, 2004). Resistance to liberalization of agricultural trade remains strong. Some progress was made to prepare the ground for Doha Round agricultural negotiations in Annex A to the Draft General Council Decision of 31 July 2004 – the so-called 'July Package'. However, the Doha Round negotiators still have much to do.

The Uruguay Round reduced protection provided to manufacturing and increased tariff bindings by non-OECD countries. These steps were traditional GATT fare. OECD tariffs on manufactured imports were reduced from a trade-weighted average of 6.3 per cent to 3.8 per cent over five years. Even so, tariff reductions were larger for intra-OECD trade in manufactures than for imports from developing countries. Developing countries' tariffs on manufactured imports were reduced by about one-third, though average tariffs remained much higher for non-OECD economies. (Developing countries remained concerned about OECD countries' tariff escalation by stage of processing.) Developing countries' tariff bindings increased from 13 per cent to 61 per cent of imports, with applied rates generally much lower than bindings.

The agreement on textiles and clothing (ATC) was a major advance, because it included a ten-year schedule to phase out VERs and other quotas imposed according to the Multi-Fibre Arrangement (MFA) by 1 January 2005. Tariffs were to be the only protection for this sensitive sector after 2004. The liberalization of QRs (quantitative restrictions – quotas) was heavily end-loaded; 49 per cent of the most significant QRs were liberalized on 1 January 2005. The effectiveness of this commitment remains to be seen, because many OECD tariffs on textiles and clothing are high, and some are not bound. Major market adjustments are expected as long-standing VER holders lose guaranteed access to OECD markets, and new competitive suppliers (especially China and India) capture increased market shares. EU and US textile and clothing producers began lobbying their governments even before QRs were removed because retailers have established new contacts with low-cost suppliers. China accepted growth limits on exports to the EU early in 2005, and the US is likely to follow suit. Interestingly, EU retailers and fashion designers have complained about the protection provided to local TCF producers.

The emotional response by manufacturers in the OECD markets was expected. Yet there is little evidence that total imports of textiles and clothing into the EU and the US markets have increased much. However, imports from China are much higher, which indicates that they are substituting for imports from other smaller suppliers that have lost their guaranteed market shares based on VERs. Most of the damage is being done to other countries' exporters rather than EU and US manufacturers. Moreover, the prompt reaction to the removal of market quotas indicates that competitive wholesalers and retailers in the OECD markets had recognized what the ATC meant for the market. Mandelson's triumphant return from China in April 2005 with his negotiated deal over imports of textiles and clothing was a betrayal of EU consumers, as well as a back-down on the ten-year-old commitment in the ATC. The US protectionism is no more honourable. The outcome is likely to be more trade diversion as Chinese manufacturers divert output through other developing countries for relabelling or final processing.

TRADE RULES

Legalized backsliding was always a weakness of the GATT. This was most apparent in agricultural policies, but it was also evident in the exceptions allowed in GATT Part II for safeguards, anti-dumping and subsidies and countervailing duties. These issues remained controversial in the Uruguay Round negotiations. The intention was to make the safeguards provisions (Article XIX) more user-friendly, so that more disruptive measures, anti-dumping duties, would be less attractive. Several major revisions were made:

1. To allow discriminatory application of safeguards.
2. To remove an exporting country's right to compensation in the first three years of safeguards action.
3. While non-discriminatory, price-based measures were encouraged, QRs could be applied for four years (with one four-year extension permitted, if measures were non-discriminatory).
4. Progressive liberalization is required beyond the first year of a safeguards action.
5. No safeguards are to be repeated within two years of a previous action.

These new provisions still allow prompt access to protection against market disruption, and it is questionable whether such measures will facilitate market adjustment.

The Tokyo Round's code on subsidies and countervailing duties contained many inconsistencies: subsidies were not explicitly defined, for example, which led to uncertainty about when countervailing duties could be used. Export subsidies on agricultural goods were excluded. The new code defined export subsidies into three categories: prohibited, actionable or non-actionable. WTO members may take countervailing action against prohibited or actionable subsidies.

Anti-dumping actions remain a problem because GATT Article VI does not define dumping and there are no agreed procedures to determine dumping. Each WTO member can impose an anti-dumping duty on an imported good if dumping causes material damage to local producers. This is an open invitation to introduce made-to-measure protection. The determination of dumping is based on calculation of the home price and the export price of an item. Any international price comparison depends on currency exchange rates and these can vary markedly over time. An appropriate selection can make a dumping determination easy. In some instances, there is no domestic price for comparison, in which case administrators construct 'normal' values as the basis for a dumping determination. Normal business practices can be declared unfair and made subject to duties (e.g., discounting obsolete models may be used to determine anti-dumping duties on new models). Anti-dumping actions are very popular with import-competing industries.

The present WTO agreement on the implementation of Article VI in GATT (1994) has many gaps. No account is taken of the public interest clause, with the main focus being the interests of domestic firms with no mention of consumer interests. With international competition now dominating it is difficult to establish predatory behaviour unless market power is assessed. These matters are politically sensitive for governments, especially when many consumer groups now seem to be captured by environmental interests rather than consumers' interests in markets. The term dumping evokes exploitation and unfairness, something bad, which misleads the public.

The only agreement reached in the Uruguay Round was that procedures and information in anti-dumping cases should be made public (i.e., transparent). Yet a major study of ten countries' anti-dumping procedures over ten years (Horlick and Vermulst, 2005) reported that transparency is at the top of the list. Because many determinations are based on confidential business information, other interested parties (overseas suppliers affected by decisions) are unable to defend their positions properly. Even when a decision is made, the overseas suppliers are not able to see the full determination, so no appeal is allowed. This indicates collaboration between the domestic industry and the administering authority, and any kind of review of decisions is rare. Anti-dumping is undoubtedly the most invidious and effective means for negating import competition. Until proper rules and statistical criteria, and a definition of dumping is devised, anti-dumping actions will ensure that liberal trade is blocked.

The insidious effect of lax anti-dumping rules has been demonstrated in the decade since the Uruguay Round came into effect. In the year to 30 June 2003, 238 new anti-dumping decisions were notified to the WTO; 67 (30 per cent) were initiations by India, compared with 76 by all OECD countries. In terms of numbers in force at 30 June 2003, out of the total of 1323, OECD members had just over half at 705; United States, EU and India are much the largest users. Many developing countries have taken to using anti-dumping measures as first-choice measures to reduce competition, because it provides made-to-measure protection.

Anti-dumping actions have been a major flaw in the GATT/WTO system since the beginning, but they have become more intrusive as most OECD tariffs have declined. This is the main instrument available to national authorities for a prompt response to sudden increases in import competition. The system is not transparent and appeals can only be made to the dispute settlement board after long delays. All three of the long-standing trade remedies continue to proliferate and all major governments are guilty of exploiting them. The US Congress has specifically excluded any negotiations on trade-remedy rules that will weaken their capacity to protect US firms against unfair competition. In the EU, trade remedy rules are administered by the Commission, which also enjoys the power. Other OECD countries, such as Canada and Australia, are also major users of trade remedies. With China and India active in world markets, access to trade remedies could become a major source of friction in trade relations and undermine further the commitment to non-discrimination. As another irritant in the global trading system, these escape clauses need to be revisited; anti-dumping will not be dealt with in the Doha Round.

WTO EXTENSIONS

The Uruguay Round negotiations extended to new areas outside the traditional GATT purview. Three new framework agreements were agreed to cover trade in services (GATS), trade-related investment measures (TRIMs) and trade relating to intellectual property rights (TRIPs). In addition, two separate agreements were concluded to prevent national standards being used as technical barriers to trade: an agreement on the application of sanitary and phyto-sanitary measures (SPS) (i.e., quarantine regulations) and an agreement on technical barriers to trade (i.e., industrial standards). A series of separate agreements relating to trade regulations were also concluded (covering customs valuation, preshipment inspections and import licensing), which were intended to facilitate trade by reducing delays.

The basic principles of the GATS follow the GATT structure; that is, most-favoured nation treatment, national treatment (non-discrimination) and prohibition on quantitative restrictions. The GATS includes specific commitments on market access. Since trade in services is restricted by regulations rather than tariffs, progress depends on identifying commitments to liberalize particular sectors, modes of supply and protective regulations. Negotiations must identify positive lists for liberalization and modes of delivery, whereas GATT negotiations identify negative listings (exclusions from liberalization). The GATS identifies four modes of service delivery:

1. cross-border supply (using mail, telecoms);
2. consumption abroad (movement of consumers abroad);
3. commercial presence (establishment of legal entity abroad);
4. temporary movement of persons (consultants, migration).

At the initial stage, many countries had long lists of services to exempt from service negotiations. However, these were quickly whittled down to specific agreements when the advantages from global participation quickly became apparent (e.g., telecoms, trade in IT products). In the decade since the WTO came into effect, expansion of service industries has promoted cross-border transactions and investment flows. International trade in services have increased faster than merchandise trade in the past decade (currently worth about one-quarter of the value of merchandise trade).

Even so, some service markets are still heavily protected: audio-visual services, entertainment and cultural sectors. These so-called cultural activities raise intense feelings in some countries. Many WTO members have been reluctant to make negotiating request/offers on services in the Doha Round. This is developing into another obstacle to progress in the Doha Round. Liberalization in services is being linked to progress on agriculture. Developing countries' interest in the services negotiations is to facilitate the temporary movement of service providers – that is, temporary migration of workers. Emerging economies are also seeking access to ICT and telecoms technology.

The TRIMs agreement is directed at host-country performance requirements that act as barriers to foreign investment that distort trade flows. It does not apply to investment policies generally. The agreement outlaws local content rules and trade and foreign exchange balancing requirements because they are inconsistent with the national treatment requirement in GATT Article III. Restrictions that limit the imports of foreign firms or constrain their exports are also banned. This agreement is modest because it simply re-affirms existing GATT rules. Some developed countries with major international corporate investors wanted a more extensive trade and investment accord, but developing countries' governments opposed any attempt to restrict their domestic policy options. This trade-link proposal is still being advocated strongly by Japan and the EU, but was effectively blocked by emerging countries (G20) at Cancun.

The TRIPs agreement proved to be one of the most controversial accords that came out of the Uruguay Round. Like the TRIMs agreement, the TRIPs agreement was an attempt to apply GATT principles of national treatment and most-favoured nation treatment to intellectual property rights (patents, copyright, trademarks, industrial designs, etc.). It is not clear why this protection was sought in the GATT/WTO, because the World Intellectual Property Organization (WIPO) manages the implementation of national legislation on intellectual property using relevant international agreements – the Berne Convention on copyright, the Paris Convention on industrial property, etc. OECD countries undertook to implement the TRIPS agreement within one year, while developing countries were allowed five years to meet basic requirements and a further five years before introducing product patents. Least developed countries were allowed 11 years to provide full protection of intellectual property rights. The effect of the TRIPs agreement was to increase royalty and fee payments from developing countries to OECD patent holders. Once these costs and payment outflows appeared, developing countries expressed serious misgivings about the TRIPs agreement. It became a serious dispute in the lead up to the Cancun meeting when it became identified as a barrier to the provision of essential generic drugs to developing countries.

WTO DISPUTE SETTLEMENT UNDERSTANDING

The review and overhaul of the gentlemen's agreement on dispute resolution in the GATT Article XXIII aroused much interest when the Uruguay Round Final Act was released. It provides for enforcement of Council decisions. A number of controversial disputes identified by environmental groups had already attracted media attention. Apart from a handful of high-profile 'green' issues, however, the vast majority of over 300 disputes notified to the WTO have been resolved without controversy, or much attention from the media. Despite the efforts of lawyers and NGOs to exploit and augment this agreement, it is recognized as a success.

In the GATT system, disputes between contracting parties over interpretations of provisions or impairment of anticipated benefits were reconciled by consultations, or, failing that, a panel of experts was asked to report on a dispute. In effect, most disputes were resolved by negotiation. A few disputes went unresolved – the major exceptions were complaints about agricultural subsidies. Retaliation was possible but rarely used, because such action would only increase the damage. Some contentious disputes (e.g., US against the EU bananas regime, US bans on Mexican tuna) caused frictions that kept the issue in the public eye while the Uruguay Round negotiations were in progress. The Understanding on Rules and Procedures Governing the Settlement of Disputes (DSU [Dispute Settlement Understanding]), therefore, was a focus of attention.

In the new arrangements for dispute resolution, if a complaint notified to the Director-General cannot be resolved by consultations between the parties within 60 days, a dispute panel is convened. This panel comprises trade experts with WTO/GATT experience, and where appropriate, scientific experts. These panels differ little from the previous GATT dispute panels. They consider all the economic and scientific evidence relating to a dispute in the context of WTO agreements. They are not confused with legal sophistries.

If the offending party does not accept the panel ruling, the panel report goes to the Appellate Body, which comprises legal experts. Paradoxically, the DSU Article 17 directs the Appellate Body to consider only points of law. In practice, however, it has found ways to review all the evidence presented to panels. On several occasions it has reversed panel decisions and criticized their processes, though it is not supposed to make law or go beyond WTO agreements. In the Shrimp/Turtle case (1998), the Appellate Body declared that

NGOs had the right to submit 'amicus briefs' (friends of the court submissions) to panels and that panels and the Appeal Tribunal could take account of them. This was highly controversial, because it supported the US position on NGOs' submissions if attached to member countries' submissions. In effect, it usurped the role of the WTO Council when considering reports on disputes because that body can only reject an appeal verdict if there is a consensus against the verdict – and that requires a successful complainant to abstain.

This capture of the dispute settlement process by lawyers casts a shadow over the negotiating process, the WTO's traditional role. The only way to reverse the claim of the Appellate Body to be the final arbiter would require renegotiation of the DSU in a new negotiating round. That is unlikely because it would re-open the debate on the whole process and risk failure. Moreover, some WTO member governments favour a more judicial approach, particularly the United States. Re-opening the DSU could lead to an unravelling of the WTO mechanism. The use of trade sanctions to enforce decisions means condoning protection, which is hardly consistent with liberal trade objectives. Only if the purpose of the DSU is to persuade member countries to comply with WTO rules, can sanctions be regarded as a means to an end. Only a handful of DSU decisions have required enforcement in the past ten years, and in some cases the offending measures have ultimately been removed.

If a guilty party does not implement DSU recommendations and Appellate rulings in a reasonable period of time, compensation or suspension of concessions may be imposed as temporary measures to enforce compliance (DSU Article 22). Compensation, meaning voluntary reductions in tariffs or other impediments, has to be agreed between the parties, but it can only be used as a stopgap. Trade sanctions have been used in several disputes between the EU and the US (e.g., EU import embargo on hormone-treated beef where the US has imposed high tariffs on selected EU exports; US Federal Sales Corporations (FSC) tax provision (a tax rebate that acted like an export subsidy for US companies) where the EU imposed high tariffs on selected US exports until that tax subsidy was removed – in both cases the exports targeted were selected carefully to avoid harming other countries' exports). One of the major objections to the DSU is that only large economies, such as the EU and the US, are able to introduce effective measures to force another country into compliance, whereas small countries lack such leverage. Moreover, trade sanctions are crude and can become contagious, with serious economic consequences (Hufbauer, 1998). It would make more sense if the DSU procedures could promote liberalizing alternatives and require a non-conforming offender to compensate the complainant by liberalizing tariffs to the same value as any trade sanctions. In both cases (trade sanctions or non-reciprocal tariff concessions of equal value), the aim is to mobilize lobbies in the offending country to persuade governments to amend policies. With tariff concessions, import-competing producers would exert pressures to retain their protection against foreign competition. With trade sanctions, the potential exporters will act to avoid losing overseas sales. But if these domestic pressures fail, trade protection would rise, which is contrary to the objective of trade liberalization and could easily spread.

Detailed studies show that trade sanctions are seldom effective in terms of achieving an objective, and require long and sustained application to be successful (Hufbauer, 1998). Water-tight sanctions are seldom possible. Rogue states will continue to trade because running sanction blockades offers large profits, while policing shipments is difficult and expensive. Trade sanctions are only an effective instrument for very large economies, such as the US or EU, where to deny access can cause pain.

One declared drawback to the DSU is that developing countries' governments lack the technical/legal knowledge and the financial resources to pursue disputes. Some developing countries have raised this as an issue for the Doha Round negotiations and proposals to provide technical and financial assistance are under review. Others have suggested the WTO Secretariat should initiate DSU cases where developing countries are adversely affected.

The idea that the WTO Council should force governments to comply with decisions is attractive to some NGOs. Most treaties lack such powers. In truth, trade sanctions are really only successful as a threat. If the non-conforming government accepts the sanction, the bluff is over. However, many NGOs (especially environmental groups) want to participate in panel hearings. They regard it as another platform for their propaganda, which argues that contravention of any environmental standards should be punished, regardless of cost. This makes sanctions seem a good idea! All presentations to WTO committees (including dispute panels) are made by governments, which are free to choose any advisers they need for their delegations. Allowing NGOs independent access to WTO committees is inconsistent with its inter-governmental character.

Above all, it is necessary to recognize that the WTO is not a legal institution. Its provisions were negotiated and drafted by governments to support the multilateral trading system; many of the negotiated articles contain constructive ambiguities that were necessary to achieve consensus on the WTO as a single undertaking. (What has been described as 'diplomats' jurisprudence' [Hudec, reported in Srinivasan, 2005].) Any subtle legal interpretation of such language is certain to upset at least one government, raise doubts about future negotiations and reduce agreements to the lowest common denominator. The DSU is about resolving disputes, not creating new international law. To allow it to be used as such will create uncertainty and confusion in international commerce. Since many lawyers seeking to muscle in on the DSU are already linked to environmental, labour/human rights and development NGOs (e.g., Foundation for International Environmental Law and Development [FIELD]) the dangers for the WTO are real.

The major achievement of the Uruguay Round was to establish unified rules of conduct in international trade. The GATT was not uniform because each contracting party acceded according to the Protocol of Provisional Application, which obliged each signatory to apply Part II Articles only to the fullest extent not inconsistent with its existing legislation. The WTO commitment undertaken should mean that all members have the same obligations under the rules. However, China's protocol of accession to the WTO is not a standard document. It has special provisions that fall into three main categories:

1. More stringent conditions on transparency, foreign investment, government procurement, sub-national government and compliance reviews.
2. Special rules apply to China's use of trade remedies (anti-dumping, countervailing duties and safeguards).
3. China has no recourse to special transitional periods available to developing countries.

These special conditions have been described as WTO-Plus and WTO-Minus obligations, both of which contradict the single-undertaking commitment of the WTO (Qin, 2003). Accepting China into the WTO, with its dynamic economic record and huge size, can be offered as an explanation for the special conditions of membership. The same problem was evident when Japan sought to join the GATT in the 1950s. However, that does not explain the special agreement on investment liberalization. Apart from the TRIMs agreement to support GATT Article III, investment has not yet been addressed in WTO negotiations. It is questionable whether this exceptional treatment should be applied to the agreement with China, after all the brouhaha that surrounded the announcement of the WTO as a single undertaking.

The WTO-China agreement has weakened the claim of uniformity in the application of WTO law. This adds weight to the claims of developing countries for special treatment, which the WTO was meant to restrict after difficulties with developing countries' commitments in the GATT. By introducing exceptions, weight is given to the WTO-Plus approach, which surfaced as GATT-Plus during the Tokyo Round, as a way for some countries to liberalize faster than the rest when negotiations became bogged down (see Chapter 6).

WTO REPORT CARD

When the WTO began to operate in 1995, there were high expectations that liberalization coupled with strengthened trade rules would provide new opportunities, after 20 years of economic uncertainty and confusion in trade rules. Unfortunately, old habits die hard. Agricultural protection was maintained, so supports and subsidies eventually began to increase. The 'peace clause' in the agricultural agreement prevented any actions under the rules of the Agreement on Subsidies and Countervailing Measures until 2003.

Developing countries became disenchanted with the WTO on several counts. No immediate returns were apparent from the agriculture agreements and the phasing of ATC quota expansions was heavily weighted to the end of the ten-year process. In addition, the TRIPs agreement (insisted on by US negotiators) bred widespread resentment among developing countries. Introduced to discourage piracy and counterfeiting of designs and patents, the TRIPs agreement also guaranteed royalties on intellectual property and extended the period of copyrights and patents. As users rather than producers of intellectual property, the TRIPs agreement obliged developing countries to increase flows of fees and royalties to OECD economies. This issue came to a head in 2001–02 when international concern to get cheap generic drugs to developing countries to treat serious diseases, such as HIV/AIDS and malaria, required exemptions from TRIPs. Patent-dependent OECD pharmaceutical companies fought to protect the TRIPs agreement.

It was not until 2003 that a WTO accord was reached, just before the Cancun ministerial meeting. That accord set out conditions under which patents could be waived to enable poor countries, without manufacturing capacity, to import cheap generic drugs to treat serious health problems. This drawn out disagreement added to developing countries' apprehensions about the WTO and was partly responsible for changing the atmosphere between the successful conclusion of the 2001 Doha meeting and the opening of the Cancun meeting two years later.

Disillusion with the WTO increased as difficulties opening a new round of trade negotiations persisted. Expectations were raised by the expansion of the GATT into a genuinely multilateral WTO. The WTO agreements even mandated reviews of certain agreements. What amounted to a built-in agenda for a new round of negotiations proposed to begin in 2000:

- New agricultural liberalization, following tariffication and reductions in domestic budgetary supports.
- The GATS was scheduled for review.
- TRIMs called for a review within five years and to consider provisions on investment and competition policy.

The Seattle ministerial meeting (1999) was poorly prepared. An agenda for discussions had not been agreed in advance and there were contradictions in prepared positions. The EU rejected serious negotiations on agriculture, while pushing for a wider agenda to include investment and competition policy – EBA, 'Everything But Agriculture'! US negotiators wanted a quick agreement, which required a short agenda. On the other hand, for domestic political reasons, the Clinton Administration wanted a WTO working party on trade and labour standards (which had EU support), even though this had been rejected by developing countries at the Singapore ministerial meeting in 1996. Many developing countries wanted more time and consideration to implement Uruguay Round commitments on intellectual property, customs practices and other trade facilitation measures. Others were smarting at what they saw as a raw deal in the Uruguay Round. The OECD members regarded this as reopening old arguments and a recipe for disaster. There was little enthusiasm among participants, and what there was suffered from the anti-globalization battles on the streets. Moreover, the traditional green room approach, where agreements were thrashed out among principal GATT players, was rejected by outside developing countries who regarded themselves as full members of the new institution, with rights to a place at the table.

The seeds for continuing confrontation were sown in Seattle. Developing countries wanted to make a protest and NGOs realized they had a captive audience for their own brand of pantomime and placard politics. The media instantly transmitted this bizarre behaviour around the world, with scant reporting of the meeting itself.

Two years later in Doha, ministers met in fortress conditions. In the aftermath of the 9/11 attack and the terrorist threat, another failure was unthinkable. The balance of influence had changed after Seattle. The developing countries' majority in the WTO outweighed the less than enthusiastic commitment of the OECD members. The Ministerial Declaration (20 November 2001) stated that the needs and interests of the developing country majority in the WTO were at the heart of the work programme adopted. Even so, EU agricultural interests were protected by a last-minute EU insertion in the text: WTO negotiations on agriculture will take place 'without prejudicing the outcome of the negotiations'. This was to haunt the Doha Development Round at the next WTO ministerial meeting in Cancun in 2003. Similar EU weasel words were included on investment and competition policy, trade and environment, and intellectual property.

A series of new headings were added to meet developing countries' specific interests:

- trade, debt and finance;
- trade and transfer of technology;
- trade of small economies;
- technical cooperation and capacity-building in least developed countries.

By including everything raised at Doha on the agenda, an agreement to proceed with the round was achieved. However, this did not represent genuine progress towards effective negotiations.

Declaring the Doha negotiations to be a development round encouraged developing countries to seek more concessions, urged on by NGOs. This diverted attention away from their own economic problems. Even in developing countries, import protectionism benefits domestic producers at the expense of consumers (especially the poor). The hardening of developing countries' positions at Cancun sharpened the North–South divide and brought about the early collapse of the meeting. This hollow political victory gained no economic advantage. The USTR (Ambassador Robert Zoellick) described this cultural clash as a return to the rhetoric of the 1970s.

Before the Cancun meeting began, most thoughtful commentators saw little prospect of progress to resolve the conflicting chapters in the Doha Declaration. Much had been promised to the militant majority of the WTO membership and any back-pedalling would cause an outcry, as the dispute over imports of cheap generic drugs for poor countries had shown. The G8 Leaders meeting at Evian, France three months before the Cancun meeting urged action on the Doha agenda, but made no suggestions. This indicated little enthusiasm for the new round of negotiations among OECD governments.

A successful Doha Round would raise world income substantially. Because OECD countries have low tariffs on manufactured imports and, in spite of high protection, agricultural output represents only 2 per cent of GDP, the benefits to developing countries will be much larger in absolute terms and as a share of their GDP. Developing countries' protection overall is much higher than OECD countries, so much of that gain would come from freer trade among developing countries themselves (World Bank, 2004). Many of the reasons for the Cancun crisis followed differences that had been papered over at the Doha meeting in 2001. Lack of progress in negotiations between the two meetings doomed Cancun to failure, while political grandstanding and NGOs' activities left little room for compromises.

The OECD countries' agricultural protectionism was confronted by the G20, comprising most of the large developing countries. Their complaint, justifiably, was that more needed to be done to reduce agricultural protection than had been offered. This was not the view of many smaller developing countries, because the ACP countries enjoy preferential access to EU markets. Their fear was that they might lose their export markets if agricultural protection was lowered (see Chapter 4). Another group comprising West African cotton producers (Mali and Senegal) had a specific grievance against US price supports to its cotton producers, which depress the world price. NGOs exploited the sympathy this generated for the poor in Africa. A special negotiating group is now dealing with this matter in the WTO. After continuing confrontations in Cancun, 90 participating countries signed a letter to the Chairman opposing OECD proposals to include negotiations on the Singapore issues (competition policy, investment, transparency in government procurement and trade facilitation).

Intransigence appeared on both sides of many agenda items. Eventually, the Chairman, Mr. Derbez, Foreign Minister of Mexico, said he saw no prospect of compromise and closed the meeting early. Unreasonably, several delegations later blamed Derbez for the failure of the meeting, though it is difficult to see what would have saved it. Acrimonious exchanges in the year leading up to the ministerial, over cheap drugs for SSA, and uncompromising positions by some important delegations were brewed into a potent mixture by NGO and media mischief-making.

NGOs were present in numbers at Cancun and worked energetically behind the scenes to strengthen anti-OECD rhetoric and to oppose compromises. The failure of the meeting did not damage the NGOs, who claimed victory over globalization, though they damaged the interests of the world's poor, whose governments seem to have been bamboozled by globophobic extremists. However, NGOs' evil intentions only succeeded because WTO rules worked in their favour. The WTO (like GATT before) works by consensus, but there are no established procedures to get to consensus. These circumstances play into the hands of troublemakers, among participants and bystanders.

AGRICULTURE, THE CENTREPIECE OF DOHA AGENDA

Possibly because of the acrimony expressed at the collapse of the Cancun meeting, even before the end of 2003, important players in the WTO took steps to restart discussions on agriculture. Brazil reconvened the G20 of leading developing countries early in December 2003 to discuss a common strategy. The principal demand remained to reduce OECD supports for agriculture.

The major developing countries in G20 (Brazil, India, South Africa, China, Egypt, Mexico, Indonesia, Philippines, Nigeria and Pakistan) focussed their attention on agricultural protection. Their perceptions of the benefits from liberalization of agricultural trade appear rather exaggerated. The G20 Ministerial Declaration in December 2003 stated: 'The elimination of barriers and distortions in agricultural trade could contribute to the economic transformation, reduction of poverty and the promotion of social and political stability in developing countries.' Reform of agricultural trade policies remains the most important and most controversial item on the Doha Development Agenda. But then it was the crux of many earlier GATT negotiations, notably in 1993. The OECD estimated that in 2003 the 16 largest OECD economies provided support worth over $300 billion to their farm sectors (OECD, 2004).

This represented one-third of all farm receipts in these countries. These transfers come from tax-payers, from consumers via tariffs, other market supports and other budgetary payments. The EU supports are worth more than those received by the US and Japanese farmers together and account for almost 50 per cent of all Producer Support Estimates (PSEs) (originally called the Producer Subsidy Equivalent) by OECD governments. EU supports are 36 per cent of farm incomes, twice the US level. However, it is not only the major exporters that have high protection. In Japan, PSEs are almost 60 per cent of farm incomes, while in small European countries PSEs are worth around 70 per cent of farm output.

This level of support gives some idea of the benefits that could accrue to poor countries from liberalization of agricultural policies in OECD economies. It would raise the prices received for their exports by allowing them access to high-priced EU markets. The Doha Declaration recognized that agricultural reform would allow improvements in market access, reductions in trade-distorting domestic supports and reduced export subsidies. However, there are many instruments used to assist agricultural sectors and to cover every avenue means very complicated agreements, where balance is difficult to achieve (see Josling and Hathaway, 2004).

The last minute EU-US agreed proposal on agriculture put to the Cancun ministerial meeting was rejected. It took almost another year to produce a new package in July 2004, and that after the US Farm Bill had raised income supports. At that stage the EU, US, Brazil, India and Australia (representing the Cairns Group of agricultural producers) met and reached an understanding on how to approach reductions in export subsidies and import barriers. This deal still required approval from all 148 members of the WTO, and some immediately called this management of the negotiations a scandal and an attempt to railroad small countries. Nevertheless, the agreed text was presented to the WTO Negotiations Committee in December 2004.

There are still three separate groups with differing views on the agricultural negotiations. The US and Cairns Group members argue that the 2004 package does not go far enough, while the EU, Japan and other high-protection OECD countries believe the package is too ambitious and biased towards exporting countries. The third group comprises small ACP developing countries that benefit from preferential access to the EU market. They fear the loss of this access if EU prices are reduced and their preference margins over competitive producers in Asia and Latin America are squeezed. Negotiations with the EU are complicated by the complex politics of revisions to the CAP, attempting to contain future budget costs *and* to separate support payments from output levels, by making annual lump sum payments to farmers rather than subsidizing production directly. French ministers believe that the EU Leaders' Conference in Berlin (October 2002) guaranteed continuing subsidies for farmers until 2013 (see De Villepin article, *Financial Times*, 29 June 2005). Major changes will take time. Simply shuffling supports between modes of payment will not open markets, and G20 governments are unlikely to be fooled. Serious negotiations still lie ahead.

Trade policy is largely determined by domestic politics, and nowhere more so than in the farm sector. Once this is understood, the continuation of so-called 'unfair' trade policies in OECD countries becomes understandable, though no more acceptable. Outlays to support farming in the US, the EU and other OECD countries (price guarantees, export subsidies, import barriers, etc.) damage the interests of poor farmers in developing countries. However, farmers in these OECD countries have political influence and they always seem to have strong political and media support. Governments and other politicians recognize that farming communities can decide who governs, so they solicit their support with handouts and concessions. Support for farmers is traditionally strong in many countries. Sympathy exists for hard work in all weathers, basic providers, etc. – even though farm technology has replaced labour. Sympathizers ignore that rents from farm supports mostly accrue to landowners. This paradox is most obvious in the EU, where consumers accept high food prices without complaint, and large transfers to farm sectors (only around 2 per cent of the workforce in OECD countries) from trade protection and fiscal transfers are condoned.

The sugar industry has become a battleground in the EU and the US as pressures are exerted by trade agreements, and developing country producers are squeezed. The WTO dispute panel's ruling on a complaint by Brazil, Australia and Thailand that EU sugar is dumped on the world market, has caused the EU Agricultural Commissioner to recommend a 39 per cent cut in the sugar price guaranteed to EU producers. Not surprisingly, this provoked complaints from inefficient producers in Italy, Greece, Ireland and Portugal. But producers in ACP countries have also protested because they will face lower prices in the EU market under their preferential Sugar Protocol. Increased access to the EU market at lower prices will reduce their present guaranteed revenue. Paradoxically, Oxfam and other NGOs object to this reduction in EU agricultural protection because it hurts some poor economies. They have demanded compensation of $400m a year to be distributed among ACP sugar producers.

Meanwhile in Washington, when the Central American Free Trade Agreement (CAFTA) was before Congress in July 2005, the American Sugar Alliance lobbied hard against any increase in sugar imports. According to reports, the CAFTA would allow only a 50 per cent increase in sugar exports to the US market over 15 years. These two confrontations show how difficult it is to liberalize trade in agricultural produce, with domestic lobbies and foreign suppliers complaining about losing rents, and development NGOs objecting to lower protection. Liberalizing trade is a slave to vested interests.

The agreement to re-open the Doha negotiations was made possible by the July Package on agricultural trade. This contained the EU commitment to remove agricultural export subsidies, which facilitates dumping of surpluses on world markets. Similarly, the US, in principle, accepted curbs on its food aid and export credit programmes, which should have similar effects. OECD governments agreed also to reduce trade-distorting domestic supports to farmers. Leading food exporters, such as the Cairns Group, also want tariffs to be cut. These decisions would fulfil commitments in the Doha Development Agenda, to raise living standards in poor countries where agriculture is important, only if prevailing ceilings on all forms of assistance are cut severely. (This should be a lesson from the Uruguay Round agreement on agriculture.) A new US proposal in November 2005, to eliminate agricultural subsidies over 10 years, has put pressure back on the EU and other agricultural protectionists to make a counter offer.

Even if price-based protections are removed, there are even more pernicious instruments available to discriminate against imports. EU farm reform programmes include references to suppliers needing to satisfy EU environmental standards. Included as a gesture to EU greens, these could provide new barriers to trade. The SPS agreement on quarantine standards could also be used to impede agricultural imports, as strict EU environment standards could block imports of manufactured goods that do not comply with regulations on whole-of-life environmental management (as, indeed, could infringements of Kyoto standards). Industrial standards and production and processing methods (PPMs) are still under review in DSU panels. In 2001, EU negotiators were insistent that trade and environment, and geographical indications should be included in the Doha Declaration.

WTO NEGOTIATIONS AS A LEVER FOR DEVELOPMENT

Agriculture was not the only stumbling block to negotiations at the Cancun ministerial meeting. The G20 Declaration reiterated the need to preserve the integrity of the Doha Development Agenda. Although many WTO members interpreted that as a positive response to the breakdown at Cancun, there is an underlying tone of using the Doha Round to lever non-trade advantages. This is consistent with least developed countries' unwillingness to negotiate on industrial tariffs or the Singapore issues until they are granted an extended adjustment period to meet Uruguay Round commitments. Many NGOs and other sympathizers who would like to convert the WTO into another development institution support them. Such single-minded pursuit of specific objectives without offering concessions is not a negotiation and it could spell the end of the WTO trade regime. There seems to be an understanding that a successful Doha Round negotiation will stand as a single undertaking. That is not consistent with developing countries picking and choosing which agreements they will accept.

This is perverse, too, because for trade liberalization to lead to development depends most of all on a country's own economic policies and institutions (Irwin, 2004). Reducing OECD countries' protection of agriculture and labour-intensive manufacturing will offer limited trade opportunities to developing countries. More 'special and differential treatment' according to GATT Part IV for developing countries' exports is unlikely to amount to much, because most OECD tariffs are low already. Only the troublesome agricultural and labour-intensive manufactured sectors remain to be opened. Serious questions arise over the benefits from trade preferences for developing countries, and whether by focussing on special and differential treatment they impede their own development opportunities. Regrettably, even some respectable development NGOs believe that promoting OECD preferences is a route to economic development for poor countries, even though preferences depend on extant tariffs that cause domestic misallocations.

The economic argument for trade liberalization is immutable and has been accepted for over 200 years. Nevertheless, to turn the tide away from competitive protectionism after 1945, the GATT had to be engineered to use trade protection as bargaining coin to buy the benefits of trade liberalization (i.e., mercantilism). Well-meaning NGOs describe the challenge of reducing OECD barriers to imports as the redistribution of resources towards reducing poverty (and helping subsistence farmers) in developing countries. On the other hand, recent experience of many developing countries shows that they benefit from reducing their own industrial protection. World Bank research predicts that if the Doha Round proceeds according to the July Package programme, developing countries will benefit proportionately more than OECD countries. This is because developing countries begin with relatively high tariffs – so have scope for larger tariff cuts – and because their exports are concentrated in highly protected industries – agriculture and TCF – where protection reductions will be large. South–South trade offers major benefits too, for equivalent liberalization (Anderson and Martin, 2005). The gains from trade come, above all, from increased specialization and improved resource allocations in the domestic economy, as well as improved access to overseas markets.

Development NGOs choose to ignore welfare benefits accruing to countries undertaking trade liberalization. They prefer to argue that the WTO system is managed to disadvantage the poor. It may represent effective propaganda to claim global injustice, but it shows little understanding of economics or the WTO system. Developing countries can gain from being passive participants in trade negotiations, but they benefit more when they reciprocate by cutting their own protection. Altruism may drive NGOs, but practical politics is the stuff of governments and international negotiations.

More than two-thirds of WTO members are now developing countries, and half of these are very poor. Since the Uruguay Round negotiations resulted in a single undertaking, they had to accept many commitments that they did not comprehend or which did not seem relevant to them. As full members, however, they exercise their rights on the WTO Council. In the GATT, their obligations had been waived under various escape clauses and they enjoyed MFN tariff reductions without having to reciprocate. However, the boundaries of trade policy were blurred in GATS, TRIMs and TRIPs, and in new areas on the Doha agenda, such as trade facilitation and environment issues.

The failure of the Cancun meeting showed developing countries that they had the power to alter the trade agenda and influence negotiation. However, several chapters in the Doha Declaration (2001) could seriously weaken the WTO, and most developing countries use that document as a creed:

1. Some developing countries want to be allowed a lower degree of commit-ment to trade liberalization than OECD countries. This approach is evident in the G20 stance in agricultural negotiations.
2. Some developing countries want to opt out of agreements in areas they consider sensitive, such as the Singapore issues.
3. Bilateral and regional trade agreements have become popular since 1990, increasing from about 50 in 1994 to 230 at the beginning of 2005. (WTO, 2005)

None of these proposals is inconsistent with existing WTO provisions. A lower degree of commitment is provided for in GATT Part IV. Four plurilateral agreements were included in the WTO framework in 1994. Additional, optional agreements are possible, with approval from the WTO Council.

Nevertheless, once permitted, two-speed liberalization, opt-outs and trade preferences create vested interests that make pursuit of multilateral liberaliza-tion and rules strengthening increasingly difficult. The multilateral approach has to be supported by commitments to domestic economic reform, too. Ideally, trade liberalization and resultant adjustment need to be accompanied by economic assistance packages to compensate losers. Even so, developing countries stand to gain most from their own liberalization; trade protection is a tax on efficient production and export activities (Clements and Sjaastad, 1984). All countries gain from liberalization according to WTO rules and negotiations. But the WTO is not a development agency.

Developing country members of the WTO are loosely divided into two groups: G20, comprising most of the large developing countries (as noted above) and G90, which includes all other developing countries, including many of the poorest from SSA. It seems to be the G90 that is holding the Doha negotiations to ransom. They reject any reductions in their trade barriers until all their demands for special trade treatment and for longer implementation periods for Uruguay Round results are met. In this they have been encouraged by the compassionate society and the movement to 'Make poverty history' to believe they have justice on their side, even if it is not good economics. The ACP countries that are in this group want compensation for any reductions in their preferential access to EU markets. The G90 ministerial communiqué (12 July 2004) criticized proposals to cut industrial tariffs and called for result-oriented, trade-related measures to help small countries. Meeting in Tanzania in June 2005, 50 least developed countries raised the ante and demanded 'a binding commitment on duty-free and quota-free market access for all their products in OECD markets, to be granted immediately'. A few days later, immediately before the G8 Gleneagles meeting, African Union leaders called for all outstanding debt to be written off and new aid to be given without conditions. It would appear that the 'Live8' demonstrations raised unrealistic expectations.

The G90 position has many supporters among the NGOs and aid agencies. Some argue that Uruguay Round agreements were 'unfair' to developing countries. The agreements on TRIMs, TRIPs and GATS have been claimed to prevent developing countries from pursuing appropriate industrial development policies (Hunter-Wade, 2004). Yet TRIMs merely ensure that GATT Article III (national treatment) is effective in all markets and GATS requires positive offers by countries without discrimination against countries that do not participate. Many of the G90 are classified as least developed economies and exempt from these agreements (31 WTO members are from the 48 least developed countries defined by the World Bank). The TRIPs agreement has been criticized and amended to facilitate developing countries' access to generic drugs, but that has little relevance to poor countries' development strategies. The same author also condemned the ending of the MFA, because it has allowed China to capture OECD markets from small developing countries that, until January 2005, had enjoyed quota protection. Any kind of competition seems to be a problem.

Arguments in this vein show no understanding of the benefits that arise from trade liberalization. Any negotiated reduction of developing countries' tariffs seems to be regarded as an unnecessary sacrifice. In which case, presumably, developing countries would be better not to trade at all. Long live autarky! Two hundred years ago, Smith and Ricardo demonstrated that this was a fallacy with the theory of comparative advantage, and ever since, this 'true and non-trivial' proposition has been demonstrated in every economic principles course. (For a thorough review of the case for the WTO and liberal trade strategies, see Anderson, 2005.) It should be obvious to everyone that having access to OECD markets still requires competitive pricing to export against competitors. High tariffs (and other import barriers) raise domestic costs and disadvantage potential exporters; effective rates of protection are much higher than nominal tariffs (Corden, 1971; Johnson, 1969). Hence, demands for preferential trade access without regard for domestic cost structures can be self-defeating.

Completion of the Doha Round would bring significant gains to most developing countries, especially if agricultural liberalization is resolved satisfactorily. Most of the G90 will gain from a successful Doha Round, and all of them will benefit from continuation of the WTO rules-based system. To convince some developing countries they will not lose from the negotiations may require some special measures to increase their market access (e.g., African cotton producing countries). This would require some form of insurance against losses. So far, this has not been mentioned by OECD negotiators, but it should not be impossible to compensate the losers. The catch comes if these G90 countries demand payment in advance. The WTO is not a financial agency. So any insurance provided would require a guarantor, such as the IMF or a European development agency. Establishing any losses from the Doha agreements would require independent assessments. Buying off unyielding G90 governments may be one way to ensure the DDA takes place, but it would be risky and difficult.

WHITHER THE DOHA ROUND?

When the contents of the Uruguay Round Final Act became known, many old GATT hands saw a danger that the WTO would become overloaded with tasks only indirectly relating to trade. The dispute settlement understanding introduced a legalistic element into the trade liberalization process, while GATS, TRIMs and TRIPs went beyond trade issues to domestic regulations. The agreements on SPS, industrial standards, trademarking and technical industrial standards required links to be made with other international agencies and took the WTO into new fields (FAO, WIPO, etc.).

The last-minute attempt to introduce an agreement on labour standards at Marrakesh by some OECD governments rang alarm bells among developing countries, even though it was rejected. It presaged the introduction of four other trade-linked issues at the Singapore ministerial meeting in December 1996: trade and investment, trade and competition policy, trade and government procurement and trade facilitation. Trade and labour standards was rejected again by developing countries in Singapore, but like trade and environment it has remained on the agenda of the EU, the US and other OECD countries, and continues to be raised.

The single-undertaking condition adopted for the Uruguay Round probably misled some developing countries with inexperienced negotiators, so that they became committed beyond their capabilities. This has triggered demands to re-programme some implementation times and increased resistance to new commitments before the Uruguay Round decisions were concluded. It has also encouraged many least developed countries to demand special treatment, including re-negotiation of Uruguay Round agreements and making prelimi-nary demands on development assistance as a pre-condition to negotiating in the Doha Development Round. The broadening of WTO negotiations has enabled international politics to contaminate the WTO processes, in similar fashion to a lawyer's takeover bid for dispute resolution (Estey, 2002).

Development NGOs and other lobby groups have taken up the develop-ment round title and are loading many unconnected matters on to the agenda. On the other hand, some leading WTO members want to improve the rules that govern the organization. Peter Mandelson, the EU's trade commissioner, has called for changes to dispute settlement procedures and to ministerial meet-ings. He has expressed frustration at the 'cumbersome and consensus-driven approach of the WTO' (*Financial Times*, 24 November 2004). His predeces-sor as EU trade commissioner – now Director-General of the WTO – Pascal Lamy expressed similar views. It is not clear what this means, but attempting to re-negotiate the GATT/WTO framework is an unlikely prospect.

Unless the Doha Round shows serious progress, WTO authority will be undermined, as additional preferential trade agreements are established. These negotiations will proceed at a pace determined by major 'hub' economies (see Chapter 6). OECD governments may be prepared to declare free trade in most industrial goods, but it is unlikely they will offer serious reductions in protec-tion for agriculture. Others might be prepared to liberalize unilaterally. Having to administer multiple tariff structures will make surveillance difficult. The advantage of non-discrimination (MFN tariffs) will be lost and reciprocity will take precedence again.

NON-DISCRIMINATION LOST

The foundation of the GATT/WTO system was to remove discrimination from trade relations and to reduce trade barriers. The principle of non-discrimina-tion was adopted as a means to establish market access. Like reciprocal tariff bargaining it had no value, except as a means to the end of liberal trade rela-tions. Non-discrimination ensured equal treatment for the contracting parties. If free trade could not be restored, at least equal treatment would discourage a return to the competitive protection that had afflicted the world trading system in the 1930s.

Unfortunately, the price for GATT acceptance in 1947–48 was the escape clauses in Part II and the Protocol of Provisional Application. Together these exceptions weakened commitments. In the early years, governments resorted to escape clauses only infrequently. The safeguards clause (Article XIX) was too lenient and at the same time too costly to employ. It was easy to apply quotas to control threatening imports, but damaged suppliers had the right to demand compensation or the right to retaliate. Countervailing duties against subsidized exports were difficult too, because widespread use of subsidies led to a cascade of countervailing duties. The third instrument was also little used, because dumping (selling below cost) made little sense in a time of shortages. These forms of contingency protection and associated trade remedies became the major issues in trade relations from 1970 onwards, supplemented by an entourage of 'voluntary' substitutes (VERs, VIEs). These measures are still not tamed. They became more common as tariffs were reduced, and bound.

This shows that far from being non-discriminatory, the GATT system as it moved into its more comprehensive WTO format, became increasingly more committed to preferences. The rise of RTAs in various forms has opened new forms of preference. This can be sourced back to several changes in trade relations. All the easy liberalization of industrial trade was virtually completed by 1994, and in areas where trade barriers remained significant (TCF and agriculture) there was no support for liberalization among major OECD governments. The majority of WTO members rejected the new sectors where liberalization offered welfare gains to OECD economies – services, investment, competition and government procurement. The trade-linked topics were rejected by developing countries in the Uruguay Round and have been denied in similar fashion during Doha Round exchanges. The GATS has shown little progress since 1996 and there has been little enthusiasm for offers in services negotiations in the Doha Round. On the other hand, recent RTAs have shown real progress in reducing domestic regulations on investment, competition, services and government procurement.

These kinds of exclusive arrangement are becoming common. Like-minded nations adopt preferential trade arrangements with neighbours or strategic partners. Hub-and-spoke systems are spreading rapidly – and are producing a 'spaghetti bowl' of trade agreements (Bhagwati, 2002). The danger from a breakdown in Doha negotiations is that the costs of trading will increase, and efficiency will be lost. Those seeking to exploit trade negotiations for development assistance should be aware of the costs that a shift from a multilateral trading system (with its many faults) to a preferential trading system could impose. Hub-and-spoke discrimination and power politics disadvantage the weak and less developed (Wonnacott, 1996).

The momentum is on cooperation among the willing using RTAs, with networks of hub-and-spoke arrangements competing for mutual benefits in national treatment and MFN treatment. GATT Article XXIV is unregulated and its impact on the global trade system is far-reaching.

REFERENCES

Anderson, K. (2005), 'Setting the trade policy agenda: what roles for economists', *Journal of World Trade*, **39**(2), 341–71.
Anderson, K. and W. Martin (2005), 'Agricultural trade reform and the Doha Development Agenda', *The World Economy*, **28**(9), 1301–27.
Bhagwati, J. (2002), *Free Trade Today*, Princeton, NJ: Princeton University Press.
Bhagwati, J. and D.A. Irwin (1987), 'The return of the reciprocitarians; US trade policy today', *The World Economy*, **10**(2), 109–30.
Clements, K.W. and L.A. Sjaastad (1984), *How Protection Taxes Exporters*, Trade Policy Research Centre Thames essay no. 39, London.
Corden, W.M. (1971), *The Theory of Protection*, Oxford: Clarendon Press.
Croome, J. (1995), *Reshaping the World Trading System*, Washington, DC: World Trade Organization.
Esty, D.C. (2002), 'The World Trade Organization's legitimacy crisis', *World Trade Review*, **1**(1), 7–22.
Horlick, G. and E. Vermulst (2005), 'The 10 major problems with the anti-dumping instrument: an attempt at synthesis', *Journal of World Trade*, **39**(1), 67–73.
Hufbauer, G.C. (1998), *Sanctions-Happy USA*, Washington, DC: Institute for International Economics.
Hunter-Wade, R. (2004), 'Held hostage by the anti-development round', *Financial Times*, 17 May 2004.
Irwin, D.A. (2004), *Free Trade Under Fire*, Princeton, NJ: Princeton University Press.
Jackson, J. (1990), *The World Trading System*, Cambridge, MA: MIT Press.
Johnson, H.G. (1969), 'The theory of effective protection and preferences', *Economica*, **XXXVI** (May), 119–38.
Josling, T. and D. Hathaway (2004), 'Thus far and no further? Nudging agricultural reform forward', policy brief from Institute for International Economics, Washington, DC.
OECD (2004), *Annual Agriculture Policies*, Paris: OECD Secretariat.
Preeg, E.H. (1995), *Traders in a Brave New World*, Chicago: University of Chicago Press.
Qin, J.Y. (2003), ' "WTO-Plus" obligations and their implications for the WTO legal system', *Journal of World Trade*, **37**(3), 483–522.
Srinivasan, T.N. (2005), 'Non-discrimination in GATT/WTO: was there anything to begin with and is there anything left?', *World Trade Journal*, **4**(1), 69–95.
Stoeckel, A. (2004), *Termites in the Basement*, Canberra: Centre for International Economics.
Wonnacott, R.J. (1996), 'Trade and investment in a "hub-and-spoke" system', *The World Economy*, **19**(3), 237–52.
World Bank (2004), *Global Economic Prospects and the Developing Countries*, Washington, DC: World Bank.
WTO (2005), *World Trade Developments in 2003*, Geneva: World Trade Organization.

6. The regional trade alternative

The fundamental principle of the WTO is non-discrimination, as embodied in GATT Articles I and III. The crucial importance of most-favoured nation treatment and reciprocity in tariff negotiations to liberalize trade was explained previously. The reciprocal bargaining over MFN tariff reductions was a device to encourage the doubtful to participate in the GATT experiment in 1947. Governments focussed attention on expected gains from increased export opportunities, while glossing over potential increases in imports. Unfortunately, that equivocation has continued to dominate trade liberalization, and it has weakened the case for free trade. Regional trade agreements emphasize the increased trade that will follow from free trade among members of a customs union or a free trade area, but neglect the trade lost by non-members and the higher costs of purchasing goods and services from partner countries, if they are less efficient than former suppliers outside the RTA.

In any international agreement there are provisions for exceptions, dealing with problems in advance of its implementation, and escape clauses, to protect participants' interests once the agreement is in effect. These caveats are used infrequently, though 'trade remedies' have become a source of friction since the Tokyo Round negotiations (see Chapters 3 and 5). Some escape clauses have compromised the principles and objectives of the GATT/WTO system. Recently, the rapid development of discriminatory, regional trade agreements, using GATT Article XXIV and other WTO agreements, have posed a major threat to the multilateral trading system.

In 1947, Article XXIV was included in the General Agreement at the request of Western European governments. The BeNeLux customs union was being negotiated at that time and other cooperative arrangements were being discussed. GATT Article XXIV permitted the formation of customs unions (CUs) and free trade areas (FTAs). This article laid down two criteria for granting a waiver from non-discrimination:

1. 'Substantially all trade' among members of a CU or FTA must be free of duties and other restrictions 'within a reasonable period'.
2. Trade barriers against non-members must, on the whole, 'not be more restrictive' than before the CU or FTA was formed.

Agreements to establish such preferential arrangements must be notified to the WTO (originally the GATT). Any preferential lowering of tariffs among signatories of a CU or FTA agreement, therefore, was regarded as trade liberalization and welfare increasing.

Two additional provisions to establish regional trade arrangements have been added. In 1979, the GATT Council decided to enact 'differential and more favourable treatment' for developing countries (the Enabling Clause). This permits the creation of preferential trade arrangements (in goods) among developing countries. Because this applies only to developing countries, tariffs and other trade measures need not be removed completely. That is, any form of preference is allowed.

The Uruguay Round Final Act (1994) included the General Agreement on Trade in Services (GATS) and Article V sets out the conditions for regional trade agreements in services:

1. 'Substantially all services' must be covered, both in terms of trade volume and modes of supply.
2. National treatment must be provided to partner countries on substantially all trade.
3. The overall level of barriers to trade in services with non-members should be no higher than prior to the agreement.

Actions under these agreements have to be notified to the WTO.

When trade flows were subject to very restrictive policies, any shift towards reduced protection was regarded as a positive change to increase trade. However, even a customs union, with its common external tariff set at the average of pre-union tariffs, means roughly half the member countries had to raise tariffs against non-member countries, while other members reduced them. The welfare consequences, therefore, depend on demand and supply elasticities. Trade creation will occur among the members of the union as mutual tariffs are reduced during the transition period. However, as external CU tariffs are shifted towards the common external tariff, some non-member countries' suppliers may be able to export more to members whose pre-union tariffs were above that CU rate, while access to member countries raising their tariffs to the common rate will decline. Both trade creation and trade diversion affect Third Country suppliers. Net external trade diversion is likely, however, because of the zero tariffs on internal trade at the end of a transition period. Viner (1950) pointed out that trade creation was only one of the effects of trade preferences.

Similarly, in a free trade area, tariffs between member countries are eliminated over a transition period, while members' tariffs against non-members remain unchanged. Hence, non-members are discriminated against in both cases, with internal trade creation and external trade diversion determined by price changes (brought about by tariff changes) and quantity changes in trade volumes determined by supply and demand elasticities (Johnson, 1965).

Assessing the trade and welfare effects of RTAs has been a popular research activity since the 1950s. Most of the early exercises on EEC and EFTA used point-to-point trade data and showed that trade creation exceeded trade diversion. This was regarded as sufficient to justify these forms of regional integration (for example, Meade, 1955; Lipsey, 1960; Williamson and Bottrill, 1971). More recent studies use continuous data sets, and some also include investment data (Ethier, 1998). These later studies indicate that net trade effects are not necessarily positive (Soloaga and Winters, 2001). The new RTAs are more difficult to assess because trade liberalization plays a small part, whereas deregulation is significant and sometimes selective.

Any regional trade agreement (RTA) according to GATT Article XXIV, therefore, undermines the GATT principle of non-discrimination. When GATT was initiated, RTAs were regarded as a means to increase trade. Governments and political lobbies favoured unification in face of military threats from the communist East. Several politically driven efforts to promote Western European integration failed in the early post-war years. In 1956, however, 'the Six' decided on a customs union within the provisions of GATT Article XXIV, and the Treaty of Rome was drafted (Camps, 1964). The European Economic Community (EEC) received wide approval in those uncertain times, though claims about economic gains from integration were probably exaggerated. This aroused interests in regional integration elsewhere. The European Free Trade Association (EFTA) was established in 1960 as a political counter to the EEC, though it proved to be no more than a 'waiting room' for membership of the EEC. Gradually, most EFTA members were accepted into the EEC in the 1970s, along with other European neighbours. (Only Switzerland, Norway and Iceland now remain in the truncated EFTA, and outside the EU, though with free trade.)

Following the European experiments in the 1960s, other RTAs were attempted in Central and South America, and East and West Africa. Some of these survived but they had little effect on trade or economic development because they lacked political cooperation. These disappointing results meant that RTAs went out of fashion, more or less until the Uruguay Round negotiations began. The lesson was that to succeed, economic integration needs some political content. In Western Europe, the threat from the communist East and determination to prevent nationalism from regenerating tensions leading to hostilities, such as had plagued the region for centuries, made economic integration necessary.

POLITICAL CONTENT IN REGIONALISM

Interest in regional trade agreements revived during the Uruguay Round negotiations, especially after the breakdown of the negotiations on agriculture in
Brussels, in December 1990. This put the GATT system under stress. While
many countries wished to continue negotiating to liberalize trade in services
and manufacturing, agreements were thwarted by the breakdown in agriculture negotiations. Provisional agreements in important and rapidly expanding
markets, such as telecommunications, finance and other service sectors were
jeopardized by the breakdown. Similarly, tentative discussions to reduce
restrictions on foreign investment and government procurement policies were
hanging in the balance. GATT Article XXIV offered an opportunity to proceed
with trade liberalization and new agreements on services, etc. with like-
minded countries, without holding back liberalization until everything had
been agreed.

While the Uruguay Round negotiations were in progress, EU members
were negotiating their next phase of integration with the Single European
Market agreement (1989). The US Administration demonstrated similar intentions when it signed NAFTA in 1992. It would pursue the preferential
approach to trade liberalization as well as the multilateral route. After all, the
discriminatory approach might incite action on the items blocking progress in
the Uruguay Round. Political interest was stimulated in GATT Article XXIV.

In retrospect, this sea change explains many of the initiatives leading to
regional trade arrangements over the past decade. Everyone in the Uruguay
Round was reluctant to sacrifice agreements already drafted among the
largest-ever number of participants in multilateral trade negotiations.
Agreements on trade in services and manufactures, progress towards agreements on trade remedies, technical barriers to trade and dispute settlement
were progressing well in the Uruguay Round. Disagreements on agriculture
were the impediment, and that remained the case until the very last moment.
Only EU and US negotiators were present when, at the eleventh hour, an
agreement on agriculture was reached at Blair House, in December 1993. It
was a 'done deal' and no flexibility was left for others to make comments or
attempt renegotiation.

However, it is worth noting that most of the supposed reductions in
protection contained in that 1993 agreement on agriculture have come to
nothing in the past decade. Overall agricultural protection has remained
unchanged. OECD research shows PSEs in 2004 were little changed since
1995 for EU and US agriculture; farmers in small European countries remain
the most protected still, while Japanese agriculture continues to be treated
like the emperor! At every stage of the Doha Round negotiations, agriculture
has been the stumbling block; only at the Doha ministerial meeting in 2001

were agricultural disagreements papered over to provide an appearance of cooperation after the 9/11 disaster. Does anyone really believe any of the major players in the agricultural negotiations can, or will, negotiate in good faith?

When the Uruguay Round negotiations were completed in December 1993, the propaganda about reduced agricultural protection was accepted. Discontent was expressed about the residual unfinished business on trade rules and 'link issues' (trade and competition, trade and labour standards, etc.), but everyone was happy that eight years' work had been concluded. Discontent increased among some developing countries' governments when the details of final agreements attached to the Marrakesh Declaration were explained. Complaints were heard that transition periods were too short to allow adjustment to changes required by some WTO agreements. Some OECD countries thought more could have been achieved without developing countries' participation and the need to satisfy least developed countries. As long as trade negotiations proceeded on a multilateral, non-discriminatory basis, however, the convoy would move at the speed of the slowest vessel – and as long as ever more reluctant players were included in the WTO, the convoy would travel ever more slowly.

Discontent with aspects of the Uruguay Round final agreement carried over to the WTO ministerial meeting in Seattle, which was intended to initiate a new round of trade negotiations. The WTO Secretariat and the OECD delegations did not expect the Seattle furore, which was one of the reasons why the meeting failed. Tensions between OECD governments and developing countries' governments continued after the Seattle meeting collapsed. After Doha, the new round was declared 'a development round' in response to developing countries' pressures. When the WTO ministerial council meeting failed again in Cancun, the prospects for new negotiations receded further. These difficulties, combined with the problems that had held up the closing stages of the Uruguay Round, increased the attractions to many governments of alternative methods for achieving trade liberalization, using regional preferential trade arrangements.

A DIFFERENTIAL APPROACH

Faced with similar stalemate in the Tokyo Round negotiations and at the 1982 GATT ministerial meeting, an academic proposal was made for a 'GATT-Plus' agreement to accelerate liberalization among 'the willing'. This self-selected group would pursue the goals of free and open trade intended by the GATT founders. They would accelerate ahead of the main convoy of GATT contracting parties, which were reduced to the speed of the slowest vessel. When the

Uruguay Round negotiations collapsed in Brussels in 1990, over the rift between the EU and Japan, and major agricultural exporters (including the US), the prospects for a 'GATT-Plus' agreement comprising all OECD economies (plus some emerging Asian economies) was shelved (Preeg, 1995: 124). Nevertheless, the advantages of differential liberalization remained an option. Interest in regional and bilateral preferential trade arrangements in the period 1990–94 resulted in 33 new RTAs being notified to the GATT (WTO, 1995).

In the decade after the WTO was established, almost 250 new RTAs (of all three modes) were notified. While WTO ministers struggled to initiate the Doha Round negotiations, regional modes of liberalization blossomed. With most tariffs among the OECD economies at low levels, the main interest in RTAs was to reach new agreements on investment and business regulation, competition policy, government procurement, intellectual property protection and liberalization of services. This is evident in recent US RTAs with Chile, Singapore and Australia, the earlier NAFTA with Canada and Mexico, and now in CAFTA.

The earliest player in the RTA game was the EU, beginning with the EEC 'Six', which has now become 25 (with others waiting in the wings), and progressing to association agreements with Africa, Caribbean and Pacific countries (ACP) (former colonies, etc.). The EU has pursued some RTAs with individual partners (Chile, Mexico and South Africa, probably because the US and Japan already had agreements with these countries). It has formed extensive RTAs with groups of countries, including in South-Eastern Europe, the Gulf Cooperation Council (GCC) and the North African states. Most recently, Economic Partnership Agreements (EPAs), designed to promote economic development, have replaced the Cotonou Agreement with ACP countries. The EU has been, by far, the most active initiator of RTAs.

US Administrations began to show interest in regional trade arrangements when progress in the multilateral arena slowed. Even in the Uruguay Round the US negotiators had pursued 'new' topics, such as intellectual property, government procurement, TRIMs and trade and investment regulations. There had been little enthusiasm for these sorties into domestic regulations in global negotiations. So the US Trade Representative's Office (USTRO) began searching for 'like-minded' partners. Eligibility has included political and security considerations, in particular, countries prepared to tolerate continuation of US domestic policies on agriculture!

Until recently, Japan had remained outside RTAs, preferring to operate through APEC, which does not require tight commitments. Japan has initiated what it calls 'new age trade agreements' (NETAs) with countries in the region. The first was with Singapore – virtually a free trader anyway – where the noteworthy feature was the complete rejection of agricultural liberalization, even though Singapore has no agricultural exports (the agreement even excludes exports of tropical fish!) Another NETA has been reached with Mexico and negotiations have opened with Korea, Thailand, Malaysia and Philippines, and Australia. A more comprehensive approach is in hand with the ASEAN, but that will raise problems over Japan's sensitivity to agriculture.

The OECD economies are not alone in pursuing regional arrangements. Developing countries have adopted three approaches. First, neighbouring countries have reached agreements to collaborate across common borders to develop in specialized activities. Examples are, SADC (South African Development Community), MERCOSUR (Brazil, Argentina, Paraguay and Uruguay) and the ASEAN. This approach follows the pattern of developing country RTAs in the 1960s. These are mostly countries seeking specialization based on market size. However, economies of scale from this approach are insignificant with global markets so dominant. Second, groups of developing countries create links to OECD markets. This includes EU-EPAs, US-CAFTA, etc. The developing countries in these groups tend to be small and poor, and still dependent on aid and trade preferences.

Third, some developing countries have adopted a 'serial' approach, attaching themselves to several major economies. For example, Chile, Mexico and Singapore have signed agreements with some of the major players (US, EU, Japan), as well as with their neighbours. These countries already have low tariffs and have enjoyed the benefits of unilateral liberalization, which they hope to exploit with tariff-free access to large markets.

ASSESSING RTAs

The major trading nations play a dominant role in setting the terms of bilateral trade agreements. The agenda includes 'new' issues that have been blocked in WTO negotiations, such as capital market liberalization, competition rules, industrial standards and regulations affecting services. These regulatory changes require 'deep' integration. This indicates, perhaps, that the lesser partners see ample economic benefits from bilateral agreements that go beyond the level anticipated in multilateral negotiations. It is also consistent with liberalization agreements being easier to achieve with fewer – and like-minded – participants. As the GATT/WTO membership has increased, the prospects of reaching multilateral agreements have diminished. Some argue that this is a natural outcome of the success of 'multilateral liberalization' over the past 60 years, which has reduced most tariffs to insignificance in many economies (Ethier, 1998).

A WTO study of regionalism (WTO, 1995) reached a somewhat different explanation. It concluded: 'There is little question that the failed Brussels ministerial in December 1990 and the spread of regional integration agreements (especially after 1990) were major factors in eliciting the concessions needed to conclude the Uruguay Round.' Following this causation, the report argues, 'it may be that governments will consider that reforms are necessary in order to put the mutually supportive relationship between multilateralism and regionalism on a more solid foundation'.

This seems a forlorn hope. In 1996, the WTO Council created a Committee on Regional Trade Agreements (CRTA) to review notifications under GATT Article XXIV, required to report annually to the Council. It has yet to report on any RTA – or to submit an annual report! Evidently, major players prefer the long-standing casual, agnostic, non-committal response on agreements. The World Bank estimates 230 RTAs were operating early in 2005. The WTO *Annual Report 2005* reported that CRTA met three times in 2004, without making any progress. It reported that the committee faced institutional, political and legal difficulties, which meant effective monitoring was impossible. It is evident that RTAs are having negative effects on third parties. The WTO Secretariat is awaiting a review of GATT Article XXIV in the Doha Round Negotiating Group on Rules.

From the 69 working parties established to examine the conformity of agreements with GATT Article XXIV before 1995, only six reported positively – and only two of these are still active. Strikingly, no agreement was reached on the compatibility of the Treaty of Rome (EEC) with GATT Article XXIV. (This is not surprising since the whole agricultural sector was excluded from the agreement [Snape, 1993].) Achieving consensus in working parties was difficult because members had different views on RTAs. These are not easily reconciled by the vague wording of Article XXIV. For example, the agreement should cover 'substantially all trade' and that post-union trade barriers should not be 'on the whole higher or more restrictive' than those before the union.

These obscurities were not relieved by Uruguay Round negotiations. *The Understanding on the Interpretation of Article XXIV* (GATT, Annex 1A to the Marrakesh Agreement establishing the WTO, 1994) clarified some points of detail but generally restated the case for RTAs. It defined some points on 'substantially all trade' and introduced requirements on the general incidence of RTAs' duties and trade regulations on trade flows. For the first time, an attempt was made to define the transition period for the formation of an RTA 'within a reasonable length of time'. The understanding states that this should 'exceed ten years only in exceptional cases'. However, no sanctions or reviews are specified. Any action to enforce Article XXIV depends on the Committee on RTAs, which has not reported on any aspect of the article, or new agreements covered by Article XXIV.

These continuing gaps in the procedures on RTAs have become more significant with the increasing number of new agreements introduced since the WTO came into effect. Tightening the requirements would revalidate the non-discriminatory clause of GATT (1994). However, the uncertainties surrounding the Doha Development Round mean that many pro-liberalization members of the WTO see GATT Article XXIV as a valuable alternative to non-discrimination. It is unlikely this escape route will be sacrificed without guarantees that global liberalization will proceed apace.

'HUB-AND-SPOKE' AGREEMENTS

Most new RTAs apply to economies that are close geographically (or politically). But in searching for trade partners, small, open and dynamic economies look for large open economies (EU and US are favourites, at present). At the same time, the major players are seeking the kinds of access they are unable to negotiate in the WTO. With a few notable exceptions (e.g., agriculture, labour-intensive manufactures [clothing, footwear, toys]), tariffs are not significant impediments to trade, but regulations affecting investment, corporate behaviour, government procurement and services can prevent business profitability and expansion. These are the main interests in new RTAs.

As the fashion for RTAs and discriminatory arrangements took hold in the 1990s, there were demands for stronger disciplines on trade preferences (Bhagwati and Krueger, 1995). Free trade areas were condemned as inherently trade diverting and instrumental in creating new interest groups opposed to multilateral liberalization. It was proposed that only customs unions should be permitted by GATT Article XXIV, to avoid new preferences being generated. Unfortunately, history has betrayed this proposal. As already remarked, trade negotiators live in the real world of politics. RTAs have become widely popular, while the Doha Round struggles.

Bargaining power is important and large economies become 'hubs', forming separate bilateral agreements ('spokes') with individual smaller countries. These 'spokes' may not enjoy free trade among themselves (Wonnacott, 1996). The 'hubs' are able to set terms and conditions for individual agreements with each 'spoke'. These arrangements remove barriers to trade in goods and services with 'the hub', and typically contain rules on investment, competition, business behaviour (e.g., environment and labour standards) and rules of origin. The 'hub' countries have strong bargaining positions over smaller and weaker 'spoke' applicants, which allows them to impose special conditions. Problem industries are usually excluded; few RTAs include trade in agricultural produce or any clothing and footwear that escape the 'rules of origin'. The exclusions reduce opportunities for net trade creation (economic benefits) under bilateral free trade agreements. Such conditions can offset competitive advantages granted to 'spokes', but they may also lead to trade and investment diversion compared with multilateral liberalization (Wonnacott, 1996).

'Hub-and-spoke' arrangements carry risks, because the 'hub' is able to enter into new 'spoke' agreements with other countries. These may give new preferences that pre-empt the benefits anticipated from earlier agreements. Each 'spoke' has an agreement with 'the hub', but there are no links between the 'spoke' countries, unless they choose separately to establish such trade links. The 'hub-and-spoke' format suits the US negotiators because each bilateral free trade arrangement can be designed to protect sensitive US agricultural interests (e.g., sugar and beef producers), which appeals to Congress.

'Hub-and-spoke' agreements with OECD economies lock in domestic economic reforms as well as attracting foreign investments from 'the hub', and possibly from Third Countries. This trade and investment diversion is at the expense of other countries. As long as small economies have to rely on the weakened WTO negotiating process, 'hub-and-spoke' FTAs will be attractive. Members of RTAs protect their market gains by discriminating against outsiders, using rules of origin, anti-dumping duties and other contingency protection (Chapter 3). Multilateralists condemn preferential trade agreements and call for stronger disciplines in GATT Article XXIV, but the GATT/WTO record speaks for itself (WTO Consultative Board, 2005). The only way back to WTO disciplines would be a return to negotiating comprehensive free trade. Failure to progress along this route is why the RTA alternative has become popular.

RULES OF ORIGIN

One of the dangers associated with free trade areas is that each country has to administer two (or more) discrete tariff (and non-tariff) systems: the preferential tariff applied to FTA partners and the standard tariff applied to third parties. If a partner country has lower tariffs on an import category, there is an opportunity for local importers to obtain that product at a lower price by acquiring it via the partner country. This 'trade deflection' requires FTA member governments to take steps to preserve their taxation sovereignty. For this purpose, all imports from FTA partners have to declare their provenance within the FTA. To achieve this, the content or transformation required within the FTA must be declared before products can be traded freely across internal borders. These 'rules of origin' can be managed to limit severely FTA trade with Third Countries.

For example, the US-Mexico bilateral FTA has strict rules on textiles and clothing. Only items produced from thread made within NAFTA receive FTA

treatment, which restricts Mexico's labour cost advantage over the US producers of cloth and clothing. In many FTAs, the rules of origin are based on 'value
added' within the area. This is often set at 50 per cent of the shipped value (40
per cent in Australia-New Zealand CER). This approach has been overtaken by
events because many complex technical products move between countries
several times, or use components from many countries, which makes a source
difficult to identify. Keeping track of value added is difficult. So, rules of origin
are expensive for firms to satisfy and many firms now forego the preferential
tariff. These 'rules' may become a protective instrument because the local
content requirement encourages local processing over imports. It protects large
'hub' economies, too, because foreign companies are likely to locate in the
biggest market to minimize problems with 'rules of origin'. Rules of origin are
also powerful instruments in the hands of ruthless border officials.

One economic effect of preferential rules of origin is that they encourage
producers to substitute higher cost inputs from FTA member countries for
cheaper imported sources from non-members to qualify for tariff concessions.
These costs reduce the gains from more liberal trade relations with FTA
members. This also feeds into investment decisions. These second round
effects may offset the gains from trade expected from the FTA.

Customs unions do not require 'rules of origin' because of their common
external customs system. However, the EU is a 'hub' for many RTAs, with
former colonies and European and Mediterranean neighbours, etc. Here rules
of origin are ruthlessly applied, often in ways that undermine the apparent
generosity of access to the EU market. All other forms of preferential trade
require 'rules of origin'. The WTO has attempted to harmonize the definition
of product change, but there are still three definitions used:

- Where a process leads to a change of tariff classification (based on the
  Kyoto Convention Customs Co-operation Council (1977).
- Where 'substantial transformation' is based on specific processes, which
  require changes in tariff definition.
- 'Value added' is the most transparent and simple measure, but verifica-
  tion is difficult and time-consuming for producers.

Because of the complexity of 'rules of origin', and because tariffs on many
traded items are low now, many traders ignore the preferences, and opt to pay
MFN tariffs. Major traders, such as the EU and the US, have multiple 'rules
of origin' for different bilateral trade arrangements, which add to compliance
costs. Although the WTO is charged to examine 'rules of origin', it is not
examining the issue in the RTA context. Despite the trade-distorting effects of
'rules of origin' in RTAs, the Uruguay Round *Understanding on the
Interpretation of Article XXIV* of GATT (1994) did not mention the matter.

'Rules of origin' stand at the intersection of two developments in international trade: on one side there is the proliferation of preferential trade agreements; on the other, the multilateralization of production, which makes determination of origin very difficult. This plays into the hands of the protectionists who can manipulate these concepts to their own ends. The only apparent solution to this complex problem would be to strengthen the non-discriminatory principle in the WTO.

THE POLITICAL DIMENSION

The slow progress with the Doha Round negotiations and the failure so far to solve the differences between developed and developing countries' positions, particularly over agriculture, has encouraged trade negotiators to continue to give their attention to bilateral and regional trade agreements. The pillar of the GATT liberalization process for almost 60 years has been non-discrimination, embodied in the principle of most-favoured nation treatment. This principle is betrayed in any bilateral or regional agreement that discriminates against non-participants. The exception provided for by GATT Article XXIV has weakened the commitment to non-discrimination since the beginning. As the going has got tougher in multilateral negotiations, this exception has become attractive to countries wishing to move faster than multilateral negotiations would allow. Only if Article XXIV is closed will it be possible to restore non-discriminatory treatment. Yet GATT and WTO reviews and working parties have not been able to enforce the conditions or restrict the formation of new RTAs. Developing countries' demands for more preferential treatment in the Doha Round places the non-discrimination principle under further threat.

The WTO Commission set up to review stresses in the world trading system, reported to the Director-General in January 2005. It argued that the WTO powers were being undermined by members' intransigence and short-term considerations. In particular, it criticized the proliferation of bilateral trade agreements, but the only solution offered was a successful multilateral trade negotiation. It is the failure to make progress in the Doha Round that is causing many governments to pursue bilateral agreements. Ironically, the Commission called for more political involvement in WTO affairs. Yet, it is a political decision – possibly out of frustration with the Doha stalemate – that drives the shift to RTAs.

Multilateralists argue that the same trade benefits, or better, could be achieved within the WTO system without the disruption of trade discrimination (Bhagwati and Panagariya, 2003). The problem is that though in theory multilateral negotiations based on reciprocal liberalization of trade barriers produce the best results, a consensus agreement among all WTO members is required. Recent experience has shown that many major members of the WTO do not want to reduce their trade protection in key sectors (e.g., EU, US and Japan on agriculture). At the same time, developing countries insist on increased preferential access to OECD markets, without reciprocity, and oppose any efforts to extend negotiations to cover their domestic impediments to trade. Until developing countries accept that most benefits from trade liberalization come from domestic liberalization, not from other countries' tariff reductions, little progress will be made with multilateral negotiations. On the other hand, RTAs can promote domestic economic reforms, economic efficiency and competitive markets, as well as fostering policy cooperation between members. When RTAs are between rich and poor countries there is a danger that the former will impose their policies. However, access to a large OECD economy attracts investment to the poor country, which must improve employment and income opportunities. Attempts to achieve multilateral agreements on foreign investment in the OECD and in the WTO have been repeatedly thwarted by NGOs, labour unions and host government concerns. An RTA allows the decision to be left for the participating governments (and domestic business and electorates) to decide.

It is a forlorn hope to expect political attitudes to change. Although regarded as the first effective 'global' agency, the WTO Council depends on consensus decisions. Nobody is going to argue for a change to the United Nations' system of worthless resolutions and voting that is ignored.

The question to ask now is whether the discrimination in the system caused by the spread of RTAs and 'hub-and-spoke' systems has already undermined the multilateral trading system? The spread of preferential trade agreements – and particularly the bilateral variety – has gained pace in the past decade. (The EU exploitation of preferential trade arrangements goes back to the beginning of the GATT.) The reasons for this were touched on above (Chapter 5) in describing the breakdown of the Uruguay Round negotiations on agriculture. For the whole of its life, GATT had struggled with agricultural protectionism. Aficionados have declared repeatedly, 'This time we will succeed'. Yet, it is evident that all the main players – EU, US and Japan – many small, rich European countries and most developing countries have embedded agricultural protection because of the weight that rural sectors exert in election systems and the power of landowners to influence decisions. Rational economic arguments are not persuasive against these groups. If real events are examined, the ineffectiveness of the Blair House agreement in December 1993 shows that even an agreement sold to the public as a major advance can be ignored. The addition of 'the peace clause', meaning five years before any agricultural discussions could be re-opened, appears to have been a contrivance to ensure that the public would not be kept informed about the process of liberalization. By the time the transition period was over, no reductions had taken place and protection was virtually unchanged. EU ministers had even decided that CAP funding should be unchanged until 2013! Agricultural negotiations among officials in the preliminaries for Doha Round have shown little progress, and developing countries' demands for better access to developed countries' markets seem to make OECD governments more obdurate.

Evidence of the past 50 years on agricultural negotiations and the subterfuge perpetrated to complete the Uruguay Round, indicate that agriculture will remain outside multilateral trade negotiations. Similar obfuscation has been evident in the TCF sector, where progressive protection was provided over 30 years by the MFA, until the Uruguay Round agreement on textiles and clothing. This provided ten years for the OECD countries to adapt to removing quota controls. Yet, when the time came, in 2005, new loopholes were discovered and protection is continuing. Why should developing countries have any faith in multilateral negotiations? Hence, it is better to proceed using RTAs, which give bargaining power to the rich and the powerful and at least the 'spoke' countries know what they are getting.

Frustrated by the hiatus in WTO negotiations, business and trade negotiators are driving the new regionalism. Acting out of self-interest, business has been provoked by interventions by aggressive NGOs and the failure of governments to confront anti-globalization in international agencies. Confidence in the WTO has been undermined by recent difficulties with Doha Round negotiations. As part of the globalization process, business has sought to integrate its production and marketing. Businesses in the US and East Asia are putting pressure on governments to negotiate bilateral agreements to gain access to new sectors (e.g., services) and to smooth away distorting domestic policies, such as investment rules, industrial and social standards. This FTA approach to liberalization is gradual and allows participants to 'test the water'.

Among OECD economies and emerging Asian economies industrial tariffs are low and many are insignificant. Hence, business wants to expand trade in services, investment flows and intergovernment cooperation (government procurement). At the same time, some major players want to avoid any liberalization in agriculture and materials processing (e.g., Japan, the US and the EU). These kinds of agreements will achieve increasing acceptance as long as major players block a genuine review of GATT Article XXIV, and developing countries block progress in the Doha Round.

Evidently, trade policies are driven by politics. For almost 60 years governments have propagated arguments in favour of the benefits from liberal – if not free – trade. Now, with many tariffs low, the charade is exposed and trading with the 'like-minded' is the solution. The free trade case is irrefutable, within the assumptions and conditions of the economic model, but who can take account of politics!

APPENDIX 6.1

GATT Article XXIV and GATS Article V

The principle of non-discrimination is fundamental to the GATT/WTO system. RTAs are an exception under GATT Article XXIV and GATS Article V. RTAs receive wide support in the WTO Council.

GATT Article XXIV sets out the conditions for trade in goods:

- Duties and other restrictive regulations of commerce must be eliminated on substantially all trade between the member countries.
- In customs unions, the same duties must be applied by each of the members against Third Countries.
- The duties applied to goods from non-members following the formation of a customs union or free trade area must not on the whole be higher than those applying before its creation.
- Agreements to enter into a customs union or free trade arrangement must be notified to the WTO.
- The adoption of an interim arrangement is possible, but this entails preparing a plan and a schedule for the formation.
- An interim arrangement must not exceed ten years.

GATS Article V sets out the conditions for trade in services:

- A regional agreement must have substantial sectoral coverage in terms of sectors covered, volume of trade affected and modes of supply.
- National treatment has to be given to the other parties in substantially all trade, and no new discriminatory measures may be introduced.
- The overall level of barriers to trade in services from non-members must not be higher than the level applicable before the agreement.
- Agreements to enter into a free trade agreement in services must be notified to the WTO.

The conditions set out in these Articles are mandatory for developed countries. Developing countries can form preferential arrangements among themselves with more flexibility under GATT Part IV and the Enabling Clause.

REFERENCES

Bhagwati, J. and A.O. Krueger (1995), *The Dangerous Drift to Preferential Trade Agreements*, Washington, DC: American Enterprise Institute.

Bhagwati, J. and A. Panagariya (2003), 'Bilateral trade treaties are a sham', *Financial Times*, 14 July.

Camps, M. (1964), *Britain and the European Community 1955–63*, Oxford: Oxford University Press.

Ethier, W.J. (1998.), 'The new regionalism', *The Economic Journal*, **108**(July), 1149–61.

Johnson, H.G. (1965), 'An economic theory of protectionism, tariff bargaining, and the formation of customs unions', *Journal of Political Economy*, **LXXIII**(June), 256–83.

Lipsey, R.G. (1960), 'The theory of customs unions: a general survey', *The Economic Journal*, **69**(3) (Feb), 496–513.

Meade, J.E. (1955), *The Theory of Customs Unions*, Amsterdam: North-Holland.

Preeg, E.H. (1995), *Traders in a Brave New World*, Chicago: Chicago University Press.

Snape, R.H. (1993), 'History and economics of GATT's Article XXIV', in K. Anderson and R. Blackhurst (eds), *Regional Integration and the Global Trading System*, London: Harvester-Wheatsheaf.

Soloaga, I. and L.A. Winters (2001), 'Regionalism in the nineties: what effect on trade?', *North American Journal of Economics and Finance*, **12**(1), 1–29.

Viner, J. (1950), *The Customs Union Issue*, New York: Carnegie Endowment.

Williamson, J. and A. Bottrill (1971), 'The impact of customs unions on trade in manufactures', *Oxford Economic Papers*, **23**(3), 323–51.

Wonnacott, R.J. (1996), 'Trade and investment in a "hub-and-spoke" system', *The World Economy*, **19**(3), 237–52.

World Trade Organization (WTO) (1995), *Regionalism and the World Trading System*, Geneva: WTO.

WTO Consultative Board (2005), *The Future of the WTO*, Geneva: WTO.

7. Promoting economic development

Programmes to promote economic development in poor countries have ebbed and flowed over the past 50 years. Not unexpectedly, economic growth of developing countries as a group has tended to follow the fortunes of the rich industrial economies. In the prosperous 1960s, alert and energetic economies in East Asia (Hong Kong, Taiwan, Singapore and Korea), which did not follow prevailing import-substitution fashion in development, grew rapidly. They attracted investment, know-how and enterprises from industrial economies and supplied labour-intensive manufactures into OECD markets. As OECD economies slowed in the 1970s, while adjusting to the oil crises and combating accelerating inflation, many developing countries following inward-looking growth strategies prospered by borrowing from commercial banks, which were flush with petro-dollars and looking for borrowers as foreign exchange regulations were relaxed. This investment-driven development came to a sudden stop in 1980 when the US and other OECD governments switched to anti-inflationary policies, which sharply reduced banks' liquidity and raised interest rates. Mexico first, then other Latin American countries, which had borrowed to pay for new infrastructure and public services, were unable to meet the higher debt servicing charges. The 1980s' debt crisis was met with debt rescheduling and IMF/World Bank support, but also brought large exchange rate depreciations. The 1980s became a period of adjustment and consolidation, with declining levels of activity in OECD economies and many developing countries.

Led by the US recovery, the global economy picked up as the 1980s progressed, while many developing economies made stuttering recoveries. As economic recovery gathered momentum in the 1990s along with renewed market liberalization, the world economy moved into 'globalization'. Economic recovery in OECD economies gradually spread to developing countries and growth reappeared, particularly in East Asia and Latin America. Private foreign investment increased across the world as deregulated capital markets increased their lending. Volatile short-term capital flows became a danger to economies where the banking systems were not well managed. Economies with apparently stable currencies and strong growth attracted speculative money flows. In 1997–98, pressures on the Thai baht led to sudden, massive capital outflows, which spread nervousness and disrupted development throughout South-East Asia, and spread to countries in Latin America (see Chapter 10). The ASEAN economies and Korea, where financial and corporate reform were implemented, recovered surprisingly quickly from the disruption and have benefited from China's surge in development. In Latin America recovery was patchy, because reforms were contradictory and unpredictable.

In Sub-Saharan Africa (SSA), the Middle East and many small island or landlocked countries, economic development, if evident at all, has been slow and erratic. Globalization has barely touched them, except perhaps via tourism. Development gaps have widened. Many SSA economies have recorded negative growth and serious health problems (malaria, HIV/AIDS, malnutrition, etc.). Their plight has deteriorated because of bad governments, civil unrest and tribal warfare. The problems of SSA economies now dominate deliberations in UN agencies, the Bretton Woods organizations and OECD governments.

NGOs and prominent media celebrities have drawn public attention to widening disparities between the prosperity in Western economies and the abject poverty in much of Africa. And, of course, it has to be somebody's fault. Like many others, the media celebrities focus on 'the gaps' but not the reasons for them. Similarly, UN agencies refer to the 'marginalization' of these economies from 'globalization', which implies some kind of conspiracy. The remedy, they believe, is the responsibility of OECD governments, international agencies and the community at large, in the name of social justice, human rights and equity.

Undoubtedly, the resources must come from these sources, but financial aid, trade opportunities and advice can only be effective if SSA governments recognize the need for, and pursuit of, institutional change to promote economic freedom and opportunities for their people. The complexities of problems in SSA countries, and other least developed economies, are subsumed by NGOs in a 'communitarian' appeal to social conscience, but self-help and responsibility are essential. The African Union (AU) meeting in Libya in July 2005, demonstrated that SSA leaders demand assistance, but on their terms. The fragility of economic and political progress in SSA is demonstrated by recent violence in Ethiopia and withdrawal of AIDS money from Uganda because of corruption. These were two countries reported as making valid institutional reforms (Mallaby, 2004: chs 8/9; UN Millennium Development Report, 2005).

Writing almost 40 years ago, the late Professor Harry Johnson (1967) described the social and political preconditions for successful economic development:

> To establish a modern society capable of self-sustaining economic growth at a reasonable rate requires, in broad terms, the attainment of political stability and a

reasonable impartiality of governmental administration, to provide a political institutional framework within which individuals and enterprises (whether working for their own gain or within the public sector) can plan innovations with maximum certainty about the future environment. It requires the establishment of a legal system defining rights of property, person and contract sufficiently clearly, and a judiciary system permitting settlement of disputes sufficiently predictably and inexpensively, to provide a legal institutional framework within which production and accumulation can be undertaken with a minimum degree of non-economic risk. And it requires the establishment of a social system permitting mobility of all kinds (both allowing opportunity and recognising accomplishment), and characterised by the depersonalisation of economic and social relationships, to provide maximum opportunities and incentives for individual advancement on the basis of productive economic contribution. This transformation is by no means complete in the most economically advanced countries, even after two centuries of industrialisation, which were preceded by several centuries of manufacturing and commercial development. It encounters strong resistance from traditional values and traditional systems of social control over individual activity and aspirations.

This explanation of the preconditions for successful economic analysis of development won high praise from Bauer (1971).

THE MILLENNIUM DEVELOPMENT REPORT

One consequence of the pressures building up for actions to relieve poverty and debt, especially for SSA countries and other least developed economies, was the UN Millennium Development Summit in 2000, which adopted the Millennium Development Goals (MDGs). These pared-down targets have become the reference points for noisy public debates, discussions at repeated international conferences and for the reformulation of international policies to assist these least developed economies. UN Millennium Development Goals (to be achieved by 2015):

1.   eradicate extreme poverty and hunger;
2.   achieve universal primary education;
3.   promote gender equality and empower women;
4.   reduce child mortality;
5.   improve maternal health;
6.   combat HIV/AIDS, malaria and other diseases;
7.   ensure environmental sustainability;
8.   a global partnership for development.

These MDGs evolved from UN and World Bank-commissioned research into why development fails, and from recent reviews of development policies by

OECD governments. This initiative has influenced outcomes of follow-up meetings:

- Doha, November 2001. WTO ministerial meeting adopted the Doha Development Agenda.
- Monterey, Mexico, March 2002. International Conference on Financing for Development.
- Johannesburg, South Africa, October 2002. UN World Summit on Sustainable Development.
- UN Special Assembly, New York, September 2005. Review of the Millennium Development Goals.

A team at the Earth Institute at Columbia University, led by Professor Jeffrey Sachs, produced a massive (3000-page) report for the UN on progress towards the MDGs: *Investing in Development: A Practical Plan to Achieve the Millennium Development Goals* (2005). This 'Millennium Development Report' (MDR) makes a strong case for revising attitudes to aid. It calls for at least a doubling of aid flows and for improving the effectiveness of aid, particularly when confronting serious poverty and social breakdowns present in SSA and other small, isolated economies. It proposes that aid should be focussed on intended outcomes rather than on policy inputs. But that still leaves the question of how?

THE EVOLVING DEBT PROBLEM

Since the debt crisis appeared in the 1980s, the Bretton Woods' agencies have become increasingly caught up with lending to lost causes without properly enforced conditionality. As flexible exchange rates and deregulated capital markets facilitated economic adjustments in OECD economies and private capital flows were liberalized, the IMF as well as the World Bank and the regional development banks became entangled in devising development programmes for developing countries with heavy debt portfolios. Simultaneously, the international financial agencies came under concerted pressures from development and 'social equity' NGOs for failing to respond effectively to widening economic disparities. (There are suggestions that the World Bank under Wolfensohn's leadership encouraged such criticism as a means of enhancing the organization's influence [Mallaby, 2004]). Conflicting interests among NGOs complicated decision-making: development and human rights groups believed more funds should be released to help the poor countries, regardless of their creditworthiness, financial management or the state of their governments, whereas 'green' NGOs wanted

investment in 'sustainable development' (Beckerman, 2003). As well as pick-
eting and harassing the financial agencies, many NGOs found joint cause
with UN agencies, which declared 'globalization' to be a divisive force in
international affairs that widens gaps between rich and poor (ILO, 2004;
UNDP, 1999).

The concentration on finance for developing economies demonstrates a
widespread misunderstanding of the development process. It is obvious that
financial aid has done little to encourage economic progress in SSA. Even debt
servicing is not achieved. Since the 1950s, when 'development economics'
became fashionable, policies have focussed on control: central planning
(including asset appropriation), compulsory saving (via taxation), large-scale
foreign aid, and control of external economic relations (to forecast export
potential allows forecasts of import capacity [Bauer, 1971]). This recipe for
control was to replace the decisions of individual consumers and producers,
without explaining why it would promote a rise in national income. Foreign
funding of these regimes, with no commitment to freedom, the rule of law or
equity, helped to entrench ruthless power elites that have prevented development (Bauer, 1982). The outcome was to divert foreign aid into corrupt uses,
especially weapons in Africa to wage war or to suppress the local population.
Aid and trade protection have turned these countries into mendicants, who
display a self-destructive claims mentality. Central planning and control have
undermined self-help, competition and innovation, and colonial-era market
institutions have been degraded. No amount of capital and other hardware of
development (technology and equipment) will be productive in generating
Third World development if it is not combined with the right institutional
'software'. So providing increases in aid flows is unlikely to help the majority
of citizens (Kasper, 2006).

The history of development assistance, what Bauer (1971) called 'government-to-government transfers' (because there is little evidence that any of
these funds reached the poor in developing countries), falls into three phases.
Initially, there was enthusiasm for helping former dependencies to become
independent. OECD countries, both directly and via the World Bank and other
development banks, provided long-term loans to build essential infrastructure,
while most developing countries pursued a strategy of import substitution
combined with socialist planning. The policy elites in developing countries
wanted more aid and more independence in its use (long-term private capital
flows were still subject to regulations that were not eased until the 1970s). In
1973, OECD countries committed to an annual target of 0.7 per cent of their
GDP – just as the oil crisis struck!

The second phase arrived with a flood of petro-dollars onto gradually liberalizing capital markets. Middle-income developing countries were able to
borrow all they wanted, at low or negative real interest rates. OECD countries

faced rising inflation and declining growth, and many of their development assistance programmes were curtailed as government expenditures were squeezed.

The third phase came when the debt crisis struck Mexico in 1980. Immediate attention was focussed on protecting the exposed financial markets and the banks by rescheduling outstanding debts. The problem spread quickly to other middle-income developing economies, especially in Latin America where economic freedom had been neglected. The serious deflations that resulted caused serious hardship in middle-income countries, as capital flows dried up and interest rates rose. Economic recovery in OECD countries was slow and uneven through the decade. Development assistance flows were increasingly tied to purchases from donor countries, which reduced their value to recipients.

When the global economy began to recover in the 1980s, confidence returned and 'the golden age' was associated with booming, liberalizing capital markets. Private capital flows returned to emerging markets; long-term capital flows increased from less than $50 billion in 1990 to almost $300 billion in 1997. In particular, the growth of foreign direct investment provided a bundle of capital, technology, expertise and access to OECD markets. However, official development assistance flows to low-income countries declined and no longer supported development in SSA and similar backward economies, which could not access capital markets. Unfortunately, the optimism derived from globalization assumed that financial markets would deal with fiscal deficits and external imbalances. Development assistance wallowed, which left the poorest economies without support, because they could not offer economic or political stability. The successful developing countries moved on strongly. By liberalizing their economies they attracted investment and became 'emerging economies' – Chile, China, India and Brazil.

As the millennium closed, attention turned to the least developed economies, many of which were recording declining income per head (World Bank Annual Reports [various]). The Jubilee 2000 campaign and the UN development goals focussed attention on poverty. Since 2000 new proposals were made to increase financial assistance for those in greatest need: debt forgiveness, mobilizing idle resources (such as selling IMF gold), schemes to bring forward future aid payments into current aid flows (UK Treasury), converting the World Bank into a grant-giving agency, financing new development assistance by taxing international transactions (airline fuel, financial transactions [Tobin Tax], etc.). The real question is whether G8 ministers can turn debt forgiveness and more grant aid into genuine development. This must depend on how SSA governments and other poor economies act to reform political and economic institutions, and use this money for reform and to react to trade opportunities (see Chapter 5).

The lessons from 50 years of aid giving are being ignored in the rush to show concern for Third World poverty in SSA and elsewhere. New aid and debt forgiveness for these mismanaged economies is the popular demand, drawing on the World Bank HIPC programme, 'Make poverty history' and various UN millennium programmes – as it had been for Jubilee 2000. They all argue that increased aid will overcome poverty.

To be effective, it is evident that future aid should be given selectively and made conditional on specific reforms. Making an announcement of a US$ 5 billion annual increase in US aid in Monterrey in 2002, President Bush said, 'We must tie aid to political and legal and economic reforms'. This was consistent with the World Bank call for targeting aid to countries' performance, not promises. This would move aid flows towards 'social and administrative infrastructure, and reduce lending for large infrastructure projects (roads, dams, bridges, etc., which were unpopular with NGOs anyway). The Bank argued that aid programmes should be owned and developed by the people who are in development, which presumably means the leaders of the recipient country. This puts a lot of faith in SSA leaders. Another suggestion is that aid should be directed to 'civil society' in recipient countries, which raises even more problems for aid suppliers. The US Millennium Challenge Corporation (MCC), which administers the Millennium Challenge Account (MCA), decides the distribution of this aid by reviewing quantitative international indices of government performance. How effective this system will prove to be remains to be seen. (The African Union has already rejected conditionality.)

DEVELOPMENT, TRADE AND AID

Traditional analysis of economic development has regarded trade as 'the engine of growth', because opening an economy to trade increased specialization in production, according to comparative advantage, and enlarged the range of goods and services available to consumers (and to producers in as much as components and other inputs could be imported). The production and consumption gains that result from trade raise incomes, while multiplier effects and realization of new opportunities impart continuing economic growth (Chapter 4).

Perversely, these traditional gains from trade did not feature in the calculations of developing countries' governments after World War II. Trade pessimism carried over from the 1930s meant that tariffs, quotas and foreign exchange regulations were widespread. Most development economists that advised the independent developing countries, therefore, chose to adopt import-substitution strategies, which were consistent with the post-war predilection for central planning and government control. Communities had accepted regulations and rationing during and after World War II, and collectivism using socialist planning was the prevailing philosophy. De-colonization brought its own problems, as new leaders sought to stamp their authority by rejecting systems left by departing colonialists. Restrictions and regulations were considered essential for nation building.

Early analysis of economic development was based on a 'two-gap' model. This structuralist model was first presented formally in 1960 (Little, 1982) and became the driving force for the UN, national aid agencies and the World Bank. The gap that became quickly apparent to newly independent states was the 'import gap', because many developing countries were dependent on imports of food, materials and capital equipment, which quickly outran their capacity to export. The shortage of foreign exchange resulted in restrictions on all kinds of international transactions. The other side of the trade gap was that domestic investment exceeded domestic saving, as inflation went unchecked and property rights were usurped. Investment in new equipment to raise productivity was essential for economic development. The saving-investment deficit quickly ran down any foreign exchange reserves and it had to be met by overseas borrowing or an aid programme, from development banks or foreign governments. Except in exceptional circumstances (famine, natural disasters, etc.), financial aid was likely to be a loan, albeit on concessional terms (over long periods at low interest rates).

In this model, financial assistance was intended to finance investment in productive equipment, which domestic saving alone could not do. (Capital equipment required foreign exchange for purchase overseas.) In due course, this was intended to increase output and allow the loan (and interest) to be repaid, assuming foreign exchange earnings permitted. However, if financial aid was used to build social infrastructure or spent on public consumption (health, education, sanitation, etc.) or armaments, there would be no imports of food or essentials, and no foreign exchange from which to service or repay loans. The stock of debt would build up as interest was added to the initial loan. It was a slippery path.

Easterly (2003) tested this 'financing gap' model to establish whether aid improves investment and growth over time. Very few countries showed a positive link between aid and investment, or between investment and growth, because of institutional defects. This was not an encouraging story for aid as an instrument for development – or to eradicate extreme poverty. Easterly did not stop at this theoretical evaluation of the 'financing gap' model. He gathered together case studies of aid experience – mostly in Africa – that supported his findings from a score of developing countries (Easterly, 2001). In Asia the story was quite different.

These results indicate that economic development must depend on a country's own economic institutions and policies. Where aid does promote growth it derives from the good economic policies pursued in that country. Burnside and Dollar (2000) established that the effectiveness of development assistance depends on conventional measures of good economic management, measured by budget balance, inflation rate and openness. Interestingly, this research showed that aid flows (multilateral and bilateral) did not seem to respond to good policy records in recipient economies, probably because institutional reforms were neglected.

COMBATING POVERTY IN AFRICA

Compared with other continents, Africa has been severely disadvantaged geographically (Sowell, 2004). Although more than twice the size of Europe, Africa has a shorter coastline and far fewer harbours. Its rivers are less navigable (apart from the Nile), because Africa has a narrow coastal plain backed by tablelands, which cause rapids on the rivers only a few kilometres from the seashore. Seasonal rainfall makes even navigable sections of rivers on the tablelands unreliable. SSA faces handicaps to development that require large investments to allow travel and trade that other continents have had for centuries. Historically, Africa was equally disadvantaged. European colonization was late, while the Mediterranean civilizations were out of reach because of the Sahara Desert. These physical and historical impediments have to be overcome with major investments that will take time.

Other causes of poverty in Africa include small markets, low-productivity agriculture, major health problems (HIV/AIDS and malaria, but many other diseases) and little access to technology because of isolation and political uncertainties. In order to break out of this 'poverty trap', the Brookings Institution and the Columbia University Millennium Development Report to the UN (*Investing in Development*) propose that a massive increase in aid flows will need to be sustained over 20 years, well beyond MDG 2015. Both these studies call for large increases in aid flows to SSA countries over this period: between 20 and 30 per cent of GDP in most SSA countries, which would more than double the present rate of aid to SSA of $19 billion per annum. However, not all SSA countries are equally destitute. Many countries have natural resources and coastal positions, and some have been progressing recently (e.g., Mozambique).

The MDR (2005) points out that a new framework is required to assess aid policies in terms of outcomes rather than policy inputs. While accepting that measuring the value of aid poses some difficulties (e.g., whether disaster aid or emergency support should be included in a measure of productive efficiency), rejecting measurement of aid flows to test efficiency of aid programmes is unlikely to appeal to aid donors. Few would dispute the report's other proposal that well-designed aid, delivered in a sustained way, 'works best when delivered to well governed countries' (MDR, 2005, 'Overview', Box 8, p. 41). But this raises more questions than it solves.

How would 'a well-governed country' be defined? It is doubtful that it would be based on economic freedom (i.e., property rights, rule of law or sound financial organization). How should its development be monitored? Evidently, many SSA governments are sensitive to assessments of their performance. Even countries with good reports in World Bank/IMF assessments within the HIPC programme (Highly Indebted Poor Countries initiative) have only recently registered stability, after many years of civil wars and bad governments (e.g., Tanzania, Mozambique) – and Ethiopia has already relapsed. The HIPC initiative was launched in 1996 and expanded in 1999. It offers debt relief to countries that pursue sound economic policies; 42 countries are participating, 35 from SSA. The Millennium Development Report lists 11 SSA economies regarded as suitable to receive enhanced aid flows because of their HIPC record, including Ghana, Mozambique, Senegal, Tanzania, Ethiopia and Uganda. (Ethiopia and Uganda have already marred their records!) These countries are eligible for ten-year lending programmes by the MDR (Box 10). This raises questions about their long-term stability.

Serious questions are raised about the value of the African Union (AU) peer review initiated in 2001 (as required by the New Partnership for Africa's Development [NEPAD]). The MDR reports that 20 countries have received favourable NEPAD assessments, including Kenya, Nigeria, Rwanda, Sierra Leone, Gabon and Congo. All these have been on the list of most corrupt and vicious regimes in Africa within the past 20 years, and some still are! None have received a favourable report from any other assessment (MDR, 2005, p. 52). An African Union approval does not give confidence. If government effectiveness is to be assessed before aid is given, an objective assessment is necessary. Mutual assessment always raises suspicions. (AU approval is suspect also because of its 'hands off' attitude to Mugabe in Zimbabwe, where one-third of the population has fled and starvation is widespread, in a country that previously exported food.)

Where good government is absent (e.g., Togo, Sudan, Zimbabwe), the MDR argues that aid should still be given, 'to improve government institutions'! The many failings of SSA governments over the past 40 years are acknowledged occasionally in the MDR, including violence and civil unrest. Nevertheless, the responsibility for poverty is laid at the door of OECD governments or blamed on shortcomings in the strategies and instruments of the IMF, the World Bank and the WTO. While 'politically correct' in UN- and NGO-speak, this attitude is a hangover from the 1960s when 'the vicious circle of poverty was alleged to be caused by the rich countries' (Bauer, 1971 quoting Myrdal, 1957). This apportioning of blame should raise warning flags among OECD governments. As the UK Commission on Africa reported, Africa must take the lead in a new partnership with OECD countries, take responsibility for its problems and take ownership of the solutions. The record of the AU in Sudan, Zimbabwe, Côte d'Ivoire, etc., has not improved relations with donor governments.

The strategy proposed in the Millennium Development Report contains much wishful thinking: 'aid is most useful if channelled to the countries that most need it . . . and channelled to the right sectors (mainly infrastructure and human capital). It works best when delivered to well-governed countries' (Box 8). The last sentence in this passage raises the key question. How can it be established that government and private institutions are capable of managing successful aid programmes? Furthermore, social rights to property defined by law and custom, rights of redress through the courts, equity and liberty are essential to promote prosperity and freedom for individuals. These institutional rules are taken for granted in most Western democracies, where they were established after centuries of trial and error. Without them, private sector activities in developing countries cannot evolve, as thinkers down the ages have demonstrated (Bethell, 1998; Schumpeter, 1961; Adam Smith, 1776 [1910] and Sowell, 1987, 2004).

While the MDR explains that 'strong civil society engagement and participation are crucial to effective governance' (p. 16) and refers to 'remarkable and dedicated civil society organizations', very little attention is given to the private sector. It is referred to as 'the engine of growth in production' and it is recognized that the private sector must provide incomes and jobs once appropriate government institutions and public infrastructure are in place. But the private sector is also admonished to support transparency and corporate social responsibility (p. 18), which seems misplaced anywhere without basic law and order! The report is strangely quiet about policies to promote private enterprise, while very 'politically correct' about civil society, social justice and human rights. Lasting prosperity, however, will depend on robust private industries. Only an optimist could believe that market competition will manifest itself by 2015, after SSA governments have been force-fed with debt forgiveness and massive public sector aid.

The verdict on the proposals in MDR *Investing in Development* is that it contains too much detail and preaching about the goals, instruments and participants, while it gives little attention to fundamental concerns about the potential of SSA countries to respond to all or any of the approaches offered.

Nevertheless, the attention of donors has been attracted. In February 2005, G7 finance ministers acknowledged the need to increase financial assistance to least developed countries, and particularly to Africa. They were divided over approaches to the problem and various plans were proposed in the months leading to the G8 Leaders meeting in Scotland. The G8 communiqué in July 2005 promised that the OECD governments would provide an additional $50 billion a year to present development aid programmes, which would then reach $79 billion by 2010. This included $25 billion additional aid to Africa, which would double the present aid level by 2010. The focus on aid in the G8 agenda had been determined by the massive programme 'Make poverty history', led by pop stars and other media personalities, as a front for some national and international bureaucracies. As expected, the aid increases were regarded as insufficient. This highly organized programme had avoided the customary anti-globalization protest, but softly, softly could not achieve the impossible demands by the organizers.

Several development NGOs criticized the aid increases immediately after the G8 meeting. ActionAid declared there was 'a yawning gulf between expectations raised and policy promises delivered'. Several other groups commented in similar tone. In truth, 'the yawning gulf' is in the practical understanding of these NGOs. The extra aid has to be phased in gradually because these economies do not have the capacities to absorb large increases immediately: health and education services need trained staff and schools; roads need surveyors and engineers; and large capital inflows need managers. On the other side, OECD governments face conflicting demands at home. France, Italy and Germany have high unemployment levels and substantial budget deficits, which means domestic priorities compete for development funds. Despite popular support for campaigns against poverty, the alternative demands nearer home are relevant too.

NGOs do have a legitimate concern about the value of the 'new' commitments. It is not clear whether the numbers in the G8 communiqué are in addition to earlier pledges or whether there may be some double counting. For example, the UK announcement in September 2004 that it will cover 10 per cent of debt payments by HIPCs in Africa will come from a provision in the existing aid budget. Moreover, in May 2005, the EU (15 members) agreed to raise aid to 0.51 per cent of GDP by 2010. This would be very close to the Gleneagles figure! The politics of aid is ruled by obfuscation.

'MAKE POVERTY HISTORY'!

We live in an increasingly complicated world of instant communications, incomprehensible technologies and jet travel. Yet slogan propaganda and mass demonstrations drive the media and policy debates – though fortunately not outcomes! The flow of research papers from scientists, technologists, social scientists, medical and health institutes, etc. is so vast that academics and experts have to narrow their field of interest. Yet vast numbers of people respond immediately to eye-catching slogans from pop stars and church charities, apparently without much thought, except compassion. Many slogans are untrue, as well as being misleading and even dangerous. They all assume there is an immediate solution – 'forgive debt', 'save our jobs', 'ban the bomb', 'no cheap imports', 'save the forests', 'nuclear free zone', etc.

Removing poverty from Africa cannot be achieved from outside. Only successful institutional development in some of the world's poorest and most badly governed countries can do that. Even if debt-forgiveness, vastly increased grant aid and duty-free access to all OECD markets could be provided, it would only help to raise living standards if necessary institutions to provide private property rights, the rule of law and democratic government were created in each African economy (Kasper and Streit, 1998; Sowell, 2004).

Forgiving outstanding government debt of SSA countries has popular appeal, according to the media. The Jubilee 2000 appeal led by the Pope, the churches and the Dalai Lama achieved wide media coverage and street support, without anyone giving it much thought, except that it was compassionate. Media reporters believed that millions of people were living in poverty because of Third World debt. Many people, who know better and know how difficult it is to reverse economic decay, failed to criticize this simple mirage in order to retain 'street credibility'. Servicing large debts is a burden. But experience shows that it is not as simple as that.

Developing countries' debt has been on the international agenda since 1980. OECD countries in the Paris Club reschedule vast amounts of official debt every year, and gradually, the World Bank and other development banks, and the IMF, have re-scheduled and 'forgiven' debt, as well as reduced interest rates charged on outstanding debts. In 1996, the World Bank and the IMF introduced the Highly Indebted Poor Countries (HIPC) initiative to provide debt forgiveness for poor countries pursuing good policies. In 1999, the G7 summit called for this scheme to be accelerated and extended. All this goes a long way to meet the demands for debt forgiveness made by Jubilee 2000. So how effective has it been?

There has been no decline in indebtedness, according to World Bank debt tables, despite these extensive schemes to reduce debt. One explanation is that countries simply borrow to replace debt that is forgiven – that is, countries borrow in anticipation of further debt forgiveness (Hughes, 1999). So debt becomes a persistent problem, regardless of forgiveness (Easterly, 2001: ch. 7). There are 32 SSA countries covered by the HIPC initiative. In the typical HIPC economy, per capita income has declined in the past 20 years, in spite of all the debt relief given. Of course, private investment flows to HIPC economies are low, so most capital inflow is from the World Bank and the

IMF. These flows are much higher than to non-HIPC economies and they are increasingly aid grants from IDA. In fact, HIPC governments continue to receive the lion's share of new disbursements to developing countries. In these circumstances, does experience suggest that poverty will be relieved by more debt forgiveness?

The history of heavily indebted developing countries does not inspire confidence in the efficacy of debt forgiveness. The levels of corruption and 'cronyism' are depressing, because funds continue to be available. But the gullibility – or duplicity – of aid givers, who continue to provide funds to governments whose policies reduce living standards, is even more disturbing. Charity offers little return, especially when the recipient governments and bureaucrats are not answerable to their own poor, who are seldom aware that any aid is given, and when outside advice is rejected.

Writing off debt alone does not improve development prospects, often the reverse. The flow of resources to finance an external deficit can raise the rate of economic development, if effective institutions and an effective strategy are in place. However, inattention of lenders to proper vetting of policies (conditionality) and their means of implementation is likely to continue in the MDG programme. The net inflow of financial resources to pay for necessary imports of equipment, food, medical supplies, etc., and to improve services, will far outweigh aid grants and loans. Another large injection of funds is required over the next decade to remove structural impediments to growth, by building roads and schools, and establishing education and health services. None of this guarantees that present governments will relieve the miseries of their populations, and not buy arms to make their misery worse.

Recent IMF research has cast further doubt on the wisdom of debt relief for SSA countries (Rajan, 2005). It argues that debt relief should be crafted according to circumstances. If a country is not able to access private capital markets and investment prospects are poor, high debt is unlikely to cause distress, because repayment is not demanded. Hence, the focus should be on net incremental resources in the short term (additionality), rather than to reduce debt. More official lending to improve social services (health, education, etc.) offers development, which means raising debt. Debt relief does not provide additional resources in these circumstances.

It is no coincidence that the deepest poverty and lowest life expectancies are found in Sub-Saharan Africa, where social cohesion and political stability are absent or spasmodic. NGOs and celebrity campaigners can point to appalling poverty in Sudan, Somalia, Sierra Leone, Rwanda, etc. But what guarantees can be provided that financial aid from any source will get to those suffering? After all, many SSA countries that are currently considered stable and reliable have emerged only recently from civil wars (Angola, Mozambique) – and some have already regressed!

What evidence can NGOs provide that debt forgiveness, which can assuage the central governments' interest payments and capital repayments, will benefit the poor? Debts forgiven leave more resources in the hands of governments or their agencies only if repayments were going to be made. The quandary is whether they will ease the suffering of the people, or simply be used for self-gratification or for military purchases by governments not subject to democratic restraints or effective institutional oversight. 'Compassion' requires effective implementation of genuine assistance. African governments are very sensitive about sovereignty when any kind of conditionality is proposed for any delivery of aid or financial contributions.

There is a naive belief that providing debt relief opens a clean sheet for an indebted country, but that only has value if the government adopts a new strategy that will instil optimism by changing laws overnight, introducing an open judicial system and removing corruption. That takes time and patience, and will irritate many in high places. It is not clear whether debts forgiven will ease the suffering of the people, or simply be used by governments for self-gratification. Some informed comments from Africa believe it is the latter.

Thomas Sowell refers to 'the tragedy of Africa':

> Forgiveness of foreign debts is always on the agenda of the political left. This would free up money for African governments to spend to relieve their people's distress, assuming that is what they would spend it for. But why would anyone think that promoting irresponsible government borrowing by periodically 'forgiving' their debts is going to help Africans? Such policies benefit the bureaucracies that administer foreign aids and enable vain people to see themselves as saviours (Sowell, 2005).

In an interview with *Der Spiegel* on 6 July 2005, James Shikwati (Kenyan economist) said:

> Aid to Africa does more harm than good. The countries that have collected the most development aid are also the ones that are in worst shape. Huge bureaucracies are financed (with aid money), and corruption and complacency are promoted. Our politicians are overwhelmed with money, and they try to siphon off as much as possible. If they (Europeans) want to fight poverty, they should completely halt aid and give Africa the opportunity to ensure its own survival.

Conceding to demands for debt forgiveness will not help poor countries unless the appropriate economic policies are implemented. If the UK liquidates $100 of debt owed by an African Developing Country (ADC), this would be paid to, say, the World Bank. In the year of expenditure, $100 would be added to UK development assistance. ADC debt would be reduced by $100 and relieved of debt servicing charges of, say, $5 per annum for that and subsequent years (but remember, the ADC was probably not required to service its debts to IBRD anyway). Economic development in ADCs would have been assisted more if a $100 grant had been delivered to its Treasury. This sum could be spent on medicines, food distributions, and so forth. Almost all World Bank financing to SSA governments is now delivered as IDA grants, so outstanding debts are not increasing. Moreover, according to the HIPC programme remaining debts to the World Bank or the IMF are being written down once an SSA country reaches a completion point. (Non-HIPCs are still required to service their debts to the Bretton Woods organizations, which seems unfair since they are more responsible than HIPC members.)

Despite these doubts about debt relief, the fundamental interest of develop-ment campaigners is in financial flows to promote development, consistent with the MDG programme. Development assistance from OECD governments can be raised, but it is still a scarce resource that has to be extracted from government revenues against competing demands for other public services. Rather than accepting debt forgiveness, the concern should be to promote development by maximizing grant aid flows to SSA. The argument for debt forgiveness is about compassion and feeling good about what you are doing. It is supported by left-leaning NGOs. In economic terms, however, it will be ineffective. The opportunity cost of such action to the donor government is nil, because development assistance values that year are raised whether the money passes to the World Bank to eliminate the debt, or goes to the SSA government as extra financial resources. However much 'conditionality' is criticized by aid recipients, no donor government will be allowed to give money away without extracting terms about its use. (It is another matter whether the conditions are met.) Development aid is not simply an exercise in charity and monitoring should be a requirement. OECD taxpayers want to know how it is spent, espe-cially if public services in the donor countries are regarded as inadequate. In France and Germany, high unemployment and large fiscal deficits add to sensitivities over outlays on development aid.

The key to the MDG 2015 programme rests with SSA governments. The UN approach is conditional on good governance and partnership between govern-ment and aid donors to build social infrastructure (transport and communica-tions) and good government institutions to support the community: farm support schemes, health services, education at all levels, etc., and to build community services. This is the critical feature of the SSA development programme. African governments are often corrupt, wasteful, indigent and violent. One report from Nairobi claims that between 1981 and 1996, nearly half the countries of Africa experienced violent conflicts between governments and opposition groups (Shikwati, 2002). Military takeovers are common. Aid flows seem to encourage violence and the misuse of aid resources. Can the proposals in the MDG programme enable aid donors and managers to incorporate SSA governments into the comprehensive programmes? That question remains to be answered.

'THE END OF POVERTY'

The lead author and Director of the MDG, Jeffrey Sachs, has produced a popular version of its argument for Penguin Books under the title, *The End of Poverty* (Sachs, 2005). This 400-page tome reads like a global travelogue that could have been titled *Travels with my Uncle*, in this case Bono!

His story traverses four continents (leaving out Australasia and the Pacific Islands), but finally focusses on the travails of Sub-Saharan Africa. Unrestrained by UN conventions, he argues that OECD development aid should be tripled, from $65 billion in 2002 to $195 billion by 2015. Sach's arithmetic for increasing OECD aid donations looks simple, but any single outlay looks simple if opportunity costs are not considered. Doubling the 2004 figure by 2010 will be hard enough, as everyone admitted after the G8 meeting in July 2005. Sachs does not make a convincing case that SSA economies could absorb so many resources effectively in a few years. The Commission for Africa cautioned that large amounts of aid could only be absorbed gradually, over long periods by small SSA economies. Sachs dismisses criticisms that some African governments and social institutions are weak and corrupt. He acknowledges that effective institutions are necessary but fails to consider the time and effort to establish them before development can begin. OECD governments' sensitivities over corruption in Africa are scorned.

This folksy presentation will do little to convince an open-minded observer that the Millennium Development Report has any substance. Its anecdotal presentation may appeal to development NGOs seeking examples to convince sympathetic audiences.

HOW MUCH AID?

There is no doubt that achieving the UN MDGs by 2015 requires a massive injection of funds, and a large act of faith that SSA governments are able and willing to reform domestic policies and institutions (rules and organizations). Most of the increase will have to be as grant funding. The share of OECD's GDP provided as aid in 2002 was 0.23 per cent. This would need to increase to 0.44 per cent in 2006 and to 0.54 per cent by 2015, to meet the MDG timetable. These are large increases, especially for the US and Japan, which have the lowest aid/GDP percentages. Governments with large budget deficits already, such as France and Germany, will need to give assurances to their electorates that the increased aid will be effective.

While charity appeals to the kind-hearted, when it lasts for 20 years and the targets are unreliable, there are likely be some second thoughts. The UN Development Programme lacks any assurances that recipient countries' governments will honour their commitment to development. The capacity of backward economies to absorb increasing volumes of aid must be monitored by the UNDP. The detail required in the Millennium Development Report will overwhelm many developing country governments, while others will refuse to comply.

Many OECD economies are already writing off outstanding debts of poor countries. The debts of the IMF, the World Bank and regional development banks now represent about 80 per cent of SSA countries' outstanding debt. The HIPC initiative has reduced such debts of some countries since 1996, but forgiving all remaining debts would upset the balance sheets of these organizations. For example, World Bank loans appear as assets on its balance sheet, so 100 per cent write-offs for SSA countries would sharply reduce its resource-base and curtail its activities. The US authorities believe the World Bank's loans are irretrievable and should be treated as 'bad debts', while the World Bank should become an aid provider, based on periodic donations in the manner of IDA (Meltzer Report, 2002). The US Administration is arguing for more effective conditionality. It claims that World Bank and IMF conditionality had been excessive, yet inadequately enforced. The report argues that the Fund's activities should be reduced to lender of last resort to emerging economies. The World Bank and the regional development banks should become providers of technical advice and facilitators of private sector financing of development. The US Administration has introduced conditionality in its Millennium Challenge Account announced at Monterrey and its Africa programme. Other G7 governments are sceptical about the resources that could be raised for a re-vamped IDA, and whether some conditionality should be attached to its grants. Various schemes for direct financing of aid, such as a tax on aviation fuel or a tax on trans-border capital movements (Tobin Tax) have already been proposed.

The Millennium Development Report relies on large increases in aid flows to poor countries, especially in SSA. Yet, as described above, there are some serious questions about how effective financial aid will be without major adjustments in the domestic policies of the aid-receiving countries. Moreover, there is still a long way to go to resolve problems with outstanding debts and devising how new grant aid should be provided to the poor developing countries.

ECONOMIC CONSENSUS?

Economic development has always been controversial and laden with political uncertainties, since the early days of economic planning and import-substitution strategies. 'The Washington Consensus' occupied pride of place as the ruling maxim in the 1990s, when competitive markets were the order of the day (Williamson, 1990). It began life as a list of reforms appropriate to Latin American economies beginning their economic recovery after the troubled 1980s' debt crises. However, the widespread acceptance of this policy guide caused its adoption as a model for all developing countries, 'a one size fits all' pattern. This was never the intention.

Early in the 1990s, Latin American economies needed to attract private capital to raise growth rates after difficult economic adjustments in the previous decade. Reduced to its bare bones, the Washington Consensus recommended the following:

1. fiscal balance to redress serious external imbalance;
2. re-ordering public expenditures and reducing subsidies;
3. tax reform to widen the tax base and to lower marginal tax rates;
4. liberalize interest rates to improve capital markets;
5. competitive exchange rates to integrate into world markets;
6. trade liberalization to open markets to competition;
7. liberalize inward foreign direct investment;
8. privatization of public corporations to increase competition;
9. deregulation of industry to establish competition;
10. establish private property rights to facilitate development.

This list was an interpretation of policy advice being given in Washington by the IMF and World Bank staffs, and by the US Treasury. Policy advice changes quickly with circumstances, and it was not meant to apply in all circumstances. Evidently, the 'Washington Consensus' did not apply to the least developed economies, which are the subject of the UN's MDG programme. However, this agenda did deliver benefits in Latin America: budgets moved towards balance, inflation fell, external debt ratios improved and economic growth recommenced. Unemployment and poverty were relieved rather less.

The Washington Consensus received widespread support, but perhaps without proper respect for differences among developing countries. The ten-point agenda was a reaction to excessive government intervention in development in Latin America, using planning, budget deficits and import-substitution strategies. The shortcomings within that agenda were revealed over time and, of course, there was a strong reaction against 'market approaches' from those with socialist leanings. In its simple, discursive form 'the consensus' did not admit to market failures, neither did it consider the fundamental institutions of property rights, the rule of law, corporate responsibility, etc.

Stiglitz has made much of market failures, such as incomplete information, risk and moral hazard, as reasons to establish strong institutions before embarking on 'competitive market models'. Yet when dealing with developing countries, government failure seems to be a much bigger threat than market failure. His criticisms of the Washington Consensus have become obsessive (Stiglitz, 1998), though it is not entirely clear how his government intervention to overcome market failure can be married with competitive markets. He claims to have a 'third way', which rejects the socialist planning model and the laissez-faire model, which is his title for the Washington Consensus. While Vice-President of the World Bank (1997–99), he changed the strategy of the Bank to meet a broader definition of development – see the Bank's annual reports during that period. He believes that successful development requires active government participation, and that public interventions should promote welfare. He asserts that it begins with analysing market failure. The strong role given to governments in the MDG programme will show whether the Stiglitz alternative can be effective, but the records of SSA governments do not give much confidence.

There will not be another Washington Consensus. Market competition is becoming recognized as globalization spreads into 'emerging' economies. The new focus is for governments to establish necessary organizations, as well as soft institutions comprising private property rights, the rule of law and civic rights. The danger of failure comes from the activities of special interest groups that focus on social welfare and big government, which would result from the Stiglitz approach.

AID CONDITIONALITY

If the proposed programmes of aid to SSA, and other backward economies, are implemented, the US Administration will insist that some kind of 'conditionality' is attached, notwithstanding objections from development NGOs, SSA governments and UN agencies. Grants of public money require proper accountability. The large increases in aid proposed have to be explained and justified to donor countries' populations. In OECD economies, there are growing numbers of citizens who remain sceptical about development aid, in spite of the overwhelming displays and publicity that development and 'social justice' NGOs organize. At the G8 meetings in 2005, the Japanese, German and French finance ministers (and Putin) were reported to be reluctant to agree to more debt forgiveness and increasing aid grants.

In recent times, development lobbying has turned against conditions being attached to aid programmes by donors. It is claimed that 'conditionality' introduces foreign cultural values, such as unaccustomed work practices and new social commitments that are inappropriate. Socialist groups complain that donors' policy preferences are imposed that advocate fiscal balance, trade liberalization and banking deregulation, which impede public sector development.

These economic policies have, not surprisingly, changed over time, which seems to be something else to complain about! Some commentators object to these 'imposed conditions', because they cause frictions in SSA economies. More careful preparation and consultation over aid programmes, they believe, would enable recipient governments to take 'ownership' of programmes. This approach is buried in the fine print of the Millennium Development Report. As a balance, it would seem prudent to provide scope for external audits and periodic reviews, especially for the massive aid increases envisaged in the MDG targets. It remains to be seen how penetrating these audits could be. It would be much safer to insist on effective audits and reviews by major donors. The Heritage Foundation in Washington has convinced the US Administration that conditionality and reviews are necessary, but it would be wrong to believe this will be easy or popular.

The EU has linked aid and human rights (defined in terms of social outcomes) in its new 20-year economic partnership agreements (EPAs) with the ACP countries, which will replace the Cotonou Agreement in 2007. The EU will include democracy and human rights clauses in each bilateral agreement. This formalizes previously 'ad hoc' withdrawals of aid from countries over violence and political unrest. There have been around a dozen instances of this in the past, many of them in SSA countries. However, it is not clear that this 'negative' conditionality works. Usually the abuse is at an advanced stage before withdrawal occurs. Trade preferences will be provided by the Everything But Arms (EBA) duty-free access to the EU market introduced in 2001.

Recently the World Bank has been persuaded by the US Administration to give attention to 'conditionality', advising that aid should be 'directed to countries with sound policies and effective institutions'. This is loosely contained in the UN proposals for MDG and is likely to be strengthened before the goals are acceptable. Large infrastructure projects have gone out of fashion, partly because they lead to corruption and partly because 'social conscience' NGOs object on environmental or cultural grounds (Mallaby, 2004). The focus has changed to strengthening government agencies and policies to support health, education and training services. The focus of aid programmes seems to be to develop public sector activities with little regard for industry or services produced in the private sector. This selection of public sector activities 'is not directly related to good policies but rather is based on political considerations' (Burnside and Dollar, 2000). This approach was given official blessing by the World Bank during Stiglitz's tenure (Stiglitz, 1999): 'The focus of the [World] Bank will be on capacity-building and consensus-building; helping the country develop the capacity to formulate its own development strategy and democratic institutions to arrive at a national consensus about those strategies.'

Whether SSA governments will accept this 'politically correct' direction of aid towards government development and democratic reforms, will be a critical issue for the MDR in SSA countries. However, at the International Conference on Financing for Development, in Monterrey, March 2002, the US President committed increased US aid 'to political and legal and economic reforms' and 'to projects in nations that govern justly, invest in their people and encourage economic freedom'. In May 2004, the US Millennium Challenge Commission announced the first list of countries eligible to receive grants; out of 16, ten were SSA countries.

'FAIR TRADE'

With attention focussed on poverty and mismanagement in developing countries by the UN Millennium Development Programme, 'Make poverty history' and the compassion brigade of churches, charities and NGOs, it is not surprising to see that 'fair trade' has been revived as another appeal to sentiment. The argument rests on two misconceptions. First, that inexperienced charity workers are in a position to know what a 'fair' price should be for a commodity, such as coffee. Second, that they should bully citizens into paying the higher price with arguments about sympathy for the poor in Africa and helping them by paying the inflated price. On top of that, spurious arguments about 'evil' multinational corporations, 'organic', environment-friendly production and human rights-approved working conditions (all verifiable) are added to the pedigree.

The intention of 'fair trade' is that poor countries' produce should be purchased at 'acceptable' prices, regardless of market circumstances. The 'fair price' is to be decided by well-meaning people drawn from churches, charities and NGOs, who have an interest in helping poor people in remote countries. Like most of the 'missionaries of compassion', they do not look beyond their actions to examine the consequences of their actions for other producers and operators in the production chain.

In its present manifestation, Oxfam introduced 'fair trade' as The Fair Trade Foundation in 1959. This movement has attracted support from charities, churches and like-minded Samaritans, and has links in many countries: the ILO claims that 17 countries in Europe and North America are associated with the Fair Trade Labelling Organizations International (FLO) (Redfern and Snedder, 2002). This 'fair trade movement' aims to provide an alternative business model to redistribute money towards developing country producers. It has also become linked with environmental and human rights issues, promoting 'green' standards in agriculture and ILO labour standards. However, belief in all good things can still create conflicts.

Raising returns to developing countries by offering higher prices depends

9

either on raising prices to consumers in OECD markets, or squeezing margins along the production chain. This requires management of the whole production process, from soil preparation and sowing to sale of the final product to the consumer. The products covered by 'fair trade' include coffee, tea, bananas and other fruit, sugar, cocoa, flowers, nuts and spices plus clothing and handicraft works. The producers are usually cooperatives or associations in developing countries, and they are members of FLO. They pay annual membership fees and undertake to supply specific products, produced according to environmental rules, at pre-determined prices. The intermediaries are traders (importers and exporters) and processors who are members of FLO and subject to standards and pre-determined prices. Final sale to consumers is often through 'fair trade' outlets but increasingly 'fair trade' products are marketed through general retailers and cafes, which purchase directly from points in the chain (e.g., coffee beans or ground coffee). The whole chain (including retailers) remains subject to 'fair trade' standards.

Coffee has much the largest turnover among 'fair trade' products (around 30 per cent of 'fair trade' turnover in Europe and North America), though its share is only around 3 per cent of world coffee sales. Recent popularity of 'fair trade' coffee in OECD markets may be based on rising production of its 'organic' coffee rather than the 'fair trade' label. This is consistent with the premium price that has to be charged to raise the returns to producers. The retail margins on 'fair trade' products are higher than for standard products. Not surprisingly, there is evidence that the supply of 'fair trade' products exceeds demand at the premium prices (Redfern and Snedder, 2002). This sales gap may account for a recent increase in government financial support for 'fair trade' producers and FLO in some EU countries. Most of this assistance is directed to promoting the 'fair trade' label to make consumers more aware of their activities. (Why taxpayers' money should be spent in that way is a mystery.) The 'fair trade' movement remains small. With present demand insufficient to clear 'fair trade' supplies, the venture is having little effect on free markets.

Even the intention of the 'fair trade' movement is dubious. If successful, prices of products would rise and consumers generally would have to pay more and would consume less. Like any interference in a commodity market (e.g., coffee), disequilibrium would appear as over-supply; because of the FLO subsidy, efficient producers would be penalized. Only by establishing a differential product, such as organic coffee, would a separate market be formed – and that would only be temporary. By subsidizing the 'fair trade' producers, governments are adding to market distortions in tropical products, just as OECD subsidies to temperate agriculture production distort prices.

Free trade is the only 'fair trade'. Imposing so-called 'fair trade' rules simply limits the right of others to compete freely. The 'fairness' of trade is determined by the perceptions of the parties directly involved on both sides of voluntary transactions. Declaring for 'fair trade' is declaring one's member-ship of 'concerned' society, which doubtless provides smug satisfaction. It demonstrates a choice to help the poor, so it matters little how ineffective and contradictory it might be! (Pressed why he favoured 'fair trade', a British friend replied, 'If it keeps Africans in Africa, I'm happy to pay more for coffee!')

The 'fair trade' argument amounts to direct consumer subsidies to selected producers receiving guaranteed prices. That encourages over-production (in the same way as CAP) and forces prices down for efficient producers. Perversely, poor SSA coffee producers are subsidized at the expense of efficient, mechanized plantations in Brazil and Central America. In an effort to extend this nonsense, it is reported that Oxfam and the churches are exerting pressure on schoolchildren to demand 'fair trade' purchasing by school canteens and their parents! Two hundred years ago, farmers and landowners used 'fair trade' arguments to fight the abolition of the Corn Laws in England. It is a traditional cry from protectionists, socialists and nationalists.

No mention is made that this 'fair trade' coffee may displace production elsewhere, reducing production and employment and causing hardship in another developing country. If poor quality coffee is purchased, to be sold as 'fair trade' coffee, it is possible that the market price will fall. That would lead to market adjustments, including reduced output. The compassionate act could lead to losses all round.

COMPASSION AND DEVELOPMENT

As often occurs in public affairs, the coming together of two independent events has focussed attention on complex issues to which there are no easy solutions. As usual, public opinion demands immediate action. The popular support for 'Make poverty history' was highlighted by the generous support aroused for tsunami victims at the beginning of 2005. NGOs and aid groups linked these together to raise popular consciousness. However, the aims were quite different. The first was to help with reconstruction and rehabilitation of those in immediate need of shelter, food and medical treatment. The second was to draw attention to long-term poverty in the world's poorest countries, in SSA and small landlocked and island economies. These problems are not susceptible to the same treatment and raise quite different issues. By linking them together, the NGOs hoped both would receive more attention.

Economic development is a long-term problem that is not responsive to emergency deliveries of food, materials and services. Financial aid will be necessary for reconstruction after the tsunami damage, but that process will generate outputs and jobs, if properly managed.

Economic development in SSA, on the other hand, depends on changing systems and processes of government, to establish new organizations and to build physical and institutional infrastructures for the first time. This is a much deeper process of reform than rebuilding damaged infrastructures and capital within a pre-existing social and political framework. The history of violence in Africa alone makes effective development a long-term operation. African governments' haste to write-off their debts and to get their hands on increased aid flows suggests they have not considered the fundamental changes that are necessary in their social, economic and, above all, political systems. Compassion is not the answer here.

It is dangerous to believe that charity will solve the problems of SSA. Economic development depends on an understanding of institutional structures and social practices, and an understanding of opportunity costs. Action on any one front depends on sacrifices elsewhere, because resources (per time period) can only be applied to one activity. Scarcity is a reality of life. Priorities have to be decided.

Economic development is much more dependent on domestic change within poor societies than on any form of financial aid, although the quality and allocation of aid is important. Without political and social reforms, new linkages within society and the evolution of effective markets, supported by strong and effective government services, any amount of financial assistance will not promote economic development.

REFERENCES

Bauer, P.T. (1971), *Dissent on Development*, London: Weidenfeld and Nicolson.
Bauer, P.T. (1982), *Equality, the Third World and Economic Delusion*, London: Methuen.
Bauer, P.T. (1984), *Reality and Rhetoric*, London: Weidenfeld and Nicolson.
Beckerman, W. (2003), *A Poverty of Reason: Sustainable Development and Economic Growth*, Oakland, CA: The Independent Institute.
Bethell, T. (1998), *The Noblest Triumph*, New York: St Martin's Griffin.
Burnside, C. and D. Dollar (2000), 'Aid, policies and growth', *American Economic Review*, **90**(4) (Sept), 847–69.
Easterly, W. (2001), *The Elusive Quest for Growth*, Cambridge, MA: MIT Press.
Easterly, W. (2003), 'Can foreign aid buy growth?', *Journal of Economic Perspectives*, **17**(3), 23–48.
Hughes, H. (1999), 'Should heavily indebted poor countries' debt be forgiven?', in I. Harper et al., *Noble Ends, Flawed Means: The Case Against Debt-forgiveness*, issue analysis no. 6, Sydney: Centre for Independent Studies.
International Labour Organization; World Commission on the Social Dimension of Globalization (2004), *A Fair Globalization Creating Opportunities for All*, Geneva: ILO.
Johnson, H.G. (1967), *Economic Policies Towards Less Developed Countries*, London: Allen and Unwin.

Kasper, W. (2006), *Economic Freedom and Development: An Essay About Property Rights Competition and Prosperity*, London: International Policy Network, Eureka Project.

Kasper, W. and M.E. Streit (1998), *Institutional Economics*, Cheltenham, UK and Lyme, USA: Edward Elgar.

Little, I.M.D. (1982), *Economic Development: Theory, Policy and International Relations*, New York: Basic Books.

Mallaby, S. (2004), *The World's Banker*, New York: Penguin Press.

Meltzer Report (2000), report of the International Financial Advisory Commission, Washington, DC.

Myrdal, G. (1957), *Economic Theory and Underdeveloped Regions*, London.

Rajan, R. (2005), 'Debt relief and growth', *Finance and Development*, Washington, DC: International Monetary Fund.

Redfern, A. and P. Snedder (2002), 'Creating market opportunities for small enterprises: experience of the Fair Trade movement', ILO working paper no. 30, Geneva.

Sachs, J. (2005), *The End of Poverty*, London: Penguin Books.

Schumpeter, J.A. (1961), *The Theory of Economic Development*, Oxford: Oxford University Press.

Shikwati, J. (2002), 'Trade not aid for the developing world', *The Age, Melbourne*, 15 November.

Smith, Adam (1776), *The Wealth of Nations: Book III*, reprinted 1910, London: Everyman's Library.

Sowell, T. (1987), *A Conflict of Visions*, New York: Basic Books.

Sowell, T. (2004), *Applied Economics*, New York: Basic Books.

Sowell, T. (2005), 'The tragedy of Africa', commentary on TCS wesite, accessed 12 July, 2005.

Stiglitz, J.E. (1998), 'More instruments and broader goals: moving towards the post-Washington Consensus', WIDER Lecture presented to United Nations University.

Stiglitz, J.E. (1999), 'The World Bank at the Millennium', *The Economic Journal*, **109**, F577–F597.

UN Development Program (UNDP) (1999), annual report.

United Nations Millennium Development Report (2005), *Investing in Development: A Practical Plan to Achieve the Millennium Development Goals*, United Nations.

Williamson, J. (ed.) (1990), *Latin American Adjustment: How Much Has Happened?*, Washington, DC: Institute for International Economics.

8. Globalization and civil society

The 1990s are remembered for the rapid spread of freemarket policies and new technologies, especially in transport and ICT. That 'new golden age', which followed swiftly on the collapse of the communist empire and the end of the Cold War, prompted optimism that the promise of peace and prosperity fostered since the close of World War II would be achieved. The economic progress was impressive for many countries, both developed and developing. However, some economies and groups within most economies faltered or missed out on the economic growth. These failures came to be regarded by many as injustices rather than as self-inflicted or chances of fortune. Even in strongly growing economies, of course, the benefits were not evenly distributed – they never are – but those who missed out blamed policies or institutional failures for their misfortune. To a minority among the malcontents and the misguided, these exceptions provided justification for opposition to the new economic order. They chose to express their discontent mostly outside normal political channels.

These antithetical groups joined with non-governmental organizations (NGOs), many of which had been formed to pursue specific interests, such as protection of the environment, human rights, labour standards or the plight of the poor in developing countries. Some of these groups became radicalized by disoriented socialists, at a loss after the collapse of the Soviet system, anarchists who were presumably angered by the success of freemarket economic policies, which they regarded as an American phenomenon, and other radicals. The free market competition associated with this economic prosperity became the target for a rag-tag of protesters, who set about disrupting inter-governmental meetings of the IMF, World Bank, WTO and G8 Leaders meetings. They also targeted the World Economic Forum meetings in Davos and regional centres, and similar international events where ministers meet with corporate and academic leaders. These became 'media events' as the complaints of this 'anti-globalization coalition' (AGC), combined with violent and provocative street theatre, elicited equal reaction from massed security forces. These tactics were successful in drawing media attention to specific concerns. An unasked question is, who pays to get all these protesters to specific locations around the globe?

The outcomes of inter-governmental meetings have become less and less relevant. Whatever is agreed is never enough for the demanders. However threatening global financial crises seem to be (see Institute of International Finance (Washington) open letter to finance ministers and central bankers, September 2005), they are less relevant than saving dolphins or dreams of utopian socialism! The meetings of world leaders are preceded by intense media speculation about their agenda and the comprehensive resolutions that should be anticipated. In reality, of course, the governments represented have little scope to deviate from their long-standing political positions, which already represent a balance of domestic political forces. Consequently, the final communiqués often present a confusing mixture of high-sounding goals associated with obscure instruments and ill-defined targets.

The G7 meetings (now G8) were convened in the 1970s to mitigate serious financial threats to the global economy. At Gleneagles in July 2005 however, the G8 agenda focussed on global warming (Kyoto Protocol) and poverty in Africa, even though international financial imbalances threaten the economic system. These were narrow NGO priorities and world leaders were co-opted to 'Make poverty history' alongside pop singers! This reduced the status of world political leaders, though it avoided violence at AGC protests in Scotland. Even so, the G8 communiqué did not satisfy many NGOs. Then, it never would.

Similarly, the discussions at the World Economic Forum in January 2005 were dominated by the same two topics – climate change and poverty – and by the attendance of leading NGOs, led by film and pop stars to ensure media coverage. 'Compassion' was the priority, while hard-nosed economic analysis typical of earlier Davos meetings, where business, public officials and academics spoke freely, was ignored. This mutation has discouraged business people and economists from attending WEF meetings.

International economic organizations have become major targets for NGOs over the past 20 years, as popular interests shifted to assertions about environmental and social issues, where analytical models have no role. Worrying economic developments are neglected or glossed over as 'technical noise' in the anti-globalization process. Undoubtedly NGOs have influenced the policy agenda. The development agenda for Africa and other areas of poverty has become a popular concern. Although a significant economic issue, it is not the only one.

Like many environmental lawyers, development NGOs tend to focus on ends, not means. For several years Esty (2001, 2002) and his fellow travellers (Charnovitz, 1994, 2000; Weinstein and Charnovitz, 2001) have attacked the GATT, and more recently the WTO, for being too concerned with trade and economic management when trade instruments could, and should, be used to pursue other goals, such as environmental protection, equitable development, income distribution, etc. These supporters of the WTO agreements as international law would expand participation in the WTO to include NGOs (of various complexions) without explaining how decisions would be reached on further trade liberalization. The available arbitrator is, of course, the dispute settlement process, which just happens to have been taken over by lawyers through the DSU Appellate Body. This would bring lawyers' win–lose outlook to trade matters, which conflicts with economists' win–win approach using cost–benefit analysis. Esty and colleagues support decisions being made by lawyers on economic matters, based on legal interpretations of articles drafted by trade negotiators.

In the development context, Oxfam (2002), Sachs (2005) and many others argue that financial aid and trade discrimination in favour of developing countries' exports will generate economic growth, without acknowledging the key role to be played by public and private institutions, which are largely non-existent in developing countries (Sowell, 2004). Similarly, unconditional financial aid is presumed to be the trigger for economic development, notwithstanding the vast amount of aid already given without success. There is much more to economic development than aid flows and export opportunities, yet these are the measures most frequently used to assess development incentives.

THE RISE OF 'ANTI-GLOBALIZATION'

Globalization has invoked two kinds of opposition. The first category opposes open internationalism and argues for protection of declining industries to maintain jobs and national independence, to promote national culture and identity, etc. (That is, mercantilism from the pre-Smith era.) The second approach favours 'global governance' and adoption of international laws to regulate globalization. Although these two approaches advocate contradictory strategies for managing 'globalization', the anti-globalization coalition of NGOs is united in its 'causes', while reconciliation of alternative and different doctrines is studiously avoided.

The fashion for the 'anti-globalization coalition' (AGC) was set by the demonstrations in Paris in 1998, against the OECD Multilateral Agreement on Investment (MAI). The MAI text had been under negotiation among OECD governments for three years because many controversial issues kept extending the negotiations. There had been little enthusiasm for a 'full-blown' international treaty from the beginning of the negotiations. The business sector wanted more openness and more uniformity for international investment in non-OECD countries (and more certain property rights in foreign countries). So when it became clear that few non-OECD governments would subscribe to the MAI, business enthusiasm dwindled. Meanwhile, OECD governments disagreed over legal and taxation issues, even as late as the OECD ministerial council meeting in May 1998 (Henderson, 1999).

Although it was the NGO demonstrations that brought the MAI to the attention of the media, it was government failure that had brought an end to the MAI saga. The broad coalition of conservation and environment groups, consumer associations, development NGOs, human rights and social justice movements, churches and trade unions, among others, that were represented at noisy demonstrations on the edge of the Bois de Boulogne in Paris in February 1998, prompted the French government to proclaim its sensitivity to MNE activities. It argued that the MAI was 'a symbol that crystallises the demands and frustrations of civil society with respect to globalisation' (Henderson, 1999). In fact, the OECD ministerial meeting in May 1998 had decided to return the draft agreement to the negotiating committee, and after three years' negotiation, this was the kiss of death. Once again governments had initiated an exercise that could not be completed, because inadequate preparation had been undertaken.

The MAI clash in Paris was probably the first occasion that a 'multi-disciplinary' demonstration of NGOs came together against a single issue. Many thousands of environmental interests had been represented at the Earth Summit in Rio de Janeiro in 1992 but they were not united against a single target. Three months after the anti-MAI protests, the anti-globalization coalition (AGC) turned out in large numbers at the 'Carnival against Capitalism' in London. NGO leaders had recognized the media power of united opposition.

The next success claimed by the AGC was the failure of the WTO ministerial council meeting in Seattle in December 1999. Intended to open the first WTO round of trade negotiations, this meeting collapsed under concerted incompetence:

- President Clinton who gave an impromptu statement to the press on the flight to Seattle where he supported the inclusion of 'labour standards' in the WTO (Clinton, 1998). (This promoted large labour union demonstrations in Seattle, which brought 'muscle' to the NGO demonstrations.)
- The WTO Secretariat and delegations in Geneva responsible for preparing the meeting of the WTO Council had not prepared properly for the new round of negotiations. In particular, they had failed to register the discontent among developing country governments about aspects of the Uruguay Round Final Act and the difficulties developing countries had meeting some commitments. It was also naive to believe that negotiations among 140 members would proceed with the same 'green room' format as earlier GATT rounds.
- The EU Commission's mandate for the new round was incomplete and offered no concessions on agricultural trade, while seeking negotiations on all the Singapore issues rejected by developing countries in 1996 (Lamy, 2000).

The lack of preparation, combined with violent and spectacular demonstrations that made good media copy, led to chaos in the negotiating room and intemperate ministerial statements. The AGC claimed another victory. This gave new vigour to demonstrations and NGO demands at major economic meetings in the following years.

NGOs' demands to participate in inter-governmental decision-making, alongside business and labour representatives, were promoted by popularity-seeking world leaders (including Clinton, who since leaving office has turned to NGOs to support his global career as peacemaker). When combined with 'compassionate' sentiments about poverty alleviation, environment protection and human rights, something in this agenda appealed to almost everyone. Even the world media struck by terrorism remains focussed on unsubstantiated statements issued by NGOs. Even countries suffering high unemployment, slow growth and unsustainable public sector deficits have governments that are more concerned about social welfare and environment issues than economic renewal. Economic development to overcome poverty, especially in Africa, focusses more on debt forgiveness, financial assistance and solicitude than economics or socio-political reforms, regardless of the corrupt governments, violence and lack of progress in SSA. The shift to 'conspicuous compassion' has occurred as living standards in the advanced economies and in many emerging economies have reached unanticipated levels as the benefits of new technologies have spread. For these people, economic concerns have diminished, while worries about pollution, environment protection, health and human rights preoccupy them.

Patrick West (2004) has summarized the prevailing view in Western Europe as, 'a culture of ostentatious caring . . . informing others what a deeply caring individual you are. It is about feeling good, not doing good'. West points out that forgiving outstanding debts of SSA countries may not help starving Africans, only 'reward their kleptocratic governments by freeing their budgets to buy more guns'. These 'compassionate objectives' are conspicuously given form in the pronouncements of the NGOs and governments.

CIVIL SOCIETY

NGOs now claim to represent 'civil society', but the term is a much older idea linked to civic responsibility and community service. Voluntary organizations were established in the nineteenth century and earlier to fill gaps in social structures, to provide recreational activities, to care for the sick and the poor, etc. These services were provided by professional associations, trade unions, the churches, private charities, women's institutes, local rescue and search organizations, sports clubs, etc., and depended on volunteers. Such voluntary social services arose to fill gaps in the market system and where government services were inadequate. More recently, 'civil society' became important in Eastern European countries as the communist system unravelled and government services broke down in the 1980s. Social cohesion in the sixteenth-century Italian city states was similarly explained (Putnam, 1993). 'Civil society' is regarded as something good and desirable, because competing, open clubs can be more effective than state bureaucracies.

Because many churches and charities have become associated with NGOs, it has been an easy step even for aggressive single-issue groups, such as environmentalists, to become accepted as members of 'civil society'. This convenient confusion enables NGOs with goals of 'global democracy' or 'zero growth' to present themselves as conduits of public participation and social progress, with well-meaning social consciences and taking action where governments are reluctant to act.

Broadly, two types of NGO can be identified, though some try to play both sides of the street (Scholte, O'Brian and Williams, 1999). 'Operational' NGOs have characteristics of 'voluntary assistance' similar to traditional 'civil society'. Development assistance groups and 'medical' NGOs are in this category. 'Advocacy' NGOs on the other hand, have commitments to 'political advocacy' and social change. Their socio-political ambitions and fund-raising activities leave voluntary services as a minor activity. These politically active groups are self-appointed and confrontational, and usually pursue narrow agendas. (Some groups, such as Greenpeace, refuse to engage in remedial action that might undermine their raison d'être.) Some NGOs lobby for specific regulations or policy positions (e.g., EarthWatch lobbied the US Administration to complain officially to GATT in the Dolphin/Tuna case [1992]).

Groups such as Greenpeace, Friends of the Earth and World Wildlife Fund for Nature (WWF) receive large donations from North European governments and from the European Commission. This encourages them to pursue specific environmental policies aggressively, and to lobby other governments for support (Kellow, 2000; Rabkin, 1999a). European Commissioners admit that around $1000 million is allocated in this way each year; almost half is allocated to humanitarian aid (*The Economist*, 23 October 2004). Many political NGOs sympathetic to 'European federation', however, receive 50 per cent or more of their funds from the Commission budget, because EU bureaucrats need such support. Not surprisingly, these NGOs lobby for consultation with 'civil society' to be a legal obligation in the EU. It is perverse that money raised from EU governments (i.e., tax-payers) should be used by NGOs to campaign for more power and money to go to their sponsor – the Commission! Such tortuous political processes are intended to weaken national governments and democracy. Negotiating power is being passed to self-appointed lobbyists with narrow objectives, who are beholden to the European Commission for their existence. More transparency is needed.

Most OECD governments provide funds to NGOs. According to reports, groups such as Oxfam, World Vision, Greenpeace, World Wildlife Fund, and other household names, receive between 20 per cent and 50 per cent of their funds from governments (*The Economist*, 21 January 2000). NGOs are, in many cases, contractors to governments, especially in the provision of official development assistance. They supply on-the-ground reports from trouble spots, as well as assisting the many casualties of wars and social disasters. When this constructive behaviour is compared with NGOs' violent and disruptive demonstrations against international agencies, it is evident that their freedom of action is not always a good thing. Maybe strings should be attached to government financial contributions. A study by SustainAbility, UNEP and the UN Global Compact in 2003, on NGO accountability, concluded that NGOs needed to become more accountable 'if they are to retain public goodwill'. Not unexpectedly, Greenpeace argued that 'membership organizations that operate in democracies are entitled to do what they want' (*Financial Times*, 26 June 2003). The size and financial strength of the NGO industry requires that its members should be as accountable as any other enterprise to legal and social standards.

Like traditional civil society organizations, at present 'advocacy' NGOs are treated as charities. This means that most NGOs do not have to produce audited accounts on incomes or outlays, or provide a mission statement. The annual incomes of large NGOs, such as Greenpeace or WWF, exceed the annual WTO budget ($120 million). Apart from financial contributions, large NGOs also franchise their brand names to raise income (e.g., Oxfam, WWF). It is an irony that NGOs that focus on 'corporate social responsibility' (CSR) have a high profile in OECD countries (Henderson, 2001).

There is no complete list of NGOs. They are being created, amalgamated and disbanded continually. In January 2000, *The Economist* reported a UN-ECOSOC estimate of more than 30,000 such organizations. Most have been established since the 1970s. Many focus on UN agencies and their activities. Since street militancy became popular, these groups have formed alliances around major topics, such as conservation, human and labour rights, and poverty and development issues. Martin Wolf (2004) has identified the irony that globalization has resulted from technological advances and economic liberalization, and its enemies now depend on the same information and communications technology (ICT) to press home their anti-globalization campaigns.

Many single-issue NGOs argue that they have a duty to fill a 'democratic deficit' left by governments, which they see as failing to meet perceived social and environmental needs. The question of competing demands on resources is not acknowledged. Many NGOs regard governments' acceptance of market competition and international liberalization of trade and capital flows as reducing national autonomy and neglecting social welfare and cultural heritage. While some NGOs would regard this as requiring more national cohesion, others choose to pursue 'global governance' and a place at the negotiating table, alongside democratically elected governments. NGOs may have national identities but they usually have strong international links too. For example, national Greenpeace organizations contribute to the over-arching Greenpeace International. This distinguishes NGOs from traditional voluntary services, which carry obligations of citizenship and legal status in specific locations in exchange for the title of 'charity'. References to 'civil society' are particularly attractive to 'advocacy' NGOs because the inference of civic duty disguises their political ambitions.

TYPES OF NGOs

Examinations of NGOs shows most of them have narrow single interests. They are focussed on a few general social and political concerns:

* conservation of natural resources (environment);
* labour standards (and human rights);
* economic development, including poverty, inequality and health problems; and
* 'public interests', such as corporate responsibility, consumer rights, etc.

Other NGO 'causes' have less relevance to globalization, but for them participation in international demonstrations is good publicity! For example: cultural protection (including indigenous rights), animal rights, religious charities, anti-war groups, etc. Anti-capitalist and radical political groups are always present.

Towards the end of the Uruguay Round negotiations, some OECD governments bowed to NGOs' lobbying to include the environment and labour standards in the negotiations. Opposition came from developing countries. A compromise was reached in the final agreement to include a provision to discuss trade and the environment, but the sensitive subject of labour standards was excluded, notwithstanding a last-minute appeal from EU and US leaders at the Marrakesh signing ceremony. The first WTO ministerial meeting in Singapore (December 1996) produced an agreement to recognize ILO 'core labour standards' but developing countries rejected further negotiations on labour standards in the WTO context. Even so, many OECD governments have continued to press labour issues at WTO meetings.

ENVIRONMENTAL NGOs

Environmental NGOs have close links with local conservationists in both developed and developing countries. At the international level, however, they work closely with the UN on global issues, such as forest conservation, fish stocks, desertification, endangered species, etc. They have played constructive roles at conferences Earth Summit (1992) in Rio de Janerio, where they contributed expertise to the Commission on Sustainable Development. A symbiotic relationship has evolved between UN agencies and some NGOs.

The environmental NGOs ignore economic costs associated with their conservation plans: but there is no such thing as a free lunch! At one extreme are the 'dark greens' that see catastrophe in economic development and oppose liberalization of international trade and investment, assuming that less efficient allocation of resources could save resources. They seek environmental impact studies before any trade liberalization or growth policies are allowed; that would make economic decisions subordinate to environmental concerns, regardless of existing international treaties. Other environmental NGOs seek to use existing WTO rules to minimize damage and pollution.

Environmental NGOs are attracted to the WTO because of GATT's record of achievement. The EU-driven intention is to use (or threaten) trade sanctions to persuade other governments to adopt international environment standards, or face discriminatory barriers against their exports. This conflicts with WTO principles to remove all trade discrimination and to dismantle all trade barriers. To allow access to trade sanctions to enforce environmental or labour standards would contravene WTO principles by opening avenues for welfare-reducing trade discrimination. Trade protection is always a 'second best' instrument for domestic distortions (Bhagwati, 1971). Adopting trade sanctions to deny access for exports from 'polluting' industries or countries not meeting 'core' labour standards, would ignore the domestic nature of these distortions and treat them as international concerns. Providing protection to industries in an importing country would reduce its economic efficiency and attract support from the domestic sector and workers that benefit from such protection, at the cost of consumers and exporters. This opens the door to increasing protection, as adherents to the precautionary principle can always find allegations of environmental damage.

Conservationists argue that because trade liberalization increases economic growth, it increases consumption of non-renewable resources, adds to pollution, etc. They choose to ignore that comparative advantage makes production more efficient, which should reduce environmental damage. Imports displace high cost domestic production, while encouraging output from efficient export industries. (For example, the EU countries import energy-intensive aluminium and other metals from Australia, Canada and South Africa, which enable them to meet Kyoto targets and still be able to produce highly worked metals.) Trade liberalization, therefore, helps to conserve the environment.

Similarly, agricultural protection, using subsidies and/or guaranteed output prices, encourages uneconomic production based on chemical fertilizers and pesticides, which pollute waterways and damage soils, native birds and animals. These policies also encourage cultivation of marginal land. Protection of agriculture in the OECD is approaching $US400 billion per annum, the same levels that existed before the Uruguay Round. Efforts to get these supports removed on environmental grounds were rejected in the WTO's Committee on Trade and Environment, and have resulted in longrunning stalemate in that committee.

In economic terms, environmental issues are largely about 'externalities' in production or consumption, which are not incorporated into private costs or benefits (Robertson and Kellow, 2001). These are domestic matters. Consequences such as pollution or contamination can be readily incorporated into production costs by introducing pollution taxes, licences or regulations. By raising prices, such imposts stimulate new technologies, decrease demand for non-renewable resources and encourage economies in use or substitution of alternative inputs. (Different problems arise over animal rights and biodiversity, where market values are difficult to establish.)

Most environmental problems are domestic matters, such as irrigation damage, urban air and water pollution, land-clearing, etc., which can be corrected by tax-subsidy policies. Trans-border conflicts over water systems or acid rain require bilateral negotiations. Global issues such as the 'ozone hole' are dealt with through international cooperation (for example, Montreal Protocol). However, the concept of global environmental standards raises serious problems. Differences in climate, resource endowments, technology, living standards, social priorities and stages of economic development mean that different weights attach to such standards. The poor will not place the same value on preserving trees as the rich, even if strict social accounting places a high value on all trees in the long term.

Some conservationists advocate global standards to overcome differences among national standards. The assumption is that these standards should satisfy the strictest requirements. On the contrary, practice shows that international negotiations usually gravitate to the lowest common denominator (Kellow, 2000). Harmonization of domestic policies and standards is not necessary to achieve the benefits of 'free trade' and comparative advantage. 'Harmonisation is more a matter of choosing to augment the benefits of free trade than of being required to harmonize.' (Johnson, 1971) Experience with GATT/WTO has shown, however, that as tariffs are reduced, distortions of international competition attributable to domestic government policies become more apparent. The EU, because it is a common market, has its own

160   *International economics and confusing politics*

commitment to internal 'harmonization'. Mistakenly, EU negotiating positions often call for international harmonization because that suits its internal strategies (e.g., targets in the Kyoto Protocol, the precautionary principle on food safety, etc.). However, 'free trade' does not require the same tax structures or social policies in all countries. Policy differences result from different circumstances and different social choices, which may create cost differences that can create mutual benefits from trade.

The links between trade and the environment are neither as direct nor as easily estimated as 'green' NGOs would like to believe. With economic growth, new technologies evolve that reduce environmental damage, while resources available for environmental conservation and clean-up increase. Trade liberalization and increased specialization are seldom sources of environmental damage. Conservationists like to blame trade because it is conveniently xenophobic, and elicits support from protectionists. This paradox reveals a conflict between the objectives of development NGOs and conservationists. The former advocate lowering trade barriers against developing countries exports to promote economic growth, while conservationists want to avoid damage to flora and fauna by restricting growth and trade. Such contradictions are hidden within the anti-globalization coalition.

More subtle approaches to tightening environmental controls are adopted by experienced NGOs, such as EarthWatch and the Sierra Club. These groups were behind two of the most controversial GATT/WTO trade disputes involving environmental issues: the Dolphin/Tuna case and the Shrimp/Turtle case.

The Shrimp/Turtle dispute began in 1996 when India, Pakistan, Malaysia and Thailand objected to a US trade ban on shrimp imports from Thailand on the grounds that Thai shrimp boats did not use turtle excluder devices (TEDs) mandated by US legislation. The Dispute Panel in this case found against the US because this action amounted to discrimination in trade, using environment policy as an excuse. The US authorities appealed against the Panel's decision and in 1998 the WTO Appellate Body reversed the decision. It decided the policy measure was an exception 'to protect sustainable natural resources, as permitted in the preamble to the GATT (1994)'. The Appellate Body also opined that the US measures were consistent with GATT Article XX (g), which permits 'measures to conserve exhaustible natural resources'. This judgement demonstrated that an import ban can be imposed even when the aim is to conserve an endangered species outside the importer's territory (Weinstein and Charnovitz, 2001). The appeal verdict, nevertheless, ruled that the US was discriminating in its selective application of the TEDs requirement. So the US made the TEDs requirement universal – even to include shrimp farming where there were no turtles!

To the lawyers on the appeal, the issue was whether turtles were needlessly endangered, and the US argument was accepted. The Thai evidence that they were breeding and releasing young turtles into the ocean to conserve the species did not influence the decision. Since imported shrimp were a small proportion of the US market, it must be assumed that the case for TEDs regulations was made at the behest of EarthWatch, the US conservation NGO, rather than to protect US shrimp fishers.

Environmental lobbies regarded the Shrimp/Turtle dispute as a triumph of conservation over trade policy. The Appellate Body did not address whether the US was entitled to apply its policy extra-territorially under GATT Article XX. Previously, it had been accepted that measures under GATT Article XX could not be applied extra-territorially (for example US-Mexico dispute on Dolphin/Tuna). One consequence of the appeal lawyers' use of 'sustainable development' in the WTO preamble without defining it, is that it creates a precedent that it will be interpreted to mean conservation, regardless of other considerations, including trade policy. The Shrimp/Turtle decision affects several sensitive issues on the continuing WTO agenda, including trade and the environment, and process and production methods.

THE PRECAUTIONARY PRINCIPLE

More general disputes are pending with the adoption of 'the precautionary principle' as an approach to environmental disputes. According to the Rio Declaration on Environment and Development (1992), a precautionary approach should be applied to protect the environment, where threats of serious or irreversible damage occur, even though full scientific certainty does not exist. However, the EU definition authorizes governments to take action even without due cause: 'The precautionary principle is an approach to risk management that is applied in circumstances of scientific uncertainty, reflecting the need to take action in the face of potentially serious risks, without awaiting the results of scientific research' (EU Environment Council decision, 17 October 1998).

This conservative approach to new scientific research was written into the Cartagena Protocol on Biosafety (2002). It requires that 'in circumstances of scientific uncertainty, action be taken without awaiting the results of scientific inquiries'. This amounts to an all-purpose excuse for market protection if there is any scientific uncertainty. It conflicts directly with the WTO Agreement on Sanitary and Phyto-sanitary Standards, Article 5 (Wilson and Gascoine, 2001).

So far, the precautionary principle has had little direct effect on economic behaviour, although it has been incorporated into several international agreements and has the potential to disrupt scientific and technological research. The biggest problem is that the precautionary principle might be used to block new technologies because they cannot be shown to create no risk, when the technology could prevent other risks. The costs of meeting the 'no risk' requirement might be prohibitive and advances for health and safety would be sacrificed. Assessing risk is always difficult; progress has a price. Risk measurement can also be subjective. Some advocates of the precautionary principle regard economic growth and development as threats to health and the environment, ignoring the benefits that progress has provided to humankind. The precautionary principle has received little attention since being adopted by the EU in the Maastricht Treaty (1992).

Some legal authorities believe that the precautionary principle is now part of 'customary' international law. One reason for this is that environment protectionists recognize that it provides scope for action on the flimsiest evidence of damage. The US authorities and other WTO signatories deny this, because it would authorize policy action without due cause (Byron, 2001). So far the precautionary principle has not been employed aggressively, but alternative restrictions have been used, such as the EU embargo on GM foods. This has been used to cajole other countries to ban plantings of GM crops because GM contamination would close the EU market to their agricultural exports.

The EU draft chemicals legislation REACH (Registration, Evaluation and Authorization of Chemicals) is raising concerns among EU and non-EU metal industries. The intention of REACH is to regulate dangerous chemicals to protect health and the environment, but many naturally occurring minerals and metals are being included in the testing procedures. The danger is that greens will employ the precautionary approach to exclude commonly used chemicals, or to require testing of all supplies. The REACH legislation was debated in the European Parliament in 2005–06. It could disrupt world trade flows and EU industrial production, which depend on imports of basic materials and commodities. The list of chemicals presented for consideration is extremely long.

KYOTO PROTOCOL STORY, SO FAR

The battle standard for the 'green' NGOs is to reduce carbon dioxide emissions that are claimed to be causing climate change. The Kyoto Protocol (1997) to the UN Framework Convention on Climate Change (FCCC), agreed at the Earth Summit in Rio de Janeiro (1992), is the focus of governments' attention. The engine driving the campaign against 'climate change' is the International Panel on Climate Change (IPCC), a UN committee of climate scientists appointed in 1988. The IPCC has produced three reports on climate change, each more pessimistic than the last. As indicated below, the selection of participants for this panel is carefully managed and it is heavily biased towards scientists.

'Green' NGOs, led by Greenpeace, WWF, etc. seek to reduce the use of carbon fuels, which are the major source of CO_2 emissions. Attempts to persuade OECD governments to raise fuel taxes failed and uniform emission targets were not politically feasible, because they were economically ineffi- cient, wasteful of economic resources and abatement costs differ among coun- tries. To reduce CO_2 emissions in the short term would entail serious economic costs in industrialized countries, lowering GDP and causing unemployment. By 1997, when the Kyoto Protocol was under discussion, the negotiators had support from 'green' parties in Northern European countries, and from the European Commission, which was promoting planned emission targets. By excluding developing countries from emission commitments, many 'sleeping partners' signed the Kyoto Protocol, which gave majority support for the EU position. It isolated non-participating OECD governments, the United States and Australia. In spite of claiming over 140 signatories, the Kyoto Protocol was not ratified until EU leaders persuaded Russia to sign in December 2004. Putin ignored advice from Andrei Illarionov (his Chief Economic Adviser) that 'Kyoto is scientifically unsubstantiated'. The Kyoto Protocol has become a sacred cow in Europe, although even its modest (EU-orchestrated) targets are unlikely to be achieved.

Although the Kyoto targets for CO_2 reductions were agreed for each partic- ipant, the EU (15 signatures in 1997) was treated as one entity and allowed to devise its own distribution of emission reductions for each member within the EU 'bubble'. This allowed South European members to increase their emis- sions substantially in the 1990 base period until 2012, because Britain and Germany had recorded large reductions in CO_2 emissions since the convenient 1990 starting date: the former by switching from coal to gas for electricity production; the latter because massive plant closures in highly polluting East German industries had reduced total German emissions. (Perversely, Germany retains subsidies on coal production.)

The Kyoto Protocol has been the focus of diplomatic exchanges about emissions in recent years, with the IPCC providing the data to inform debates on CO_2 emissions. The latest IPCC report, in 2003, was the Special Report on Emissions Scenarios (SRES), which contained four 'families' of alternative future situations (comprising 40 separate scenarios). The IPCC emphasizes that these are not forecasts or predictions. The key figures seem to be reached by resolutions and voting by selected scientists. Even so, the green propaganda uses them as predictions, without qualification. (For someone who lived through the London 'smogs' of the 1940s and 1950s, the possibility of rapid recovery from air pollution is real.)

The findings of the IPCC reports show a wide range of consequences for the global climate from increasing carbon emissions, between 1.4 degrees C and 5.8 degrees C by 2100. One worrying feature is some detected differences between chapter contents in the SRES and the chapter summaries provided to national authorities for discussion. This suggested political interference was one factor among many that worried the House of Lords' Economic Affairs Committee in its report into *The Economics of Climate Change* (House of Lords, July 2005).

Another complaint from that Lords' committee (comprising eminent academics and former ministers) was that the IPCC had given little attention to economic costs and benefits that would arise from climate change. The IPCC focussed on damage and disruption. Criticisms of IPCC modelling by economists had been dismissed out of hand. Castles and Henderson (2003), supported by Maddison (2003) before the Lords' committee, questioned the use of market exchange rates when making inter-country comparisons of GDP growth, when economic and statistics' experts recommend purchasing power parities for projections over long periods. The 'unofficial' IPCC responses (Grubler et al., 2004; Nakicenovic et al., 2003) were masterly examples of obfuscation, but did little to answer the Castles and Henderson criticisms. The Lords' committee made clear that it considered that more needed to be done to take account of the statistical queries, especially since the IPCC is 'the monopoly provider of information and advice to governments' (Zillman, 2003).

While the relationship between emissions and climate change undoubtedly is a scientific matter, once different types of adaptation to climate change are allowed for, economic cost–benefit analysis becomes important. The scientific risks in measuring temperature change from measured CO_2 emissions are speculative enough. Social adaptation to consequences over time will depend on technology and investment, as well as government policies and public services. Climate warming has positive consequences, which do not seem to be taken into account in IPCC analyses. Warmer climates will be welcome in some regions, crops will flourish and new areas of land will come into cultivation. These have to be set against negative effects from higher sea levels, melting glaciers, droughts, damage to fresh water supplies, etc.

The IPCC aversion to open debate and the protective position adopted by many scientists towards outside comment is puzzling. Over the next century many new technologies will evolve from the efforts of scientists and engineers. And if IPCC projections are believed, there will be strong pressures to find energy-saving equipment and new energy sources. The driving force for the development of these technologies will be the economics of the market. Laboratory science only becomes new technology if there is a market for the equipment or product. Even in terms of carbon taxes or emissions controls, adjustments will be achieved through economic effects, which will feed back into technologies in the laboratories. As the Lords' report explains, the CO_2 problem needs economic analysis and governments should put aside dirigiste approaches, such as allocating pollution permits and planning. As *The*

Economist (8 November 2003) stated: 'You might think that a policy issue that puts at stake hundreds of billions of dollars of global output would arouse at least the casual interest of the world's economics and finance ministries. You would be wrong.'

The political/IPCC mindset has been strongly influenced by green NGOs' pessimistic prognostications on the effects of CO_2 increases. They demand reductions in CO_2-producing activities regardless of economic costs, to restore some 'ideal' level of CO_2 in the atmosphere – probably last seen in 1400! (Green NGOs work on single issues, so they do not even acknowledge that CO_2 is the source of plant growth, which is another of their interests.) There are ways to adapt to climate change, while at the same time seeking to reduce CO_2 emissions. After all, IPCC reports show that the effects of CO_2 emissions today will not cause climate change for decades. Current warming is the result of earlier CO_2 emissions. Allowing freedom of action to developing countries so that their development is not adversely affected, which is why they were left out of the Kyoto exercise, will impose severe limits on affluent countries that could cause political imbalances. Who would like to forecast the consequences of that? Lomborg (2001) has argued, for example, that resources committed to reducing global warming would be better spent providing clean water and sanitation in poor countries.

The Lords' report contains an extremely thoughtful and objective assessment, based on the committee's vast experience in public affairs. Its opinions should be given careful consideration. It expresses concern about the objectivity of the IPCC process, which may have been subject to political interference that has affected the completeness and balance of IPCC reports. Proper assessment should compare monetary costs of global warming damage with their benefits. Although likely to be negative, the committee considers that adaptation to climate change should be taken into account in economic analysis. It recommends that Treasuries and Finance Departments should participate in the work of the IPCC. If economic risks are ignored, hasty action on climate change could bring disaster. The current focus on emissions targets by environment departments does not take sufficient account of adaptation, new technologies and their diffusion.

The analysis by the House of Lords' committee has received little coverage in the media, probably because it has a balanced approach. Interestingly, however, only a few weeks after the Lords' report was released, a new independent approach was announced. The governments of the United States and Australia (the two key OECD countries that refused to sign the Kyoto Protocol on economic grounds) plus Japan (a Kyoto member), India, China and South Korea have signed the Asia-Pacific Climate Pact. Together these countries already account for half the world's CO_2 emissions and half the population. The aim of this pact is to devise new technologies to improve energy efficiency in member countries, without imposing targets for reducing CO_2 emissions. The Kyoto targets are unlikely to be met in 2012 and they will only achieve minor reductions (Singer, 2004), partly because the fastest growing economies (China and India) are not subject to CO_2 targets. The Asia-Pacific approach is designed to make technology the answer to climate change, rather than the UN-EU approach using central planning.

LABOUR STANDARDS

Employment and wage levels have always been associated with trade policy, often in the context of the short-term impact of trade liberalization creating unemployment in import-competing industries, seldom mentioning increased long-term employment created in export industries, and better resource allocation. The labour case for protection is more organized because labour unions have been a prominent force in domestic politics since the Industrial Revolution began. Globalization revived old arguments about job and wages protection, with workers in 'old' industries in the OECD countries apprehensive about competing imports from emerging economies. This was anticipated because labour-intensive industries in OECD economies have remained heavily protected. TCF industries only lost their quota protection on 1 January 2005, when the ATC finally took effect, and within a few months quotas were reintroduced. Remaining tariffs are still significant, and EU and US authorities have already sought 'safeguard' protection or 'voluntary' export restraints. This shows the continuing influence of employment issues in rich countries' politics. Recently, the employment wages questions have also emerged in OECD countries' service industries as 'out-sourcing' has increased, but data suggests this is insignificant (OECD, 2005).

In the globalization debate, labour issues have mutated into the broader question of 'labour standards'. This is prominent in the EU 'Social Charter', and so on the EU trade negotiating agenda. The presentation that EU labour standards should apply universally ignores the question of poverty in developing countries, as well as gains from trade for importers and exporters. Human rights and high living standards are desirable but impossible without financial and economic foundations. Economic analysis is required to put such humanitarian considerations into perspective.

NGOs pursue 'labour standards' for mixed motives. Labour unions focus on wage levels and job security in OECD industries. Other NGOs, however, use labour standards as a stick to beat MNEs. Here the wage comparisons are between OECD rates and payments to workers in developing countries, not between wages earned in MNEs and elsewhere in the developing country economy. These campaigns have received wide media coverage in OECD countries. The aim is to show MNEs as exploiters of cheap labour by comparing, say, an LDC wage with the US wage. The implicit assumption here is that we live in a friction-free global labour market, which is nonsense.

Wage levels are determined in local labour markets, but the differentials are important in determining 'Mode 4' service delivery, which is increasing strongly. Average wages are determined by labour productivity. Rich OECD economies have many skilled workers and employ high levels of skill and capital per worker. Developing countries, by definition, lack both human and physical capital. Hence an international wages gap exists, which is not the skilled–unskilled wages gap as measured in OECD economies.

Actual wages for different workers in an economy are determined by demand for and supply of that kind of worker, and the scope for them to respond to wage differentials by changing jobs, retraining, etc. The relevant comparison between countries is average wages (i.e., cost of labour) rather than comparisons of wages for the same job in different countries. (If workers in Vietnam or Bangladesh could achieve OECD productivity levels in clothing factories, they would earn OECD wages, but they would lose their competitive edge, and ultimately their job!)

International trade tends to equalize wage rates in two ways:

1. Labour is attracted towards industries enjoying comparative advantage (labour-intensive production in developing countries); because wages rise as demand for outputs rise, workers shift towards the higher paid and more productive jobs.
2. As average labour productivity increases from these labour movements, average wages tend to rise in trading countries.

Confusing labour standards and wage levels/price comparisons tends to obscure the differences, but the key element is poverty. If developed countries were serious about 'core' labour standards they would be introduced without imposing economic costs on the poor. 'Competitiveness' in trade is a function of both wages and productivity. Trade offers gains as long as comparative advantage exists.

Advocates of 'core' labour standards comprise two groups:

1. humanitarian supporters of basic ILO rights;
2. protectionists who believe that all workers in an industry should receive the same wage in all countries if 'fair' trade is to exist.

The International Labour Organization (ILO) was founded in 1919 and is the only organization remaining from the League of Nations. Workers' rights are a major target for labour unions but enforcement is extremely difficult, even though many countries have signed ILO commitments. Labour unions in OECD countries claim that multinational enterprises exploit workers in developing countries by paying low wage rates and providing poor working conditions. However, there is now reliable evidence that most MNEs operating in developing countries pay higher rates than local employers. Even so, it is claimed that unemployment among unskilled workers in OECD economies is rising because of low cost imports from developing countries. In other words, 'workers' rights' are really an instrument of trade protection. This brings NGOs arguing for 'labour standards' into conflict with development NGOs who want more export opportunities for developing countries. Workers in developing countries who suffer most from bad working conditions are employed in non-traded sectors, where trade sanctions have no direct effect.

Even if enforcing labour standards is intended to improve working conditions in developing countries, trade sanctions are unlikely to be effective in achieving that. Increasing tariffs (or quotas) in developed countries inevitably reduces employment opportunities and living standards in developing countries, and drives up prices in rich countries. This forces workers to work 'illegally' under even worse conditions in the informal sector. The choice is not one well-paid job or another, but a reliable job or the streets!

Once again, an analysis of NGOs' objections to globalization shows serious contradictions with other NGOs' objectives. Pursuing 'core' labour standards may appear to be consistent with basic human rights, but its effects are inconsistent with economic development in developing countries, and may even worsen wage inequalities in OECD economies. It is evident that trade policy, in the form of a 'social clause', is not an appropriate instrument to encourage labour standards as set out by the ILO. In a review of the EU proposal for a 'social clause', Sapir (1995) concluded:

> There is no denying that poor social conditions are an important problem, on both ethical and economic grounds. The root of the problem, however, lies much less (if at all) with alleged artificial labour standards aimed at raising competitiveness (so-called 'social dumping') than with poverty itself. As a result, the introduction of 'social clauses' in trade agreements is more likely to reinforce the problem than to solve it.

This is consistent with the theory of second best – 'protectionist trade policy is rarely the best instrument to remedy economic or social problems' (Bhagwati, 1971).

DEVELOPMENT NGOs

Development NGOs are concerned with poverty and raising economic performance in developing countries. They have a strong interest in operational matters and, on-the-ground assistance, which requires funding. They play a major role in delivering financial aid, and providing support activities and technical services. Their enthusiastic proselytizing for development aid is usually the result of practical experience.

'Advocacy' NGOs are equally impassioned, but sometimes they get carried away and become economically unsound. They often advocate protectionism and import-substitution strategies for developing countries while demanding preferential access for developing countries' exports in OECD markets. (These policies were analysed in Chapter 4.) Similarly, they argue that development aid should be unconditional (Chapter 7). Some development NGOs (e.g., Oxfam) also argue for 'fair trade'. At first sight, it appeals to the kind-hearted, but it can disadvantage efficient commodity producers also (Chapter 4). 'Fair trade' is also an obfuscation in the hands of politicians and the media, where it indicates something not quite free trade but evades use of the word 'protection'.

The approach to aid and financial assistance by development NGOs is mixed and confused. Debt forgiveness provides only a transient gain, and in many instances serves to sustain corrupt regimes. Development depends on new capital inflows and the question is how long donors will continue to provide money if there is no evidence of development. This is not a question of repayment. Badly run economies – Zimbabwe, Sudan, Sierra Leone – are not candidates for development assistance, though they may still get food aid, health funding, etc. NGOs cannot pretend that development will occur – in these (and other) disaster cases – even if finance is made available. In many instances, economic damage is caused by bad policies, not absence of assistance or opportunities. An inventory of shortcomings in development programmes is not evidence of damage from globalization, if it is self-inflicted by governments or rulers. UN targets, like the Millennium Development Goals for advancing welfare in developing countries, will elicit little progress on development until 'government failures' are corrected. History is redolent with programmes to help developing countries, but experience shows that economic development begins with self-help.

'PUBLIC INTEREST' NGOs

Multinational enterprises (MNEs) find themselves increasingly the targets of adverse publicity campaigns by human rights, labour rights and environmental NGOs that blame corporate behaviour for one thing or another. These alleged transgressions are used to threaten corporate images. The creeping influence of 'international law' is evident in these attacks. Globalization of product and service markets has created demands for international social and environmental standards, with strong support from UN agencies and other international bureaucracies. The EU has led this process with the EU Charter on the Fundamental Social Rights of Workers (1989) (Social Charter), which is supported by a series of directives. The US also has new legislation on corporate conduct.

Government legislation to influence corporate behaviour may be regarded as an attempt to protect the corporate sector from the excesses of NGO campaigns, which asserts that business controls the financial and economic activities of society, and it possesses more power and influence than world governments (Klein, 2001). The advocates of corporate social responsibility (CSR) are drawn from a range of NGOs because MNEs make easy and popular targets. Attacks on malpractices and exploits of MNEs have been common for many decades and all types of NGOs seek opportunities to embarrass them. These 'villains' of environmental damage, pollution, workers' exploitation, corruption, price gauging, appropriation of natural resources, monopolists, etc., are soft targets because they seldom receive credit for anything they do. In particular, their financial success makes them the enemy of socialists, churches and anti-profit propagandists. Governments are seldom prepared overtly to support high-profit companies. Consequently, all NGOs recognize that they can use corporate behaviour (of MNEs in particular) as a lever to impose their policies on communities. Unfortunately, the 'corporate social responsibility' (CSR) agenda is less about correcting MNE shortcomings than a means to foist inconsistent and often conflicting NGO strategies on a naive public. Worse, they tend to reduce economic efficiency generally, with particular damage by discouraging private investment in poor countries.

The CSR programme has been facilitated by the willingness of many corporate bureaucrats to pay lip service to arguments for 'stakeholder' capitalism. The rush to 'good corporate citizenship' in 2002 followed a number of spectacular corporate collapses (including Enron), which put the reputation of the corporate world under a cloud. The Confederation of British Industry (CBI) commissioned a report on CSR at that time, which was adopted by its president and other business leaders, and recommended to all members. Adoption of such a vague concept, with open-ended demands from many and varied NGOs, has the flavour of political expediency, rather than commitment. 'Stakeholder' corporatism does not mean simple discussions with society to negotiate over problems. Corporations are already regulated by the marketplace and by governments with laws and regulations. CSR is applied by 'civil society' using naming and shaming, otherwise known as blackmail! The techniques adopted include demonstrations and disruption of shareholders' meetings, as well as demands for so-called 'triple bottom-line accounts'.

NGOs claim such actions are necessary because governments fail to protect citizens from corporate excesses, especially since programmes of privatization and deregulation were adopted. There is little recognition that public enterprises were able to disguise their shortcomings behind a bureaucratic screen, supported by governments. To most NGOs, leaving order and discipline to the spontaneous order of the market is anathema. They choose also to ignore the growth of corporate regulations in recent years. CSR is an instrument to increase leverage and influence over the corporate sector for political purposes (e.g., bypassing government to achieve environmental controls, improve workers' rights, increase financial contributions to NGO finances, etc.). These objectives say more about NGO political ambitions than 'stakeholder' interests. Governments and the courts should decide what controls are required to modify corporate behaviour. If these public institutions are bypassed, democratic processes are usurped by unelected groups of malcontents.

In the period following the Enron collapse and other corporate failures, CSR and its 'stakeholder' version of capitalism became widely accepted, on the assumption that it would safeguard corporate reputations. In practice, many large companies continued to be severely criticized by NGOs. This should be no surprise because CSR activists work on the assumption that companies can balance all 'stakeholders' interests – shareholders, local communities, employees, conservationists, consumer groups, governments – so that they are all satisfied. In changing circumstances, reconciling conflicting interests requires compromises, which are usually reached by governments and translated into policies or laws. CSR activists cannot do this. In many instances there is no way to satisfy all CSR 'stakeholders'. A company like Nike, accused of labour exploitation in developing country workshops, may work to resolve problems (i.e., paying wages above the local level), but transformations in the global labour market will ensure that responses create frictions. Jobs will continue to shift from OECD economies to poorer countries with lower wage costs, and labour unions in OECD will protest by complaining about low wages and conditions.

Even so, CSR has been promoted by international agencies with alacrity. While NGOs are more or less tolerated by affluent countries' governments, they are enthusiastically welcomed by international agencies, such as the United Nations, OECD and the European Commission, as collaborators in the campaign to strengthen 'global governance'. One of the designers of the UN Global Compact (2000), John Ruggie, has commented: 'The corporate sector has become trapped by its own success, in a world of proliferating problems.' Corporations have global reach and capacity. They can make and act on decisions faster than governments or agencies. Therefore, society is demanding that they should cope also with social problems. This argument contains convenient jumps in logic. Then, Ruggie asserts: 'Corporate, social and environmental reporting must become standard operating procedure.' After complaining that corporations dismiss CSR, he goes on to argue that 'they should contribute to public sector capacity-building where it is lacking. This implies supporting a balanced system of global rulemaking.

One wonders how national governments react to this NGO-MNE joint venture with UN agencies. The UN Global Compact evolved from a Kofi Annan (UN Secretary General) speech at the Davos World Economic Forum in January 1999. He called for the private sector 'to support core values on human rights, labour standards and environmental practices'. The Global Compact was launched in July 2000. Its reports indicate that several committees have been established, but membership is small, with companies heavily outweighed by NGOs and UN agencies (UN Global Compact Office, 2002).

This kind of muddled thinking with an appeal to generosity of spirit has become common, especially in discussions about proposals to establish 'global governance' or 'international law'. David Henderson has undertaken a thorough analysis of this approach in several public presentations, most rigorously in his IEA Hobart Paper (Henderson, 2001). Beginning from Adam Smith, he re-establishes that if producers and consumers act out of self-interest, the outcome through the operation of 'the invisible hand' serves the public interest better than any social planner could do. The triumph of the market is taken for granted by many, but it is not universally accepted. Social welfare is still widely believed to come from government policy, combined with generosity within the community. Hence, corporations are called upon to be good citizens and to meet the needs of not just shareholders – by maximizing profits – but satisfying all their 'stakeholders'. Henderson argues that by taking their eye off the ball, such corporate behaviour weakens innovation and profitability, and reduces long-term corporate wealth creation. Worse, it fails to understand how profit-based capitalism works. Profits are an incentive for firms (and individuals), and trade between sellers and buyers makes both parties better off.

As mentioned above, CSR is an attempt to capture corporations to do NGOs' bidding and to displace government. Without strong government, where would democracy be, and law and order? Moreover, by sacrificing profits to meet CSR demands (e.g., conservation, workers' rights, pursuit of development in poor countries, support for global rulemaking, etc.) firms act against their customers by raising costs and prices, and reduce shareholders' returns (lower profits). These detrimental effects are passed on to suppliers and employees, and ultimately they reduce government tax revenues. Moreover, profit-making competitors will capture these losses by 'socially responsible' firms. So, the 'politically correct' firms will either have to abandon CSR, or force non-participants to adopt CSR by lobbying the government. The latter is the route that NGOs would advocate. They believe that getting some major corporations to help them to lobby for changes to legislation, CSR would become widely accepted. Yet governments must see that financial transfers to NGOs under present rules amount to transfers of government revenue; MNEs would earn lower profits as NGOs receive non-taxable contributions from MNEs that support CSR.

David Henderson's conclusion is that CSR campaigns form part of 'new millennium collectivism'. This danger needs to be recognized before 'stakeholder' capitalism takes hold. CSR is a radical doctrine, which receives strong support from 'public interest' NGOs hostile to market economies. Encouraged by a perceived decline in the power of national governments and the fashion to support 'global governance', NGOs are seeking to use corporations to further their goal of so-called 'sustainable development'. Never sympathetic to economic analysis (or institutions), NGOs see 'sustainable development' as a socio-political concept that is well-defined and widely accepted. They ignore the economic rejection of this NGO aphorism.

Beckerman (2003) points out that the original definition of 'sustainable development' defined it as meeting the needs of the present without compromising the ability of future generations to meet their needs. But 'needs' is a subjective concept. Moreover, when since 1820 has a generation not enjoyed higher living standards than the previous one? Shortfalls have occurred only when state planning has destroyed open competition and property rights. After the Brundtland Report defined sustainable development, it was interpreted as 'a requirement to preserve the environment intact'. This was soon abandoned. The acute poverty in which many of the world's people live put the 'greens' on the spot. A new 'weak' definition of sustainability was devised based on maintaining the level of human well-being. This is much closer to the economic definition of 'welfare' and allows human capital to substitute for natural resources. To all intents and purposes, therefore, the concept of sustainability has no practical value.

NGOs' alarmist predictions about the state of the environment, the dangers of globalization, social injustices, 'marginalization' of poor countries, etc. have been repeated until most people, including corporate managers, shareholders, and many governments, have weakened and accepted them. Many of the 'predictions' are not well-founded statistically, often exaggerated and motivated by self-interest. Unfortunately, the media profits and prospers from bad news and sensational projections, but only a select few expose errors or the weight of self-interest in CSR. The NGOs live a charmed life with their propaganda and carefully selected statistics accepted without question – presumably on the basis that their activities are well-intentioned. The sentiment of compassion and social welfare that prevails in the Western democracies facilitates these NGOs' messages.

NGOs AND GLOBALIZATION

The four categories of NGOs discussed here comprise the key players in the anti-globalization campaign. However, there are many small single-issue NGOs acting nationally or locally that suffer the same preoccupations. Many enjoy being associated with high-profile activities.

The anti-globalization posture suits NGOs, but they do not show uniform attitudes. In fact, there are evident conflicts between their objectives. Development NGOs have differences with advocates of workers' rights. Labour unions in OECD countries promote strategies that would impede developing countries' exports and discourage flows of MNE investment going to developing countries. Similarly, environmental NGOs subordinate economic growth to 'sustainable' development, which could disadvantage indigenous groups or poor countries wishing to exploit natural resources. CSR NGOs seek to put all the adjustment costs from programmes of conservation, social welfare and public infrastructure on to the corporate sector, usurping the role of national governments in the process.

Nevertheless, many NGOs collaborate to oppose globalization and to undermine markets, while agitating to centralize control over economic, social and political activities, at the national or global level.

THE UNITED NATIONS CONJUNCTURE

NGOs' participation in international meetings began with the blessing of the United Nations. Article 71 of the United Nations' Charter provides for consultations with NGO representatives. This was first recognized by the UN Economic and Social Council (ECOSOC). NGOs with an established headquarters and branches in at least two countries were eligible. The UN agencies quickly saw advantages from this because NGOs can lobby national governments, whereas UN agencies are not supposed to solicit support from member governments. This creates a symbiotic relationship between UN officials and NGOs. Successes at the Earth Summit in Rio (1992) encouraged environmental NGOs to believe they could influence UNEP meetings. However, incidents at some meetings where accredited NGO representatives protested against unpopular governments, led to the withdrawal of privileges and tighter security on NGO delegations (Paul, 1999). Some governments proposed a 'code of conduct' for NGOs in the UN, and steps were taken to close opportunities for NGOs to influence decisions. Nevertheless, NGOs are still useful for UN officials, while NGOs enjoy status from advising UN committees and meetings.

References to 'global civil society' are particularly attractive to 'advocacy' NGOs, because the inference of civic duty masks their political ambitions.

Many NGOs regard themselves as accountable only in terms of their political ambitions. Any collateral damage to the global economy, national economies or governments is incidental. As conduits for public participation and advocates for social progress they can influence the international agenda, as they have shown at the Earth Summit (1992) and other environmental negotiations.

An alleged 'global democracy deficit' is their latest mission. This has become a major theme within the UN system (see ILO, World Commission report below).

Globalization is criticized for delivering unequal distribution of benefits among and within countries. Yet some governments refuse or are unable to adopt the necessary policies to redistribute benefits, because of organizational or regulatory failure in their political systems. Unfortunately, this sense of failure results in shooting the messenger without hearing the message. Many developing countries have benefited extensively from economic reforms. That should send the message to non-performers that they need to change. Market failures or regulatory imbalances that impede globalization usually result from domestic shortcomings. Rather than opposing successful strategies and rules that promote globalization, it would be more appropriate for NGOs to promote social and political changes in non-performing countries.

The prejudices against globalization in UN agencies have been evident in successive reports by 'World Commissions' since the 1970s:

- Independent Commission on International Development Issues, 1980. *North-South: A Programme for Survival* (Brandt Report) (Pan Books, London).
- World Commission on Environment and Development, 1987. *Our Common Future* (Brundtland Report) (Oxford University Press).
- Commission on Global Governance, 1995. *Our Global Neighbourhood* (Oxford University Press).
- World Commission on the Social Dimension of Globalization, 2004. *A Fair Globalization: Creating Opportunities for All* (ILO, Geneva).

Annual reports of UN agencies (UNCTAD, UNDP, UNESCO, etc.) are similarly directed at the faithful, with little reference to economic and political realities. Unfortunately, once statements appear in official reports, UN officials and NGOs adopt them as dogma and policies are advocated to realize them. An elegant turn of phrase can develop a life of its own.

One example of this misleading philosophy was evident in the UN Development Programme Annual Report 1999 (UNDP, 2000). This contained an assessment of globalization 'as a dominant force in the 20th century's last decade'. Yet the emphasis of the report turned to the adverse effects: 'growing marginalization of poor nations and people, growing human insecurity and growing inequality . . .'. Globalization was described as damaging poor countries, causing deprivation, exclusion and shrinking opportunities. The report prescribed international and national remedies, but its major recommendation was concerted action to establish stronger global governance, to provide 'globalization with a human face'. 'The world is rushing headlong into greater integration – driven mostly by economic forces and guided mostly by a philosophy of market profitability . . .' This quotation had the authority of a UN agency. It played into the hands of groups wishing to revolutionize national and global governance.

If globalization was so decisive in the 1990s, why was its effect so uneven? Some developing economies (especially in East and North Asia) grew faster than any of the OECD countries. Other developing economies did not grow at all, mainly because of bad policies, civil wars and other conflicts. The report did not attempt to explain this divergence. It implied that globalization was responsible for the 'marginalization' of many African countries, but not apparently for the strong economic development in Asia.

As economics would predict, liberal economic policies generate economic growth and dispersed prosperity. Globalization resulted from the removal of government interventions of many kinds, and the creation of free markets. Reviewing globalization, the ILO World Commission (2004) argued for fairer rules so that 'globalization [should be] subjected to better governance at all levels'. It continued: 'globalization must shift from a narrow preoccupation with markets to a broader preoccupation with people', although it does not explain how the two differ. It did not examine the globalization process. The 'preoccupation' of that Commission was with inequality. Not why it happened but that it was 'unacceptable'. As already noted, the laggards suffer from fundamental political failures that prevent market forces from taking effect. The benefits of globalization cannot be distributed while these faults exist.

In recent years, UNDP annual reports have become somewhat more open-minded. However, the damage was done by the 1999 report. When the NGOs (or World Commissions) hear the words they want to hear, they do not forget them!

ANTI-GLOBALIZATION: A UNIFYING ROLE

NGOs have cooperated in attacks on international economic organizations and the free-market system they support. This encouraged many international agencies to review their 'administrations'. Some have established informal meetings with groups of NGOs. Others have adopted some NGOs onto their committees. In 1997, an Advisory Group on the environment reported to the OECD Secretary-General that 'all global ecosystems are in decline', and it went on to declare that 'governments are losing much of their traditional influence . . . democratic elections are losing much of their significance' (OECD, 1997). This sensational opinion was not refuted. The OECD established a new consultative group with environmental NGOs, alongside the long-standing advisory committees, BIAC (business) and TUAC (labour unions). This did little to help democracy, but the increased workload did increase the employment expectations of OECD staff.

Such responses could only encourage the new NGO cry for 'participatory democracy', to replace 'representative democracy'. They argue for 'global governance' by depicting national governments as weak and unrepresentative in areas such as development, the environment, human rights, etc. By seizing the moral high ground on such media-sensitive social issues, they are able to undermine governments. It is easy to claim that more should be done by raising targets or reducing time-scales. NGOs seldom consider alternative demands on the same resources (opportunity costs), second round effects of regulations, or the interests of other 'stakeholders', businesses, consumers, overseas competitors, etc. And they seldom say how alternative policies should be designed and implemented. These NGO strategies weaken national governments, while they strengthen NGOs' public profiles.

The WTO dispute settlement process provides openings for NGOs to intimidate governments by using its evolving system of 'case law'. Many environmental NGOs are led by lawyers (e.g., Foundation for International Environmental Law and Development [FIELD]) who seek to exploit these new opportunities. They argue also that WTO dispute panels should refer points of law to the International Court of Justice (Cameron and Campbell, 1998). This is an attempt to use the WTO dispute settlement provision as a 'house of litigation', which environmental lobbyists would support strongly.

The new 'legalism' in WTO proceedings already causes tensions (see Chapter 5). WTO Dispute Panels are composed of trade experts, while the Appellate Body comprises legal experts. This leads to tensions between Panel recommendations and Appellate Body decisions on appeals. Any attempt to use precedent could cause further problems. 'Case law' is accepted in Common Law countries, but countries subject to Roman or Islamic law, or any other system, have difficulties. Using WTO procedures to create 'international law' is supported by NGOs, who could use it to browbeat national governments. Most international disputes now revolve around interpretations of international treaties – so-called 'international law' (Rabkin, 1999a). Some NGOs try to use these 'international' interpretations to influence decisions in national courts. Human rights advocates employ UN statutes. Environmental NGOs have declared an intention to use WTO rulings in the same way. When NGOs pursue their goals by drawing on 'international law', elected governments' sovereignty is threatened because NGO-promoted public demonstrations are often used.

For governments to confront these claims requires courage because they face political risks that NGOs do not face.

The WTO dispute settlement process offers other opportunities for NGOs too. In disputes about quarantine or environmental regulations, panels need to measure risk, assess it and determine how to manage it. Some NGOs can provide expert advice. If the scientific evidence does not suit their case, however, NGOs can emphasize social or cultural risks to achieve the political outcomes they want. This occurred when the EU blocked GM food imports and hormone-treated beef imports. The WTO Secretariat is not equipped to undertake its own risk analyses because of its restricted budget. So the Dispute Panels rely on outside experts, but they still have to choose between alternative opinions (Wilson and Gascoine, 2001).

According to Marceau (1999), interdependence between nations now requires coherence in international law across the whole range of national policy and international treaties. The interference of lawyers in WTO dispute settlement appeals raises the question whether 'public international law' should be applied to disputes over trade and the environment policies.

This problem has been analysed by Rabkin (1999b). Traditionally, international law refers to relations between nation-states. Rabkin argues that this has changed since the European Union has integrated relations between nation states and intruded into national legal systems. The (unelected) European Commission drafts many EU regulations, which get almost automatic approval by EU ministers. These go beyond commitments on EU treaties. They are enforced by the European Court of Justice, which in many areas supersedes national courts. The NGOs are encouraged to lobby the Commission in Brussels or the European Parliament. They bypass national governments because they offer only indirect access to EU law-makers (Rabkin, 1999a). This European legal system has become accepted, allowing 'law' to take effect with little legislative review. This topic is taken up again in the next chapter.

NGOs 'CHAINED'

NGOs have freedom to pursue any goal they choose and, as mentioned above, without any requirements to publish mission statements or to submit financial accounts because they are treated in most countries as untaxed charities (Johns, 2004). Governments could demand the same accountability for NGOs as they require from business and political parties, which is what many NGOs most resemble. Because most NGOs are 'international' this would be facilitated by international cooperation, but governments could act alone. Company laws are being reviewed and amended currently in many OECD countries and

NGOs should be included in these reviews. In 1998, the OECD adopted Principles of Corporate Governance aimed at establishing common standards of behaviour for governments and public policy. A code of conduct for NGOs was proposed in ECOSOC in 1988.

In many European countries, environmental groups are now identified as political movements. After election to parliaments, frequently they have joined coalitions with established political parties. 'Green' parties and their links to environmental NGOs should be open to inspection. Such transparency for NGOs would provide the public with information to make judgements about their motives, alliances and funding (Adair, 1999). Claims of 'global' status by groups, such as Greenpeace, Friends of the Earth, World Vision and Oxfam, should not exempt them from scrutiny. The opinions and strategies of NGOs are seldom scrutinized, even though many of their claims are misleading, ill-informed or false. The idea that 'public interest' NGOs have legitimacy that does not extend to business or government should not prevent scrutiny of their operations. The record of NGOs activities at the UN and other international agencies shows many of them are politically ambitious and support 'global governance' (UN, 1996; Robertson, 2001). Seeking participation in inter-governmental meetings is part of the strategy of the 'advocacy' NGOs. Electorates should know what their intentions are.

Establishing a code of conduct for NGOs is justified to redress the balance for governments and business (Adair, 1999). It should require:

- obligations to be legally constituted (with identified aims and objectives), to disclose audited financial records, fund-raising and expenditures;
- a commitment to act within relevant national laws; and
- an ethical approach to money, resources and information (including suitable refereeing of scientific claims.

The Commonwealth Foundation has produced Guidelines for Good Policy and Practice for NGOs. This research, in conjunction with the UNESCO proposal and the SustainAbility review (2003) (mentioned above), would provide a framework for a code of conduct to be drawn up by inter-governmental agreement in collaboration with major international agencies. It should apply to all NGOs wishing to participate in public policy discussions at the national or multilateral level. Among other things, such a code would be prudent for NGOs receiving or administering public monies. A code of conduct establishing appropriate standards of behaviour, accountability and transparency would bring NGOs up to the standards they require of others.

Governments have been reluctant to act against traditional 'civil society' organizations when questions of taxation or disclosure are raised at the national level (Johns, 2004). Yet many NGOs skulk under the heading of charity to benefit from tax-free donations and grants. Moreover, the functions of charities have changed. Rather than providing aid and assistance to the poor and disadvantaged, many domestic charities now lobby for more welfare payments and assistance, at tax-payers expense. They have become politicized. These changes make the traditional role of charities and civil society groups more questionable. This should make the case for NGO reporting and public scrutiny more acceptable.

REFERENCES

Adair, A. (1999), 'A code of conduct for NGOs: a necessary reform', IEA. Environment Unit working paper, London.

Beckerman, W. (2003), *A Poverty of Reason: Sustainable Development and Economic Growth*, Oakland, CA: The Independent Institute.

Bhagwati, J. (1971), 'The generalized theory of distortions and welfare', in J. Bhagwati et al. (eds), *Trade, Balance of Payments and Growth*, Amsterdam: North Holland.

Byron, N. (2001), 'Risk the environment and MEAs', in D. Robertson and A. Kellow (eds), *Globalization and the Environment*, Cheltenham, UK and Northampton, MA, USA: Edward Elgar, pp. 27–40.

Cameron, J. and K. Campbell (1998), *Dispute Resolution in the World Trade Organization*, London: Cameron and May.

Castles, I. and J.D. Henderson (2003), 'Economics, emissions scenarios and the work of the IPCC', *Energy and Environment*, **14**(4), 415–35.

Charnovitz, S. (1994), 'The World Trade Organization and social issues', *Journal of World Trade*, **28**(5), 17–33.

Charnovitz, S. (2000), 'Opening the WTO to nongovernmental interests', *Fordham International Law Journal*, **24**(1), 173–216.

Clinton, W.J. (1998), remarks by President Clinton, at the commemoration of the Fiftieth Anniversary of the GATT/WTO, White House press release, 18 May.

Esty, D.C. (2001), 'Bridging the trade–environment divide', *Journal of Economic Perspectives*, **15**(3) (summer), 113–30.

Esty, D.C. (2002), 'The World Trade Organization's legitimacy crisis', *World Trade Review*, **1**(1), 7–22.

Grubler, A. et al. (2004), 'Emissions scenarios: a final response', *Energy and Environment*, **154**, 11–24.

Henderson, J.D. (1999), *The MAI Affair; A Story and its Lessons*, London: Royal Institute of International Affairs.

Henderson, J.D. (2001), *Misguided Virtue: False Notions of Corporate Social Responsibility*, Wellington: New Zealand Business Roundtable.

Johns, G. (2004), 'Charities reform in Australia', *Agenda*, **11**(4), 293–306.

Johnson, H.G. (1971), *Aspects of the Theory of Tariffs*, London: Allen and Unwin, Ch. 16.

Kellow, A. (2000), 'Norms, interests and environment NGOs: the limits of cosmopolitanism', *Environmental Politics*, **9**(3).

Klein, N. (2001), *No Logo*, London: Flamingo.

Lamy, P. (2000), 'Post Seattle: what next', speech at the European Institute, Washington, DC, 17 February.

Lomborg, B. (2001), *The Skeptical Environmentalist*, Cambridge: Cambridge University Press.

Maddison, A. (2003), *The World Economy: Historical Statistics*, Paris: OECD.

Marceau, G. (1999), 'A call for coherence in international law', *Journal of World Trade*, **33**(5), 87–152.

Nakicenovic, N. et al. (2004), 'IPCC SRES revisited: a response', *Energy and Environment*, **14**(2&3), 187–215.

OECD (1997), 'Guiding the transition to sustainable development: a critical role for the OECD', report of high-level advisory group on the environment to the secretary-general, 27 November.

OECD (2005), *Trade and Structural Adjustment: Brochure for MCM 2005*, Paris: OECD Secretariat.

Oxfam (2002), *Rigged Rules and Double Standards: Making Trade Fair*, London: Oxfam International.

Paul, J.A. (1999), 'NGO access at the UN', *Global Policy Forum*, accessed at www.globalpolicy.org/ngos/jap.

Putnam, R.D. (1993), *Making Democracy Work: Civic Traditions in Modern Italy*, Princeton, NJ: Princeton University Press.

Rabkin, J. (1999a), 'Morgen die welt: the "Green Imperialism" ', *IPA Review*, **51**(3), 8–9.

Rabkin, J. (1999b), 'International law vs the American Constitution', *The National Interest* (spring), 30–41.

Robertson, D. (2001), 'Civil society and the WTO', in Peter Lloyd and Chris Milner (eds), *The World Economy: Global Trade Policy 2000*, pp. 29–44.

Robertson, D. and A. Kellow (2001), *Globalization and the Environment: Risk Assessment and the WTO*, Cheltenham, UK and Northampton, MA, USA: Edward Elgar.

Sachs, J. (2005), *The End of Poverty*, London: Penguin Books.

Sapir, A. (1995), 'The interaction between labour standards and international trade', *The World Economy*, **18**(6); 791–803.

Scholte, J.A., R. O'Brian and M. Williams (1999), 'The WTO and civil society', *Journal of World Trade*, **33**(1); 107–23.

Singer, F. (2004), 'A 2004 view of the Kyoto Protocol', *Energy and Environment*, **15**(3); 505–11.

Sowell, T. (2004), *Applied Economics*, New York: Basic Books.

UN (1996), *NGO Review*, accessed at www.globalpolicy.org/nvos/ng1snv96.htm.

UNDP (2000), *Annual Report 1999*, New York: UN.

UN Global Compact Office (2002), report on progress and activities.

Weinstein, M.W. and S. Charnovitz (2001), 'The greening of the WTO', *Foreign Affairs*, **80**(6), 147–56.

West, P. (2004), Conspicuous compassion Centre for Independent Studies occasional paper 91, Sydney.

Wilson, D. and D. Gascoine (2001), 'National risk management and the SPS agreement', in D. Robertson and A. Kellow (eds), *Globalization and the Environment*, Cheltenham, UK and Northampton, MA, USA: Edward Elgar, 155–68.

Wolf, M. (2004), *Why Globalization Works*, New Haven, CT: Yale University Press.

Zillman, J.W. (2003), *Bulletin of the Australian Meteorological and Oceanographic Society*, **16**, 85.

9. A system under siege

Earlier chapters in this volume explain that many important decisions and fortuitous developments established the strong global economic conjuncture at the millennium. That is now threatened by opportunistic attacks from disparate NGOs, rehabilitated socialist policies and empire-building by burgeoning international agencies. These ambitious forces seem oblivious to the history of the middle years of the twentieth century, when chaos, disunity and collectivism threatened the world economy. Not only the OECD countries have achieved unexpected economic prosperity after the confused and desperate policy dilemma of the debt-depressed 1980s, but also many emerging economies of Asia and Latin America. Even the two sleeping giants, India and China, have awakened and are becoming major players on world markets. The inflation and debt-driven hiatus of the 1970s and 1980s has been largely forgotten. Where are the celebrations for the globalization and prosperity achieved since the dim, dark days of the 1930s and 1940s?

In the 1970s, economics and economists were criticized for not being able to offer strategies to give stable economic growth, even in the OECD economies. The sparring between Keynesians and 'market' economists was a sporting target for politicians, media commentators and fringe political groups. Much heat and tension was generated at OECD meetings and working parties in the 1980s, between a group of European governments' representatives focussing on social welfare and government-managed economies, and a US-led group of 'marketeers'. The 'good guys' won that policy debate! However, President Chirac and several EU colleagues at the EU Summit in July 2005 reminded us that 'Left–Right' disagreements couldn't be resolved by mere economic experience! The 'anti-Anglo-Saxon' market economics theme has become a fashion for some European politicians and EU bureaucrats.

The globalization of the 1990s was founded on open, competitive markets, many prised open by the new 'enabling' technologies. The late twentieth century's golden age matched the late nineteenth century's Belle Epoque, which had been stimulated by trade and capital liberalization, and by new technologies in transport, power and communications (Bordo et al., 2000). The benefits also spread to peripheral economies in Asia and Latin America, as they had in the nineteenth century (Nurkse, 1962).

The institutions and principles that were the foundations of post-World War II economic recovery, and the continuing prosperity since, have come under attack increasingly in the past decade. Yet membership of international organizations has grown, as has the number of these agencies. Everyone wants to be a member of the club – though many want to change the rules and by-laws.

New members of inter-governmental organizations seem more interested in 'modernizing' them to take account of perceived new problems than in meeting their obligations. In this, they get explicit support from UN officials and independent international commissions that promote 'participatory democracy' rather than the efficiency of the organizations. Their aims are centrist and socialist; they require major redistributions of both power and wealth, with cooperating governments replacing markets in a managed economic system. These politically sympathetic aspirations, expressed by UN officials among others, encourage and promote unofficial social groups (NGOs), believing they can become part of new global governance that will embrace all international agencies. Supranational agencies, such as the European Commission, already encourage NGOs' participation in their deliberations.

Such presumptions are undermining democratic systems, as well as the Bretton Woods system on which much of the present economic well-being and stability was founded. The pressures on the IMF and the World Bank were examined in Chapters 2 and 7. The WTO/GATT record and its present parlous state were reviewed in Chapters 3 to 6. The rise of civil society was considered in Chapter 8.

The well-meaning club of developed governments that established the postwar system in the closing years of World War II designed the management structures to provide effective management of the world economy to restore order and stability. The numbers of representatives on the executive boards of the IMF and the World Bank were restricted to facilitate management, and have increased only as major economies have taken on responsibilities (e.g., Germany, Japan and China). Most directors on these boards represent groups of countries. That way control over lending policies and major financial decisions rests with the members with the largest commitments and market security to back borrowings. Like all prudent financial organizations, the Bretton Woods twins respond cautiously to changing circumstances. Even so, policies have changed and some OECD members are concerned about World Bank and IMF activities (Chapter 7).

The protection of national interests in the GATT was provided by safeguards and escape clauses incorporated into the General Agreement, and by the 'consensus' rule on GATT Council decisions. These provisions have been maintained in the WTO. NGOs and many developing countries (G90) would like to change decision-making to allow them to use their numbers to force decisions on disputes and disagreements delaying the Doha Round. Given the weight of developing countries' representation, the OECD governments are unlikely to accept changes to Council decisions that could be used against their interests.

In the past decade, it has become evident that new forces are evolving that seek to change the balance that has allowed the global economy to develop strongly over the past half century. The institutional structure since 1950 has been similar to that in the second half of the nineteenth century, with a balance of political power that allowed economic progress to be achieved, based on new technologies and liberal trade and investment regimes. This pattern has been disturbed by political changes that could interfere with economic relations, especially terrorism and demands for redistributions of incomes and wealth by anti-globalization groups.

The key change, however, is the rise of new international forces that favour 'global governance' to over-ride policies of national governments. Unelected committees appointed by international agencies meet to examine issues and recommend changes to organizations and rules, especially inter-governmental agencies. In the past, most of these independent commissions have reported to the United Nations (or one of its agencies), which have no powers to take action. Now, however, there are so many UN agencies supporting new treaties that reports commissioned by them are able to exert pressures on reluctant signatories or to manoeuvre changes in rules by simple majorities. Greenpeace and other NGOs attempted this during the negotiations of the Basel Convention (1989) on dangerous chemicals, and revisions to the texts in 1995–96 (Kellow, 1999). In similar fashion, ratification of the Kyoto and Cartagena Protocols were achieved by signatures from non-OECD countries that are not subject to the provisions of these protocols.

In recent times, UN agencies have promoted recommendations from study groups using their own media experts, often supported by NGO propaganda machines. Such exercises are everyday activities for NGO promotion campaigns. For the most part, national governments are reluctant to confront 'civil society' or to contradict its propaganda. Much of the political discussion surrounding globalization, ending poverty in SSA countries, extending debt forgiveness, curtailing CO_2 emissions to reduce climate change, etc. turns on complex economic analysis, which is not displayed in UN debates.

There are good reasons to leave such matters in the economic agencies. First, the economic welfare of most of the world's population has improved markedly over the past 50 years, sometimes erratically, but progressively they are living healthier, longer and more comfortable lives (Maddison, 2001). Continuing these trends by promoting development in the poorest countries is important, though developing countries should accept responsibility, too. Second, international economic organizations should be required to report on trade and aid issues before any UN councils deliberate on them. Finally, where poor countries have bad records on human rights, economic management or corruption, specific commitments should be imposed before new finance is provided, to show they are in earnest about policy reform. The deference given to SSA sovereignty over aid funds allows them to resile from their agreements, without penalty. The grant aid given to SSA countries in the past 20 years has shown little return, while debt levels have risen notwithstanding debt forgiveness. Standards should be set and monitored as finance is provided. The only alternative would be to provide aid directly to poor communities and bypass governments, which would be very difficult, dangerous for recipients in some cases and would require new methods of delivery.

GLOBALIZATION: FREEDOM OR CONTROL?

The clash between economics and politics tends to devolve into the choice between freedom to choose or to concede that right to others. Globalization is about open markets and competition with minimum government interference, but this is anathema to political activists who, whatever they may claim, are about imposing their will on the community. Economics offers choices, opportunities and material advancement to individuals, whereas political activism promises control and stability as perceived by others. The state has the capacity to monopolize both military and political power but it has always had problems controlling merchants and intellectuals. Until philosophers such as Hume, Smith and others attacked mercantilism in the late eighteenth century, nation states controlled commerce for political and military reasons. Since the Age of Enlightenment, however, commerce has advanced living standards, while the role of governments diminished as nineteenth-century internationalism spread. The credentials of economics became established because the role of the market was both accepted and rejected at different times by politics of the Right and the Left (Coleman, 2002).

Unfortunately, nationalism and state rivalry made a comeback early in the twentieth century and economic forces receded before political ambitions. That undermining of economic prosperity by war and nationalism should be a warning to all.

Globalization is unacceptable to many political commentators because most of them are nationalists as well as centrists, preferring the power of the collective community to the individual freedom and the choices provided by economics. Economic nationalism is the only strategy acceptable to political forces because it gives control over the economy, even though its failings are obvious to everyone familiar with comparative advantage and the operation of markets. Many political commentators still attack globalization as amoral because it encourages self-interest, and communication with foreigners.

Politics can be corrupt, nepotistic, sectional and downright crooked, as history reminds us, and many of the present regimes in SSA countries amply demonstrate. A government can pursue policies that satisfy the social and political objectives of the most principled NGOs (human rights, environment protection, etc.), but in doing this they could simultaneously undermine an economy and the well-being of its citizens. The key question is whether environmental regulations are worth it, but opportunity costs are a mystery to the single-minded environmentalist. If the alternative to globalization and freedom of choice is a political vision to restore moral order and communitarianism, surely we need only to look back at the 1930s, or to the record of genocide and corruption in Africa or the former Soviet Union.

The fundamental flaw in the argument that politics is more 'moral', egalitarian and socially conscious than globalization and economic rationales, is that the self-interest is present in both systems. Politicians are no less self-interested than businesspeople or consumers, whatever they may say. History shows that economic freedom and choice work well, whereas political control leads to conflict, violence and catastrophe. Liberalization of economic systems over the past half century has brought rising living standards, good health and longevity far beyond the dreams of its Bretton Woods founders. Without exception, the alternatives to liberal economics have failed, and recently many countries have resiled from socialism to adopt market economics, with excellent results. Of course, there can be 'market failures' that require remedial actions by governments (e.g., information breakdowns in labour and capital markets). But equally there are 'government failures' where pricing policies, over-manning or maintenance delays in providing public services are costly and dangerous.

The case to contain or moderate globalization, as presented repeatedly by UNCTAD and UNDP in their annual reports, makes even less sense than the domestic conflicts between economics and politics. International economic agreements have been used to moderate policies that have influenced international transactions since 1860 (Cobden-Chevalier Treaty on trade between England and France [Haberler, 1936: p. 374]). The Bretton Woods system, WTO, OECD, BIS, G7, etc., were established to coordinate economic policies at the global and regional levels. Power still resides with these economic agencies. UN efforts to extend this coordination to include developing economies led to the establishment of new, less influential agencies, such as UNCTAD, UNIDO, etc. UN efforts to expand its management base and to introduce political considerations into the post-war economic system have been resisted so far.

The Millennium Development Report (2005) has the same flavour as reports from many UN agencies. It acknowledges the many failings of SSA governments over the past 40 years, but then chooses to ignore them. The weaknesses in government and repeated civil unrest are excused, so that the responsibility for economic collapse can be laid at the door of the OECD governments, and the strategies and instruments of the Bretton Woods system. This is consistent with many earlier attempts to influence the Bretton Woods system's market-oriented decisions. The UN's goal is to introduce political influence into globalization, using its 'social compact' approach to economic development, as proposed in many UN agencies' reports in recent years (UNDP, 2000). NGOs work closely with UN officials to exploit joint interests in this stratagem.

UN officials, like any bureaucracy, respond favourably to new opportunities that offer more funds, more staff and more influence. For their part, NGOs pursue issues that extend beyond national borders, for example, water pollution, chemical waste, climate change and forest preservation. Bringing such issues to UN agencies satisfies their ambitions to expand, while raising the public profile of the promotion-conscious NGOs. There are outstanding examples of the UN promoting NGOs' interests. For example, the UN Global Compact (2000) provided NGOs and labour unions with a forum in which to confront multinational enterprises. In the same way, UNEP and the Cartagena Protocol to the UN Convention on Bio-diversity are open to NGOs' participation, an example of participatory democracy. NGOs also participate at meetings of the IPCC, Kyoto Protocol and major conferences, such as the Earth Summit (1992) and Global Environment Summit in Johannesburg in 2003.

This cooperation with NGOs has stimulated some UN agencies to attack the Bretton Woods organizations, by coordinating with NGO anti-globalization activities. This complies with recent directions to the UN:

> to achieve fairer rules, ... to make globalization a positive force for all people, ... to shift from a narrow preoccupation with markets, ... to promote coherent policies in international institutions, ... to strengthen contributions from civil society organizations to increase 'participatory democracy'.

These phrases are taken from the latest World Commission report (ILO, 2004). These political aspirations are common to reports of UN World Commissions (see Chapter 8).

Many annual reports from the UN stable – UNCTAD, UNDP, ILO, etc. – follow the same pattern. They reject or seriously question the effectiveness and justice of economic liberalism, usually identified as globalization. To reduce inequality, they propose an alternative interventionist (collectivist) approach to be masterminded by the UN, supported by 'participatory democracy' to ensure social justice. Inevitably, these approaches depend on large resource transfers to developing countries, usually without any more than simple faith that such transfers will prove to be beneficial. There is no mention of domestic reform measures or institutional development, although trade preferences and financial aid have little value without domestic structural adjustment. The UN's MDG programme has caught a tidal wave of compassion at the beginning of the millennium.

The UN's first attempt to interfere in the Bretton Woods system was made in 1961, when the UN General Assembly declared the 1960s to be 'The UN Development Decade' and adopted a resolution entitled 'International trade as the primary instrument for economic development'. When the UN Conference on Trade and Development (UNCTAD) was opened in Geneva in 1964, the confrontation between the UN General Assembly and the more narrowly controlled Bretton Woods agencies was engaged. The developing countries, supported then by the Communist Bloc, were bidding to reshape the management of trade policy to the design of the UN majority. Fortunately, the GATT contracting parties headed off the scheme by incorporating Part IV into the General Agreement in 1964 (see Chapter 3). This helped to thwart the attempt to establish a managed international economy with discriminatory trade arrangements to promote development. Further efforts to use UNCTAD in the 1970s were handicapped by East–West divisions in UN politics, developing countries' inability to coordinate their negotiating positions, and an inadequate Secretariat. The confrontation in UNCTAD continued throughout the GATT Tokyo Round negotiations, but came to an end with the onset of the debt crisis in 1980 and the global recession.

Similar attempts to interfere with World Bank and IMF management have failed, because the 24 member executive boards in these institutions are not susceptible to UN political pressures. This has not stopped the UN from deciding to set up agencies to duplicate their activities – for example, UNDP and UNIDO, as well as UNCTAD.

The main attacks on the IMF and the World Bank have come from NGOs. However, ILO (2004) refers to allowing 'greater participation of developing countries in reforming the international financial system', and 'the Bretton Woods institutions should establish a fairer system of voting rights giving increased representation to developing countries'. This is regarded as necessary to achieve democratic participation. Yet the World Bank's role is to finance development and to protect the financial commitments of national governments to secure the Bank's borrowings on capital markets.

The UN solution to all problems seems to be voting according to sovereign status; one vote for the US, one vote to Rwanda! And then, hopefully, a vote for the WWF! Is this realistic? All the World Commissions' reports (cited in Chapter 8) reach similar conclusions, spiced up with calls for organizations to be 'accountable to the public at large', which presumably means participatory democracy. But democratically elected governments provide the only legitimate voices for sovereign states. Already too many representatives in the UN assembly have dubious or uncertain legitimacy, and lack democratic mandates. Extending participation to any group of malcontents or usurpers would not strengthen democratic participation.

The international economic organizations and the UN system are administered quite differently. UN General Assembly decisions are based on majorities of sovereign states. The UN Security Council redresses the balance of power by granting vetoes to five countries: the US, China, Russia, France and the UK. Boards administer the Bretton Woods organizations, with members representing countries according to contributions. In other words, those who provide financial resources to implement them make decisions. This is a source of tension in international affairs – much as Treasury/Finance Departments are targets for line departments in national administrations. While national governments find it difficult to confront NGOs, the UN agencies are happy to collaborate with them because they have overlapping agendas. Moreover, NGOs are adept at using media propaganda, which UN agencies welcome – as demonstrated with the UN Millennium Development Report (2005).

THE UNITED NATIONS' INFLUENCE

At present, the United Nations' family is in some disarray. Unilateral action by the US in Iraq, after the Security Council refused to sanction military action; the scandal following from the inquiry into the Iraq oil-for-food programme; the report by the UN High-Level Panel on Threats, Challenges and Changes, and the failure of the UN Summit meeting to endorse the Secretary-General's programme for a more centralized UN, with more power and authority; all these setbacks have reduced confidence in the organization as a guardian of global order. Reform of the UN will be difficult because of the many differences among the membership. NGOs and EU officials, with support from some governments, will be expected to bid for more global governance, once the summit is over.

The UN High-Level Panel, in its December 2004 report, focussed on the role of the Security Council in global security. Without Security Council approval, no state should use force to defend itself unless the threat is imminent. Moreover, even defensive force against a threat requires approval. Likewise, armed forces should not be used to prevent genocide without Council approval (Kosovo, 1998; Rwanda, 1994). Without such tight conditions, the Panel claims, 'the risk to global order of unilateral action is too great'. Yet a moment's thought shows there is no single definition of justice. Justice varies according to culture, religion and perspective on an issue. Does this mean that an enlarged Security Council would never be able to agree to approve the use of force?

In recent years, many resolutions have been put to the Security Council (on Kosovo, Rwanda, Sudan). They have been either blocked or ignored, and many approved resolutions ignored by recalcitrant governments (e.g., Iraq, Sudan, Serbia). Does this impasse expose the irrelevance of the Security Council? If the UN Security Council cannot define international law, how can the Secretary-General invoke it to resolve disputes? Is it likely that the General Assembly could help?

BOX 9.1   DIPLOMATIC VICTORIES COUNT!

The diplomatic games at play in the UN Security Council reveal the extent to which some governments will go to draw the US into their net of 'global governance'. In February 2005, the Security Council received a report of systematic killing in Darfur, Sudan where 70,000 people were estimated to have been killed. This was described as 'crimes against humanity', because if called 'genocide' the Security Council would be required by its Charter to take action. China and Russia allegedly have interests in Darfur that would make them unwilling to permit military action. So, it was proposed that the UN should send lawyers from the International Criminal Court (ICC) to Sudan. However, that could only happen when the US agreed to support the ICC. An offer of US troops to go to Sudan was rejected. This meant that the UN Security Council put a backdown by the US on the ICC ahead of the thousands suffering in Sudan. Evidently, a diplomatic win over the US was more highly valued in UN New York at that time. A diplomatic success over US policy would be perceived as a step closer to achieving 'global governance', while a resolution on the disaster in Sudan would not. The UN Security Council's inability to act on the Darfur massacres repeated the disaster wrought by the 1994 slaughter of 800,000 Tutus in Rwanda.

The UN is largely impotent, with Security Council vetos leading to actions without approval, and inaction resulting in chaos. Major states will act, and always have when push comes to shove. In 1998, when the European governments proved incapable of agreeing to enter Kosovo to stop genocide, the US led NATO forces against Yugoslavia, without Security Council authority. (The UN Charter does not authorize intervention on 'humanitarian' grounds.) The US government believed similar conditions applied in Iraq. Other major (and minor) governments on the Security Council disagreed. Over 100 non-aligned UN members declared against intervention in Iraq. Shortly afterwards, President Chirac declared he wanted 'a multipolar world in which Europe is the counterweight to US political and military power' (Glennon, 2003). Evidently others had similar misgivings (Russia and China).

Writing in December 2002, Samuel Brittan in the *Financial Times*, argued, 'the UN is far from providing a satisfactory system of international law'. The General Assembly has an absurd system of one vote for each of almost 200 countries, ranging from China and India at one extreme, to Andorra and San Marino at the other! The Security Council gives more weight to large countries, but it is hardly an international court of justice. It consists of governments jockeying for position, as indicated above. Brittan continued, 'The use of vetos in the Security Council has less to do with justice than international rivalry'. He continued that UN principles mean more than UN votes. By nature they are 'midway between legal and customary restraints'. But with international balances changing, none of the five veto powers are likely to get unanimous support in the Security Council. That means international action in any crisis has become unlikely. (The UN history in Rwanda and Kosovo showed the direction things were going.) At the time of writing, Brittan was still hoping for 'a coalition of the willing on Iraq', but he was not expecting it (Brittan, 2005).

It is common to hear government ministers (more often opposition politicians), media commentators or NGO propagandists refer to 'international law' to support an argument. The impression is given that this imparts gravitas and closes the argument. But what is international law? Technically, it should refer to a ratified treaty, and preferably one that the country in question has signed. On the other hand, most international treaties do not have penalty clauses that enforce them. Any penalties will take years to decide, and are usually followed by appeals, reviews, etc. By the time all these procedures are completed, the damage will have been done and the contestants will have moved on. (Several WTO disputes have reached verdicts that penalize an offending party, but the instrument of redress is trade sanctions, which cause as much damage to the complaining economy as to the offending party, and still the infringement will be uncorrected. Most treaties do not even have this degree of sanction.)

So anyone invoking 'international law' must be bluffing or hoping public censure will shame the offending party into contrition. It is interesting that Kofi Annan uses that term. At the UN Assembly in September 2004, Annan appealed to world leaders 'to rally behind the rule of international law' (*Financial Times*, 22 September 2004). He did not explain it, beyond saying, 'All must feel that international law belongs to them, and protects their legitimate interests.' That does not tell us much! The appeal at the UN is for 'agreement' to act in an agreed way. As has been shown, even in the Security Council that proves very difficult. There is no process available under most treaties to exact punishment.

While the administration and the functions of the United Nations inspire heated debates, the organization has always been underfunded – at least in terms of its programmes – and seldom raises adequate forces from members to police 'hot-spots'. Nothing is likely to change because major players do not need the UN, though some will use it ruthlessly, while the smaller countries lack the necessary resources to act.

The exception seems to be a core group of countries in the EU, supported by the European Commission, which has aspirations to establish 'global governance' in its own image. Increasingly, the UN bureaucracy is dominated by activist Europeans, raised in the hothouse atmosphere of Brussels, who believe that EU regulations and taxes should be imposed on all countries to facilitate the activities of UN agencies. One model is the Kyoto Protocol, which indulges European interests. (This has been described as 'a predatory trade strategy masquerading as an environmental treaty'!)

The UN Secretariat's response to the December 2004 High-Level Panel's report has identified the usual selection of key issues to place before the General Assembly: Iraq, new security threats, poverty reduction goals, human rights, terrorism and UN management issues, especially expanding the Security Council. The Secretariat has included several proposals to increase its powers, such as a Human Rights Council, a strategic UN military reserve, more powers for the Secretary-General, etc. This list could occupy the General Assembly for several sessions.

While security issues got most attention in the High-Level Panel's report, little progress is likely because of the differences explained above. A more pertinent concern in terms of MDGs and the Millennium Development Report is the question of 'failed states', of which there are many. The West African states (Sierra Leone, Liberia, Côte d'Ivoire, Guinea, etc.) are infected by civil wars, coups and economic crises. National failure usually appears as civil unrest or tribal fighting, which brings it to the attention of the Security Council. Abuse of power also leads to misappropriation of aid funds and development lending, maltreatment of the population, starvation, neglect, etc. This kind of 'state failure' should be a major concern for the United Nations itself, and its agencies. The tragedy of SSA countries needs more than money to resolve it. But the failures begin with bad leadership, non-existent personal security, no property rights, crony-ridden officialdom and inadequate public services. All add to the burdens of urban and rural dwellers. The UN Charter regards the right to sovereignty as 'natural law', but disparities among states make a mockery of that! Procedures for dealing with 'failed' states should allow censure under declarations on international order, human rights and genocide. Aid flows alone cannot overcome regime-induced poverty and disorder. A politically legitimate framework needs to be established to deal with these kinds of breakdowns. The United Nations is the obvious home for such a facility, and the old concept of 'trusteeship' could be revived, under the control of a strengthened UN Security Council, to deal with insurrections in SSA states. Australia has recently intervened in Solomon Islands to stop corruption and civil unrest, and similar action is in hand for Papua New Guinea, if local factions can be persuaded to accept help to restore law and order. The needs of SSA are not dissimilar from those in the South-West Pacific.

GLOBAL GOVERNANCE: THE EU MODEL

The European Union, like the European Economic Community before, is based on discriminatory trade policies allowed under GATT Article XXIV. This provides an exception to the basic principles of the GATT and the WTO (see Chapter 6). However, the EU went much further than harmonized trade policies when in 1992 it established the Single European Market (SEM) with the Maastricht Treaty. The original six members of the EEC have now risen to 25, following the latest expansion of EU membership in 2004.

The EU has used its bargaining power as the world's biggest trading entity (40 per cent of world merchandise exports) to establish bilateral, reciprocal trade arrangements with many countries. It began with discriminatory trade agreements with its EFTA and Mediterranean neighbours, then spread to association agreements with former colonies (consolidated into the Lomé Convention in 1975, which was replaced by the Cotonou Agreement in 2000). Bilateral trade agreements with Eastern European countries, as they returned to democracy in the 1990s, were a preliminary to full membership. In addition, the EU has negotiated new discriminatory trade agreements with Mexico, South Africa and its neighbours, and it is negotiating with the MERCOSUR group. Such discriminatory trade agreements make a mockery of the multilateral trading system. (EU MFN tariffs apply to only half-a-dozen trade partners!) However, RTAs have become the mechanism of choice for liberalization (as explained in Chapter 6), and any serious WTO review of exceptions allowed by GATT Article XXIV is unlikely. The European Commission's political influence reaches far beyond its geographical boundaries.

Market deregulation that began in the 1980s among EU members called for policy coordination and formal treaties to maintain unity, while discriminating against non-members. The Single European Act (1987) contained a far-reaching programme of legislation (279 directives) to remove all physical, technical and fiscal obstructions to the free movement of goods, services, persons and capital within the EU. This moved the EU into deeper integration and required common policies on standards, regulations and competition across the membership. Since harmonization of policies proved difficult, European governments opted for 'mutual recognition', leaving competition among rules and market forces to resolve themselves. Even so, important common policies were agreed.

The Maastricht Treaty (1992) set the seal on political union by formalizing details for economic and monetary union, and incorporating the Charter of Fundamental Social Rights. The Maastricht Treaty updated the Treaty of Rome, including increasing the powers of the European Parliament and the Court of Justice. Further amendments were made in the Treaty of Amsterdam (1997). The drafting of an EU Constitution in 2004 was intended to be the ultimate step towards federation, until national electorates were invited to ratify it.

As EU members accepted political unification, the power of the Commission increased. Directives, regulations and decisions are adopted, which over-ride national legislation. The Council of Ministers or the European Parliament approves them, but this is usually little more than a formality. European Commission staff draft most of these documents, and many are passed by EU Councils 'on the nod'. The European Court of Justice interprets the basic treaties, so the supranational powers of the European Commission are very real. However, there is a contradiction at the heart of the EU. Electorates want national parliaments to be accountable for laws and policies, but the EU legislation transfers that power and sovereignty to the independent, unelected Commission. It is this model that some European bureaucrats would like to transfer to the UN agencies, to establish 'international law'.

The Commission's search for common standards among EU member countries, after the Single European Market was established, generated an interest in extra-territorial application of its rules. When EU standards were established, the Commission applied its influence to get other countries to adopt similar rules. As NGOs increased their influence, a natural alliance grew up to extend EU standards into international agreements on environmental matters and social conditions. Many international NGOs are based in and financed in Europe, and they cooperate with the European Commission in many ways (Rabkin, 2000). They have also exerted influence on EU positions. For example, Greenpeace is alleged to have persuaded the EU to support the Basel Convention, which prohibits trade in hazardous chemicals (Kellow, 1999).

Whether European standards are suitable for other geographical regions is seldom questioned. Nor is the suitability of 'global standards' for matters where national standards might be more appropriate. The drive for political influence often overwhelms EU pursuit of optimum solutions. Environmental problems would be expected to vary according to geographical or climatic conditions. What is appropriate in crowded, temperate Europe may not be suitable in a tropical location. (European countries have banned use of dioxin chemicals, but then, malaria-carrying mosquitos no longer plague them.) Moreover, economic circumstances are relevant. In poor countries with low living standards, sparse populations and weak institutions (organizations and rules), environmental conditions have low priority. They cannot afford them. Yet European Commission negotiators often propose European social standards for global agreements, even though they are unlikely to be enforced. If the standards are restrictive, centrist NGOs welcome them.

The European Commission's association with NGOs was cemented at the 'Earth Summit' in Rio de Janeiro in 1992, when the EU's concept of 'sustainable development' was adopted into the Rio Declaration at the end of the conference, though never properly defined. EU delegations also collaborated with environmental NGOs at negotiations for the Basel Convention, the Kyoto Protocol and the Cartagena (Biosafety) Protocol. The latter two are still controversial. The role of NGOs in mobilizing support for EU positions among member countries and developing countries has been important (see Chapter 8 above). (Rabkin [2000] estimates that 10 per cent of the Commission's budget is distributed to NGOs who lobby for support of EC policies.) This alliance is particularly significant in the UN context.

Developing countries face pressure from the European Commission's negotiators to adopt EU labour and environmental standards. Under its 'Everything But Arms' (EBA) initiative, the Commission offers increased preferences in the EU market to developing countries that adopt these EU standards. However, the rules of origin applied to developing countries' exports under the EBA initiative appear to be more restrictive than under the Cotonou Convention (Brenton, 2003). The Cotonou Convention (2000) offered tariff concessions worth 790 million euros a year to ACP countries to reward countries that signed ILO conventions and adopted the International Tropical Timber Organization's standards. GSP schemes are covered by GATT Part IV, which provides exceptions to WTO/GATT's principle of non-discrimination. These extra preferences double the margin offered on some industrial products and increase preference margins on agricultural exports by up to two-thirds. The European Commission submits proposals for these special preferences to labour unions, traders and NGOs for comment, before making a decision.

Australia and New Zealand provide duty-free access for most imports from low-income developing countries in the Asia-Pacific region without conditions.

EUROPEAN DEMOCRACY

EU governments, supported by the Commission in Brussels, aspire to spread their supranational institutions into 'global governance', via the UN system.

On the other hand, Americans do not see any source of democratic legitimacy beyond the nation state, and probably few major players outside the EU would favour such centralization either (e.g., Japan, Russia, China, India and most other large developing countries). Europeans are committed to regulation and harmonization of policies, whereas, in principle, the US authorities prefer open market (and federal state) competition, with rules adopted only where 'market failures' (or domestic lobbying) make them necessary. This philosophical difference between market competition and social welfare states has been weakening the North Atlantic Alliance since the Cold War ended.

The EU commits member governments to accept uniform interpretations of its regulations, directives and decisions, which over-ride national legislation. (European Commission recommendations and opinions are not binding, but can easily be made so.) In the event of differences about this legislation, it is referred to the European Court of Justice, which interprets European treaties and adjudicates on disputes (Treaty of Amsterdam [1997]). This court supersedes national courts and national parliaments. This system of law-making does not allow national legislatures to review or amend these 'edicts' from the supranational commission. This is especially worrying because it is doubtful whether the EU ministerial councils (meeting on different areas of responsibility) have time to give thoughtful scrutiny to all Commission proposals during their brief meetings in Brussels. Certainly, they receive much less scrutiny than is normally applied to parliamentary bills in national legislatures.

The European Parliament can discuss and comment on draft regulations, directives and decisions. However, national electorates show little interest in the five-yearly elections for Members of the European Parliament (MEPs), recording low voter turnouts. Hence, that assembly has many unrepresentative factions because electorates seem to treat European Parliamentary elections as an opportunity to 'protest' against national governments, without risking a change of government. (There is a disproportionate number of 'greens' compared with national parliaments.) Hence, the European Parliament has a strong socialist bias, which favours centralized rule-making.

The complex processes built into the whole EU system of integrated government, which most Europeans probably do not understand, account for the lack of voter interest in the European Parliament. This complexity disguises the power of the Commission in Brussels, supported by the European courts. This confusion is intensified by the Commission's power to write legislation, which is seldom mentioned, and the unwillingness of national governments to own up to the power they have ceded to Brussels. It is the practice of EU governments to adopt a common position on policy before international meetings, which reduces EU flexibility in negotiations, and hence greatly reduces the value of the meetings. Effectively, the EU offers an ultimatum: accept what we offer, or no agreement. At the same time, EU countries unhappy with the compromise are unable to declare their alternative views. This 'take it or leave it' stance seriously affects the WTO trade negotiations. At UN meetings, where NGOs attend, the Commission's position is likely to be supported by these groups, and by many developing countries beholden to the EU for trade preferences and development aid (ACP countries).

If European electorates were made aware of the power and influence exerted by the Commission and the restrictions imposed on their national governments, they would perhaps give more attention to the European Parliament as a participant in the inter-governmental processes of the EU. Political propaganda from those with vested interests in the EU construct seriously reduces democratic processes in Europe.

The European Court of Human Rights has for many years been the final court of appeal against sentences and verdicts pronounced by national courts. It has a record of many 'politically correct' reprieves that have amended national courts' sentences.

The power of the European Court of Justice would become even more dominant if the European Constitution drafted in 2004 were to be adopted. The President of the ECJ declared (June 2004) that the new constitution would allow that court to make rulings on foreign policy and to enforce the Charter of Fundamental Social Rights (1989) in all EU member countries. This Charter is controversial and has not been adopted by all EU countries (e.g., UK and Ireland), because it entrenches workers' rights, including collective bargaining, rights to strike, social protection, etc.

The 'Social Charter' is also unacceptable to non-European countries. In 1995, Australia sought a Framework Agreement on Trade and Cooperation with the EU. The EU demanded that its EU Charter of Fundamental Social Rights should be included in the agreement. When the Australian government refused, the 'friendship' agreement became an EU–Australia Joint Declaration. Probably this was not an attempt to colonize Australia, but a requirement of EU trade unions to prevent competition from Australia's 'cheap labour'!

The President of the ECJ went on to say that the ECJ distinguishes the EU from all other international organizations: 'It is a system where the rule of law prevails, politics is subject to law. Political authorities are not completely free to act as they please' (*Financial Times*, 18 June 2004). This is controversial, to say the least. It appears to advocate judges making law rather than administering it. Transposed to the UN context, this approach would raise the profile of the International Court of Justice (ICJ) and the controversial International Criminal Court (ICC).

In most democracies, parliamentary processes can delay new legislation, if it is thought to be inappropriate (e.g., a House of Review [Upper House] may seek amendments to government legislation). In such instances, some judges may take the initiative and re-interpret statutes. This 'judicial activism' is common among judges with strong social interests (e.g., human rights), even though the government's commitments may be different (Kirby, 2004). In common law countries, where judges are appointed for life – and are difficult to displace – any criticism may be declared to be 'contempt of court'. However, 'judicial activism' can set a precedent, and changing the law will be difficult and time-consuming. Respect for the law was not intended to protect judges' licence to re-interpret laws. If allowed to pre-empt debate in parliament, a judge's verdict could undermine authority, increase risks and reduce efficiency throughout the economy and the legal system (*Quadrant*, January–February 2004). Yet the President of the ECJ appears to be asserting that right under the draft EU constitution.

Judicial law-making by the ECJ in Luxembourg has already occurred with several controversial decisions on corporate taxation, where decisions on cross-frontier transactions have been disputed (*The Economist*, 28 August 2004). Corporate tax rates promise to be a major issue for the ECJ (even if the EU constitution is not ratified), because major economies have different tax rates and systems. Most EU governments wish to retain their fiscal independence. The EMU fiscal balance target is already a burden for some. EU lawyers and judges may have other ideas.

Undeterred by the opposition to the EU constitution, in September 2005 the European Commission won a verdict in the ECJ that allows the Commission to pursue criminal cases against individuals and firms breaching EU rules. The ECJ verdict concerned a dispute over EU environmental legislation, but the Commission commented that the decision created a precedent that opened the way for actions using other legislation. The case began in 2001 but the ECJ ruled that, although criminal sanctions did not fall within EU powers, criminal sanctions were justified 'when the application of effective, proportionate and dissuasive criminal penalties by the competent national authorities is an essential measure for combating serious environmental offences' (*Financial Times*, 14 September 2005). This verdict has been enthusiastically received by EU greens. Evidently, the ECJ did not need the new constitution to enforce EU legislation.

The danger of majority voting in the EU (as proposed in the EU constitution) was that the introduction of new regulations would be easier and could interfere with freedom of contract. In the same way, allowing judges in the ECJ to decide how articles in the constitution should be interpreted could reduce competitive freedom. Lawyers and economists have quite different attitudes to policies and regulations, especially if it involves competition. Lawyers look at laws and regulations as win–lose, whereas economists look at policy in terms of cost–benefit analysis for the economy as a whole, seeking a win–win outcome. This dichotomy leads to confusions among policy-makers, and if judges have the last word on regulations or agreements, economic consequences could be serious.

The profusion of EU directives, regulations, decisions etc. issuing from Brussels supersedes national equivalents. But where is this explained? (The UK government announced in the House of Lords that in the period 1973–2003, 101,811 directives, etc. had been issued by the European Commission, and adopted! [*IPA Review*, June 2003]). The Commission and its supporters justify their interventions in terms of 'market failures' and 'externalities'. Market failures can cause externalities resulting in pollution, unbecoming consumer choices, unequal income distributions, etc. Of course, the EU establishes regulations to promote 'harmonization'. All are manifestations of the same thought patterns that produced socialism's hopeful yet unhappy experiments (Centre for the New Europe, 2000).

If that is not comprehensive enough, the EU adoption of 'the precautionary principle' (1992) provides an all-purpose justification for regulation on almost any excuse! If there is a presumption of liberty, it is up to the person arguing for restriction to show there is harm, not for the person wishing to act to show no damage will result – on grounds of costs alone! One does not need to be reminded that 'the precautionary principle' began life among environmentalists.

This brief excursion to review the processes within the EU, the role of the ECJ and changes hidden behind the draft constitution show the extent of its supranational powers. After nearly 50 years of policy harmonization, the European Commission is well placed to understand the intricacies of international diplomacy and the role its civil society allies could play. The EU has set the pace of harmonization in the areas of their choosing, and that experience leads many Europeans to expect others to follow. The EU weight in UN agencies is substantial. In addition, the European Commission has cultivated the interests of NGOs centred in Europe. It has cooperated with them in common interests, such as the UN Convention on Bio-diversity (1992) and its Cartagena Protocol (2001), and the Kyoto Protocol (1997). The influence exerted by these combined forces means that only the strongest outside governments could resist 'the conventional wisdom' and the propaganda campaigns.

WHAT IS INTERNATIONAL LAW?

The United Nations Organization is a voluntary association that depends on nation states accepting commitments embodied in the UN Charter. It is naive to believe that majority support for a motion or undertaking, in the UN

General Assembly or any other forum, will ensure compliance. The default position in international law is that if a restriction or requirement cannot be authoritatively established, each member is free to act as it chooses. For example, with respect to the UN Security Council, no state should believe the UN Charter protects its security (Rabkin, 2000).

With new global treaties and UN resolutions multiplying, the question of when to comply becomes important. Conventionally, UN treaties had been regarded as guides to international 'good behaviour', promoted by 'moral suasion'. Now, however, new UN treaties create powerful secretariats that monitor behaviour, and comprise NGO activists as well as UN bureaucrats. These bureaucracies (with some legal support) argue that compliance with these treaties should be enforced (ILO, 2004). They suggest a system of supervision should be incorporated into environmental treaties, which initially would offer advice and assistance, graduating to recommendations, then 'naming and shaming' non-compliers and, ultimately, to enforcement using sanctions. Such supranational powers are contrary to the accepted understanding of sovereignty. For example, if proposed after the initial treaty has been ratified, there would be opposition and a threatened breakdown. If included in the initial draft, the treaty would be less likely to be agreed. And, who knows what could happen with judicial activism? References to 'international law' are used loosely as a threat, although what that means is uncertain.

The earlier UN Commission on Global Governance (1995) praised NGOs for their 'vital assistance to the UN in the conduct of its work, providing independent monitoring, early-warning and information gathering services . . . that serve as unofficial or alternative channels of communication . . .' (see Rabkin, 1999). But whom do NGOs answer to as representatives of 'planet Earth'? These advisers to UN agencies play a role in UN deliberations and are regarded as contributing to global governance. This seems to be an acceptable development for the EU Commission and some of its member governments. But are other countries being consulted about this? The EU has already granted powers to its courts, which reduce the influence of its national electorates. UN governance would be even more remote from voters, making lawmaking the prerogative of bureaucrats. The rejection of the EU constitution by France and the Netherlands in 2005, and the withdrawal of referenda in other EU countries have been interpreted as the first rejection of EU integration. Subsequent inhibitions about EC proposals on the trade in services, foreign investment restrictions and national welfare programmes suggest further reservations may be developing

George Monbiot (self-styled advocate of the 'Global Justice Movement' and proposer of a global parliament with 600 members, each representing 10 million people!) would make everyone abide strictly by UN conventions and treaties (Monbiot, 2003). This approach would centralize government at the

UN in the hands of communitarian bureaucrats. While this may seem reasonable for some EU citizens, other nations, including most developing country governments, would not wish to relinquish their independence.

Legal institutions move slowly and tend to consider problems in static circumstances, rather than commercial terms that allow for changing markets and technologies. New international treaties are proliferating and they are seldom assessed for compatibility. The media and social activists regard any document signed by groups of countries as 'international law', with the implication that this is a 'higher' law than national legislation. Yet, as demonstrated earlier with respect to the UN Security Council, no means of enforcement exists, short of war. Safer to stay with national laws and organizations.

Even so, the European experience has shown that supranational authority can develop from coordination (harmonization) of policies around common goals, as set out in the Treaty of Rome (1956) and progressively elaborated. The European Economic Community evolved without serious conflicts, although the specific conditions set down in GATT Article XXIV were not met with the adoption of the Common Agricultural Policy or increasing protection for labour-intensive manufactures, such as textiles and clothing. Internal competition was increased and maintained through successive expansion in the membership. However, EU environmental regulations have been introduced that increase costs and disadvantage EU producers. This increases pressures for domestic subsidies or to impose charges on imports from countries without the same environmental standards. The EU has advocated imposing trade penalties against non-compliance with international standards, in the same way as protection against imports from 'cheap labour' suppliers. (In 2004, the New Economics Foundation (London) recommended that trade sanctions should be applied against countries that did not accept Kyoto targets for CO_2 emissions. Fortunately, the EU trade commissioner, Pascal Lamy at that time, rejected this suggestion.) The EU and US negotiators have raised the issues of trade and labour standards and trade and environment repeatedly since the Uruguay Round final agreement in 1994. They were among the 'sticking points' at the Cancun meeting. Developing countries are alerted to the danger of this discrimination.

The UN programme presented at the UN Summit meeting in New York in September 2005 contained far-reaching proposals to strengthen the UN structure. This included a hastily drafted response to the criticism of the Iraq 'oil-for-food' scandal, which has jeopardized progress at the Summit; namely, to review the ambitious Millennium Development Goals agreed in 2000 (discussed in Chapter 7). The fundamental differences between the Security Council, the General Assembly and the UN Secretariat cannot be resolved in a few weeks, beginning with unseen drafts. The balance of power in the UN is a delicate matter. Many middle-income developing countries regard the

202 *International economics and confusing politics*

General Assembly as the only place they can express their interests, whereas the Secretary-General wants more control to prevent another Iraq scandal, and the US Administration is unwilling to open its chequebook while having to submit to UN criticism. Trying to resolve all these problems in a few weeks was impossible, and it is not clear that all aspects of the UN Secretariat's proposals were desirable.

The global system is still under siege. Much has still to be done to make the UN capable of tackling the urgent security threats and humanitarian crises, with many autocratic regimes frightened of outside intervention. Before the UN could become effective in this way, the Secretariat and its subsidiary agencies must be overhauled. The outstanding problem is to restore enthusiasm for the Millennium Development Goals agreed in 2000.

REFERENCES

Bordo, M.D., B. Eichengreen and D.A. Irwin (2000), 'Is globalization today really different from globalization a hundred years ago', in M. Richardson (ed.), *Globalisation and International Trade Liberalisation*, Cheltenham, UK and Northampton, MA, USA: Edward Elgar.

Brenton, P. (2003), 'Integrating the least developed countries into the world trading system: current impact of EU preferences under the EBA', *Journal of World Trade*, **37**(3), 623–46.

Brittan, S. (2005), 'The flaw in the UN', in *Against The Flow*, London: Atlantic Books, pp. 40–42.

Centre for the New Europe (2000), *Rights, Risk and Regulation*.

Coleman, W.D. (2002), *Economics and Its Enemies*, Basingstoke: Palgrave-Macmillan.

Commission on Global Governance (1995), *Our Global Neighbourhood*, Oxford: Oxford University Press.

Glennon, M.J. (2003), 'Why the Security Council failed', *Foreign Affairs*, May–June.

Haberler, G. (1936), *The Theory of International Trade*, London: Hodge.

International Labour Organization, World Commission on the Social Dimension of Globalization (2004), *A Fair Globalization Creating Opportunities for all*, Geneva: ILO.

Kellow, A. (1999), *International Toxic Risk Management*, Cambridge: Cambridge University Press.

Kirby, M. (2004), 'Beyond the judicial fairy tales' (and editorial comment), *Quadrant*, **xlviii**(1), Jan–Feb.

Maddison, A. (2001), *The World Economy: A Millennium Perspective*, Paris: OECD.

Monbiot, G. (2003), *The Age of Consent*, London: Harper Perennial.

Nurkse, R. (1962), *Patterns of Trade and Development*, Oxford: Wicksell Lectures Blackwell.

Rabkin, J. (1999), 'International law vs. the American Constitution', *The National Interest*, Spring, 30–41.

Rabkin, J. (2000), *Euro-Globalism: How Environmental Accord Promotes EU Priorities in Global Governance – and Global Hazards*, Brussels: Centre for the New Europe.

United Nations (2000), *Global Compact*.
United Nations (2004), Threats, Challenges and Changes, High-Level Panel.
United Nations (2005), Millennium Development Report.
UN Development Programme (UNDP) (2000), annual report.

10. Economics and international politics

Globalization through economic integration was the focus of attention at the turn of the twenty-first century, much as it had been in the wake of growing international trade and technical innovation 100 years earlier. In both periods, advances in technology provided the impetus for new forms of transport and communications. The development of new products and services promoted international commerce and capital transfers, and opened up new markets and new territories. One hundred years ago, radical political forces and nationalism that led to two World Wars destroyed 'La Belle Epoque'. Economic well-being was sacrificed on the altar of political ambition.

Will it happen again? Many signs suggest such an outcome is possible. The North Atlantic Alliance is divided over 'global governance', which affects the management of the international agencies established after 1945, while rapid economic developments in other parts of the world (especially in Asia) are altering the economic landscape. At the same time, the political balance is threatened by terrorism and religious zealotry, which fall outside the scope of this rubric.

'Globalization' and 'the new economy' are being challenged by different political responses to growing economic interdependence. Some anti-globalization critics disapprove of the distribution of the economic benefits, within societies and between them. These echo national socialist and communist rhetoric from an earlier era, though the protagonists would probably deny such parallels. In many instances, these groups hide behind the cover of civil society, as protectors of the environment or purveyors of social justice. Such groups cooperate at the international level as an anti-globalization coalition, where they become entangled with anarchists and anti-capitalists committed to violence and disruption.

Other political opposition comes from groups seeking to control global economic forces with direct policy measures, or from old-fashioned nationalists who choose to deny the economic lessons of history. Those seeking global governance are dangerous to free trade and capital flows, because their strategy is to establish so-called international law through the activities of proliferating international agreements and organizations. UN agencies and other international agencies are willing collaborators, because such agreements enhance their activities and their influence. In some cases, the instrument may be a protocol to an existing agreement (e.g., the Montreal Protocol on Substances that Deplete the Ozone Layer [1987], which is attached to the 1985 Vienna Convention for the Protection of Substances that Deplete the Ozone Layer). In other cases, a new treaty may be needed to establish a new agency, such as the Treaty of Rome for the International Criminal Court (2002).

The vigorous expansion of the European Union, to encompass increasing membership with more comprehensive policy harmonization, has encouraged many European commentators to promote global governance, which means integration imposed from above. They try now to colonize the rest of the world with this top-down integration. This seems misguided for several reasons. First, the 25 countries that comprise the EU are from common historical, political and constitutional backgrounds, whereas many differences exist among the 190-plus members of the UN. Second, most UN members would not accept an international court that could over-rule national governments and domestic courts in the manner of the European Court of Justice. Third, senior UN officials and several UN agencies advocate participatory democracy, where civil society is included in decision-making. While the European Commission and some EU governments may think they could exploit such participants, this would not suit most governments, democratic or otherwise. Fourth, many developing countries' governments regard UN decisions as 'voluntary', and often excuse themselves from implementing them by invoking 'special and differential' treatment. This could lead only to disarray and confusion.

The list goes on. A cynic might say that EU proposals on 'global governance' are another attempt to persuade the US Administration to listen to European wisdom on global affairs! A more serious challenge to 'global governance', however, must be how to draw Russia and China into its orbit – not to mention other major developing countries, such as India, Brazil and Iran. The EU countries have difficulties coordinating their own policies on foreign affairs (e.g., Kosovo, Iraq), and they have shown little inclination to engage China or Russia on such matters. On the other hand, their stance on 'global governance' does endear them to the many NGOs based in Europe, which expound interventionism to achieve narrowly defined objectives. These groups are generally opposed to international economic integration, often violently so. NGOs' liaisons with international organizations, mostly in the UN family, are doubtless enhanced by EU support.

International meetings and liaisons are carried on at many levels and proliferate in ways that governments seem unable to control. Though all standards and requirements established at such meetings should be analysed or examined by national legislatures, the volume of such proposals is becoming overwhelming. In these terms, global governance is already in place. Officials from the UN and other international agencies meet with NGO activists, international lawyers and sympathetic officials from national governments (and the European Commission) and conspire to promote integration from above, often against market trends. These groups can combine with corporate elites and international bureaucrats whose future prospects are tied to expanding the activities of their organizations. Sometimes NGOs' representatives even participate in the drafting of international agreements. Because NGOs are lobby groups, often with narrow interests and no concern for second-round effects or the general interest, they are effective negotiators. Similarly, other non-governmental participants (including UN officials) are not responsible for the implementation of agreements, or to any democratic processes either. This global governance has been described as 'post-democratic' because it has little to do with liberal democracy (Fonte, 2004). Governments do not easily amend rules and constraints introduced into international agreements by NGOs' activities at conferences, even if they are supported by a democratic outcome (e.g., a referendum or a legislative decision).

Experience shows that international conferences rarely provide effective outcomes because reaching compromise wording is often regarded as a measure of success and takes priority over content. Ineffectual compromises result. Only large and influential countries are able to block agreements, and even they can suffer intense media pressure. For example, the US Administration (among others) has been widely criticized over its rejection of the Kyoto Protocol and the International Criminal Court, although its reasons get little consideration. When many lesser governments are unlikely to stand by their commitments, such political shenanigans are unacceptable. Compliance need not follow from signing an agreement, yet enforcement is virtually impossible. This raises serious questions when such agreements are referred to as 'international law'.

Advocates of more top-down integration using global governance seem not so concerned by non-compliance as by non-participation, perhaps because that appears to represent resistance to internationalism and the transfer of decision-making to international committees. The kind of chaos this process can produce was evident in the EU's 'relaunch' of the Lisbon Agenda (2000) in March 2005. Five member governments insisted that the relaunch communiqué should contain strong commitments to 'Europe's social model and environmental objectives, especially biodiversity, sustainable development and energy efficiency' (*Financial Times* 14 March 2005). Yet the Lisbon Agenda is about industrial reforms, competition and economic growth. The EU's socialist petticoat was showing! Such manipulations indicate that uncoordinated governance can inflict substantial costs on economies committed to economic growth, high employment and development. Newly industrializing, developing countries with strong competitive industries should be warned what policy harmonization could mean in terms of restraints on competition.

POLICY RETROGRADATION

It has become fashionable among neo-Keynesians and other policy interventionists to question globalization and to play down its importance. Integration-
from-below was the intention of the post-1945 system drawn up at Bretton
Woods. The policies of the Bretton Woods organizations, however, are now
being used by 'retrograde' political economists to argue for the adoption of
national economic policies to ensure 'continuous and sustainable expansion of
aggregate demand with flexibility to counteract external shocks . . . [which
requires] . . . governments pursuing active counter-cyclical policies . . . [rather
than] . . . resorting to deflationary policies to counter inflation' (Kitson and
Michie, 2000). Such attempts to restore Keynesian demand management policies, while rejecting independent monetary policy and stable fiscal policy, are
difficult to comprehend when data are available to compare the past decade
with the 1970s and 1980s. When the same source proceeds to call for 'an
effective national industrial and technology policy' (i.e., picking winners), it
is clear this 'tried and failed' strategy is coming from 'planners', who are looking for a return to the comfortable economic policies followed in Western
Europe in the 1960s, when exchange rates were 'managed' and capital movements regulated.

In another volume, Michie (2003) concludes that the 25 years up to the
mid1970s were 'much more successful' than the past 25 years when 'powerful interests have benefited'. This ignores the effects that 'cheap' money and
fiscal deficits in the 1970s generated inflation that led to debt crises in developing countries, as well as widespread fiscal and monetary chaos in the 1980s.
The uncertainty created by inflation has been quickly forgotten. The adjustment in macroeconomic policies that followed the inflation helped to generate
renewed economic integration and growth in the 1990s. The spread of multilateralism and prosperity just as the socialist system collapsed was no coincidence. That system focussed on outcomes (social distributions) in the interests
of the rulers, rather than on inputs, incentives and efficiency to raise productivity. The critics argue that markets can fail, but without acknowledging how
often government coordination has failed to attain promised objectives. The
dangers inherent in 'the new political economy' are demonstrated in Michie's
admission: 'The problems witnessed in today's global economy are not just
technical, economic ones. They are also political. Devising new structures of
world economic governance requires . . . that this be recognised' (Michie,
2003). In other words, he asserts that globalization is a political (distribu-
tional) problem that cannot be left to market forces. As always, the assumption
is that powerful bureaucrats in the socialized system will be more effective
than market competition, something experience does not verify.

The most extreme and ridiculous attacks on globalization proliferate on the

Left. The New Economics Foundation has produced some exasperating read-
ing (e.g., Pettifor, 2003). Its grotesque and unsupported projections of
economic collapse use strange associations, such as likening the post-1945
economic chaos with the 'problems' of present-day globalization! It is obvious
these 'young bloods' did not endure post-World War II shortages, reconstruction or rationing. The solutions proposed include:

- taming financial markets with capital controls and credit restraints;
- 'upsizing' the state sector to empower governments;
- 'downsizing' the single global market to 'localize' production (and to
  forego specialization gains).

All this is to allow national economic planning and 'to maintain our life
support system . . . [and] a sustainable mechanism for allocating fuel emissions'. This moves us into a system of total control; the realm of Gaia! This
nightmare exercise concludes that all we need is political will! With so little
understanding of economics and emphasis on politicking, this witless argument shows that political extremists are still with us.

One of the leading criticisms of globalization and its adherence to the
market system is that the role of government in OECD economies is declining. It is claimed that privatization and competition have weakened the
economic role of governments. Recent OECD data on government expenditure shows otherwise (Table 10.1).

In general, Table 10.1 shows that shares of government expenditure in total
expenditure (GDP) have changed little in the OECD as a whole, or in the euro
area. The most recent peak in the share of government expenditure occurred in
1992–93, in the trough of the most recent general recession. This is what
would be expected, because as activity levels decline, fiscal 'automatic stabi-
lizers' take effect. More significantly, perhaps the five most rapidly growing
economies (average growth above 3 per cent per annum) show declining
shares for government expenditure in GDP. (Even the UK, with growth just
below 3 per cent per annum, shows no rise in government expenditures until
2003). On the other hand, slow growing economies show mostly strong
increases in government outlays.

However this table is viewed, it shows that the 'economic planners', who
claim that emphasis should be given to government participation in the economy to maintain stability, receive no support from this OECD data. In countries with low growth and high unemployment (France, Germany, Spain),
government expenditures increased faster than output, because of the social
welfare preoccupations of these countries. In strongly growing economies,
shares of government expenditure in real GDP declined – sometimes rapidly
(Ireland, Canada, Australia, New Zealand, Netherlands). Several economies

Table 10.1   Government expenditure in GDP

| | Real GDP Average Annual Growth Rate 1992–2004 | | Government Expenditure | | | | | |
	Total	Per capita	1987	1990	1993	1996	2000	2004
United Kingdom	2.9	2.6	43.6	42.2	46.1	43.0	37.5	44.4
United States	3.3	2.2	37.0	37.0	38.0	36.5	34.0	35.6
Canada	3.4	2.4	46.1	48.8	52.2	46.6	41.1	39.4
Japan	1.4	1.4	31.5	31.7	34.2	36.3	38.2	36.7
Australia	3.9	2.7	38.9	36.2	39.8	37.9	35.7	35.7
New Zealand	3.8	2.7	53.6	53.3	46.0	41.0	38.5	38.2
Sweden	2.6	–	62.3	63.5	72.9	65.2	57.3	57.5
Switzerland	1.2	–	–	30.0	34.8	35.3	34.0	36.0
Euro area:	1.8	1.4	48.9	48.7	52.9	51.5	47.1	48.6
France	1.9	1.5	51.9	50.7	55.3	54.9	52.5	54.5
Germany	1.2	1.0	45.8	44.5	49.3	50.3	45.7	47.8
Italy	1.5	1.4	50.8	54.4	57.7	53.2	46.9	48.7
Netherlands	2.3	1.7	58.4	54.8	56.0	49.6	45.3	48.9
Ireland	7.3	6.2	52.0	43.2	45.1	39.6	32.0	33.9
Spain	2.8	2.5	41.0	43.4	49.4	41.8	40.0	41.0
Portugal	2.0	1.8	40.0	42.1	47.8	45.8	45.2	48.0
Total OECD	2.7	2.3	40.4	40.3	43.1	41.9	39.2	40.6

Source: OECD Economic Outlook (Volume 2004/2, December).

that averaged GDP growth above 3 per cent per annum over the period 1992–2003 are running up against capacity constraints, which is another reason why increases in government activity should be unwelcome.

It is interesting that 'interventionists', who believe that governments should manage the economy, seldom consider the supply-side. The evil they see in 'globalization' is really the efficiency achieved from increased competition in labour, capital and commodity markets. Aggregate supply was not part of Keynes's analysis, which was designed to combat severe unemployment and under-utilized industrial capacity. Excess aggregate demand early in the 1970s generated severe inflation and, ultimately, debt crises when monetary policies had to be tightened. The remedy applied in the Anglo-Saxon countries and East Asia during the 1980s was aimed at making the supply-side more elastic, using deregulation, competition and efficiency to facilitate supply growth. 'The retrogrades' fail to mention that demand management fails when supply structures are inelastic. These commentators discuss parts of Europe where unemployment has risen and growth has slowed. The reasons for this appear on the supply-side, caused by generous social welfare programmes (pensions and unemployment benefits) and featherbedding of labour (job guarantees), as occurs in France and Germany. These policies create distortions and make labour and other markets inflexible.

Ultimately, the political economy pessimists are likely to claim their diagnosis is correct, because OECD economic expansion, which has been strong for at least 12 years, eventually must run up against bottlenecks. By that time, any stimulation of aggregate demand would be futile and inflationary, because there will be little unused capacity to redeploy. Most of the sad socialist economists in Europe choose to ignore the strong economic development underway in India, China and other Asian economies that has been stimulated by multilateralism and institution-strengthening domestic policies. On the other hand, the world's least developed and slowest growing economies in former Soviet Asia, the Middle East, Sub-Saharan Africa and badly governed nations in Latin America, have heavy-handed governments, tribal rivalries and inadequate social and economic institutions, and hence poor economic growth.

It is the open and institutionally strong economic systems that benefit from multilateralism and free movement of goods, services and capital. If countries are 'marginalized', as reported by UN agencies (ILO, 2004; UNDP, 1999), the reasons are to be found inside those countries. Often they are ruled by corrupt dictatorships or are subject to civil unrest, both of which are associated with inadequate institutions (domestic organizations and rules for social behaviour) and poor public sector infrastructures.

Economics has demonstrated the benefits of liberalism since the Bretton Woods meetings initiated international market integration in 1944–47. Many political scientists and some governments, however, see globalization as generating inequalities, and preventing 'emancipation, cooperation and solidarity', choosing to discount economic benefits. Economic integration offers human improvement, material benefits, new opportunities and, above all, reasons for optimism. Politics promises control and security for those in power, but a sense of disempowerment, dependency and pessimism for others. If the past 200 years teach us anything, it is that 'power corrupts' (Lord Acton, 1887). Allowing politicians to subjugate economics has left a string of disasters. The power of the collective community and imposed order is inferior to the freedom of the individual to choose when seeking prosperity and opportunity. Yet, many socialists still regard private property rights as 'theft', even after the abject failures of centrally planned economies.

The rise of the anti-globalization coalition (AGC) indicates that the world will have to endure another face-off between freedom and control. As Santayana (1905) remarked: 'Those who cannot remember the past are condemned to repeat it.' When it is only 15 years since the fall of communism, one must wonder about Alzheimer's disease among the young, rather than amnesia. But then there is a sad neglect of history studies! For example, when a Nobel laureate in economics, Joseph Stiglitz, states that globalization has eroded the ability of the state to cushion individuals and society from the impact of rapid economic change, and that 'the root of this problem lies in the global political system', it gives reason for pause. When he argues that 'the IMF and the World Bank must become more transparent and their voting structures must be changed to reflect the current distribution of economic power', it requires comment. These statements appeared in an article by Stiglitz, which reviewed the report of the ILO (2004), *A Fair Globalization: Creating Opportunities for All* (Stiglitz was a member of that commission) (*Financial Times*, 25 February 2004).

There were many highly contentious comments in Stiglitz's article. Even the brief extract above raises serious questions:

- What is meant by 'the global political system'? International relations cover an ever-widening canvas, but this sounds like global governance.
- How should the 'voting structures' of the IMF and the World Bank be changed? And why? Would major subscribers to the IMF and the World Bank relinquish control to major debtors?
- What is meant by 'basic democratic principles'? The UN system? How many UN members can be classified as 'democratic'?

Stiglitz offers no explanations for his demands, nor does the ILO Commission report. To add to the confusion, he refers to 'damage done by globalization as a result of institutional and policy failure, . . . managed to erode the state's ability to provide macroeconomic stability and social protection'. Nowhere does he mention the spectacular economic development in China, India and the South-East Asian economies. Neither does he refer to the record of state control in the Soviet Union and Eastern Europe.

Many of the issues raised by Stiglitz have been examined in earlier chapters, along with attempts to overcome slow economic development in SSA and other 'low income' countries. Major efforts to promote development must be appropriately directed. They should be applied to domestic weaknesses, especially government, justice and law, property rights, openness and essential public infrastructure. For most of the world's poor, international trade and financial matters, as well as UN activities, are remote and incomprehensible. The survival of these people depends on markets and entrepreneurs, and the process must begin at home by establishing social rules and organizations, and an effective government infrastructure to allow markets to evolve. Above all, developing countries must act for themselves to obtain benefits from trade liberalization.

The alternative that state socialism should cushion individuals and society from the effects of economic change has been exposed by history. The record of socialism is discouraging. Those who favour a statist approach must remember that organizations (including governments) are no wiser than the people that operate them – and they are no smarter than the people in the marketplace! Indeed, they are normally less motivated to seek solutions and less capable of uncovering relevant information than decentralized, self-motivated market processes.

PROMOTING FEAR

Most commentators and writers attacking 'globalization' are pessimists about the future of the world economy and foresee serious conflicts arising from uneven economic growth, widening income gaps and environmental disasters. In most cases, however, these Jeremiahs show little understanding of history and the interdependencies among economic, technological, political and legal determinants of social welfare.

Environmental degradation, which features high on NGOs' lists of future disasters, is predicted to cause economic chaos, food shortages and starvation that will create wars and social breakdowns; increasing scarcity of basic mineral resources and oil will exacerbate frictions. (This is a re-run of the Club of Rome's Project, The Predicament of Mankind (Meadows, et al., 1972). Even if such scarcities appear, they will become apparent over long periods of time through rising prices. Markets react creatively, whereas planning governments resort to controls and rationing. Moreover, technology, which is widely acknowledged to be behind 'globalization', would come into play. GM crops may be anathema now to 'green' NGOs, but such unfounded beliefs will be quickly swamped as prices of 'organic' fruits and vegetables rise and their quality drops. Most disaster scenarios will play out in a 30 or 40-year time-frame (if not further into the future). Yet NGO propaganda portrays them as occurring instantly, without allowing markets or technology (or society and government policies) to react. This is evident in the marketing of IPCC reports and the Kyoto Protocol (Chapter 8).

As globalization proceeds, the pessimists assume an increasing gap will develop between rich and poor, which will increase tensions and lead to conflicts and breakdowns. Fortunately, the world is not divided into 'haves' and 'have nots' according to country. China and India are growing much faster than any OECD countries and poverty is declining rapidly (Bhalla, 2002). They are closing the 'GDP per capita' gap, much as Singapore, Taiwan, Korea and other countries have done over the past 40 years. But it is not national income figures that matter. The wealthy and increasingly influential residents of China, India, etc. will have interests that align with the same cohorts in OECD countries to advance their status and living standards. On the other hand, developing countries that might threaten the international order are likely to be led by power-hungry dictators, who show little interest in the welfare of their own people anyway.

NGOs use scare tactics to get public support in the rich countries, always putting the worst interpretation on possible future events or contracting the time-scales. They argue that, eventually, one or more environmental disasters will bring down the economic prosperity that globalization provides (see Diamond, 2005, where tenuous historical evidence is mischievously compiled to foretell disaster, in the mode of the Club of Rome (Meadows, 1972)).

In anti-globalization campaigns, the environment plays a key role, especially climate change, which has been styled into the scourge of a sinful world. Yet, even if warming occurs, some regions of the globe will benefit from more rain and warmer weather; similarly, land area will increase as snow-lines recede, while rising sea levels will flood some low-lying areas. What will be the balance? Environmentalists indulge in 'dismal' science at every turn, seeking to protect everything rather than showing confidence in new technologies, institutional change and good management to optimize living in a world of 10 billion people in 50 years time. As OECD countries are learning about ageing populations, the march of demography is unrelenting. The question is how to manage environmental, social and economic systems while shaking off historical prejudices against nuclear power generation, genetically modified crops and new technologies, which must be released from the shackles of the 'precautionary principle'. Bullying and threats will not achieve protection of the environment in developing countries. It will follow from economic development and competitive pricing, based on property rights and the rule of law. When environmental protection is discussed, it nearly always depends on government intervention, land confiscation or exclusive regulations, all infringing property rights. Political processes and social controls replace individual responses and initiative. On the other hand, 'market environmentalism' has shown other approaches can be effective (see PERC [Property and Environment Research Center] website, Hoover Institute, Montana).

Many of these melancholic commentaries begin by building 'globalization' into a straw man that is vulnerable to firebrands from the Left. Multilateralism has been restored as a feature of the international economy, as it was in the nineteenth century. However, it is not complete. It suits politicians (especially those in opposition), NGOs, labour unions, anti-capitalists and nationalists to portray 'globalization' as an irrepressible force led by multinational enterprises and profiteering capitalists. But the statistical evidence does not support this.

Countries that adopted the 'Anglo-Saxon' model of market competition

have experienced strong economic growth since 1992, but other OECD countries performed much less well than over the previous cycle.

A brochure prepared for the 2005 OECD ministerial council meeting
suggests that structural change in OECD countries (as a group), as measured
by the employment shift from manufacturing to services, has declined in the
past 20 years. Another OECD study, however, shows that the booming 'Anglo-
Saxon' economies recorded sharply increased productivity from strong take-
up of ICT and new technologies, and structural adjustment in the 1990s
(OECD, 2001).

TRADE PROSPECTS

Trade liberalization has contributed to economic growth since the 1950s, when
European trade benefited from relaxation of import quotas under the auspices
of the OEEC, as well as tariff reductions negotiated in the GATT. Opening
protected markets continued in the 1960s, both through GATT negotiations
and regional trade agreements, according to GATT Article XXIV. Since the
beginning, however, agriculture and TCF manufactures have been excluded
from liberalization, and for most of the past 60 years both sectors have
received increasing protection, of one sort or another, often in contradiction of
negotiated agreements.

In spite of promises and undertakings to liberalize, and the substantial tariff
reductions achieved in other sectors, the history of protection of agriculture
and TCF in many OECD economies shows that trade policy remains primarily a political matter. The economics of trade liberalization is repeated every
time a new round of trade negotiations commence, but this is dissembling
because whatever liberalization is agreed (promised) on agriculture or TCF, it
is repudiated. If any confirmation is necessary, the failure of the Uruguay
Round agricultural agreement to reduce tariffs and domestic production
supports since 1995, and the back-pedalling over TCF import quotas since
January 2005 should be sufficient. The confusion surrounding the preliminary
stages of the Doha Round demonstrates the aversion to negotiations on agriculture by many OECD governments.

Trade policy is regarded as an economic matter, but experience shows that
politics is much more important in determining how and when changes will be
made. Writing almost 30 years ago, Jan Tumlir and his GATT colleagues
argued: 'Trade rules exist to protect the world against governments' (Tumlir et
al., 1977). Unfortunately, GATT rules are no longer respected as Tumlir had
hoped. Producer interests outweigh consumer interests, which contradicts
Ricardo's argument that countries are not in competition because there are
mutual benefits from trade. Since the WTO expanded trade agreements

beyond the GATT agenda, political interference has been pushing economics aside. Moreover, lawyers are abrogating decisions by dispute settlement panels of trade experts. This is playing into the hands of NGOs and other UN agencies. Some lawyers go further and argue for the WTO to 'expand rule of law obligations for all governments' (Yeutter and Maruyama, 2003). This would create a goldmine for international lawyers, but it is doubtful if it will improve trade relations or solve economic problems.

National politics has important allies in its efforts to dominate trade policy. The evidence is to be seen in the lists of trade protection measures and the variety of preference schemes still poisoning trade relations. These and other exceptions to GATT/WTO principles speak for themselves.

The WTO has reached a crossroads. Accessible trade liberalization has been mostly achieved as far as market economies are concerned. There is little hope of achieving genuine liberalization in the two problem sectors, agriculture and TCF. Tariffs on most other sectors are low and could be eliminated without much pain. Now the main barriers to liberal trade are 'behind the border' domestic policies; for example, government procurement rules, investment regulations, licensing arrangements in services, labour standards, environment standards and technical standards. OECD countries are getting around these problems with RTAs, because bilateral negotiations are much simpler than multilateral negotiations. Moreover, for major players, such as the US and EU, the results are more congenial. With this alternative, slow and painful progress in a full-scale WTO round is much less attractive.

Since January 2005, new pressures are being exerted on trade policy from OECD governments and NGOs supporting the 'Make poverty history' campaign. UN agencies promoting the Millennium Development Goals are also pressing for additional trade preferences for SSA and other poor countries. The economic case for such preferences is taken for granted, even though most of the target countries are unlikely to be able to exploit them.

This strategy of unassessed concessions is in keeping with demands from NGOs. It derives from the same arguments used by Monbiot (2003) for replacing the WTO with 'a fair trade organization':

- a sense of injustice;
- loss of 'democratic powers' to defend the environment;
- erosion of 'cultural integrity' and regional identity;
- losing jobs to cheap labour overseas.

These objectives form an oddly contradictory agenda. Monbiot believes the solution is to redistribute purchasing power, rather than finding ways to permit people in developing countries to become more productive and independent in order to participate in the global economy. In most cases, the source of the problem is in the poor country, which is not organized to create income. It is the same reason that debt forgiveness and more aid funds will not create prosperity without changes in the recipient country, as experience has shown time and time again. Monbiot is a non-economist who knows all the answers.

Imposing requirements on poor countries from outside can only be a temporary expedient. Creating trade preferences for developing countries can only work if their socio-political systems allow enterprise to take advantage of them. This means establishing property rights, the rule of law and honest government, not charity, trade preferences and exhortation.

In summary, the effects of eight rounds of trade negotiations have amply demonstrated the case for free trade and the exercise of comparative advantage. But many people (especially government officials) do not believe what the evidence tells them. So even in trade, where 'globalization' is incomplete, officials feel threatened as import-competing industries and their workers lobby them for more protection. The mercantilist mentality survives.

CAPITAL MARKETS

Only in capital markets has 'globalization' been widely achieved. Almost all capital flows among OECD economies have been liberalized and many non-OECD governments have followed suit. The principal benefit has been to international investors and to host economies with investor-friendly institutions that receive benefits from the capital inflow, and the associated package of resource inputs from multinational enterprises. These financial, technical and managerial resources have promoted development and absorbed parts of the host economies into international activities. OECD labour unions complain about exploitation, but many developing countries have benefited from this aspect of globalization.

De-restricting capital markets has opened new opportunities in emerging economies and has contributed to their economic growth. It has also raised growth rates in market economies with new opportunities. The stagnating developing economies of SSA and West Asia have been less favoured by MNEs. Most of these countries lack the social and political infrastructure and economic stability to support new ventures. Some critics of MNE activities regard this as a shortcoming of the capital market and refuse to acknowledge the difference between aid flows and private investment, notwithstanding the massive outstanding debt of many of these countries. The solution to poverty in SSA economies, however, requires constructive domestic policies before external assistance of any kind can have any lasting economic benefit.

Stiglitz (2001) and Bhagwati (2004) have blamed the international capital market liberalization for the Asian financial crisis in 1997–98. These two eminent economists argued that when liberalizing short-term capital markets, appropriate prudential regulations should be in place. This ex post rationalization is irrefutable and undoubtedly was the reason for much of the pain and damage caused. After 30 years of export successes, these countries had a sense of invulnerability that led them to accept large inflows of speculative short-term capital inflows without reviewing prudential requirements or ownership profiles in their financial organizations. Stiglitz has blamed the IMF for the financial 'run' that put severe pressure on exchange rates in Thailand, Korea, Malaysia and Indonesia. He argued that the Fund encouraged this financial deregulation. (Rogoff [2003] has vigorously disputed this.) Bhagwati makes the general case against financial deregulation without suitable regulatory procedures. Perhaps financial deregulation was too rapid in the mid-1990s, but some Asian governments participated in some strange financial dealings too.

Prudential requirements were always a banker's responsibility before governments took over supervision of the banking sector. So some of the blame must rest with inadequacies in commercial banking and central bank supervision. The economic consequences of the Asian financial crisis have now receded, thanks to globalization. But much pain was caused. While governments and central banks are held responsible for financial regulation, short-term capital flows are likely to be restricted, though commercial banks have responsibilities too.

The Asian financial crisis created serious disruptions but the recovery was less painful than it might have been, because their export markets remained open. Globalization aided the recovery.

HOW SIGNIFICANT IS GLOBALIZATION?

Globalization has become 'an issue' because NGOs and left-wing political sympathizers have used it as a convenient stalking horse for their narrow environmental, social and political goals. As indicated above, international market integration from below is still at an early stage. Nationalism remains strong and international links for many countries are limited (or non-existent). The leading exceptions are the EU countries, where integration from above by the Commission and the ECJ, is augmented by political and social integration from below by powerful NGOs. In the long run, the spread of regional trade agreements may induce closer economic links on a broader scale. That remains to be seen.

Research undertaken at the Brookings Institution shows that national economies have internal linkages that are much stronger than the flows between nations, as measured by trade in commodities and services, capital movements, migration and information flows of research development (Helliwell, 1998). By comparing merchandise trade flows among Canadian provinces with those between Canadian provinces and individual US states (1988 to 1996), and after adjusting for differences in size and distance, this research showed that inter-provincial trade flows were 12 times those between provinces and states. Bilateral trade between Canada and the United States increased sharply after their Free Trade Agreement (1989) came into effect; before that inter-provincial trade had been much higher. When this analysis was applied to OECD countries (using input–output tables to estimate total domestic sales of merchandise), internal trade densities were estimated to be ten times higher than bilateral trade among OECD countries. Interestingly, internal trade intensities within the EU countries were still six times higher than trade between the member countries. On the other hand, the border effects for a sample of developing countries were very much stronger (up to 100 times) and largely explained by differences in GDP.

For trade in services, which were not formally liberalized until the GATS (1994), the Helliwell study showed that Canadian inter-provincial trade was up to 40 times more intense than trade in services between these provinces and US states. Since services trade depends on proximity and familiar institutions much more than merchandise trade, this is no surprise.

There are several explanations why internal trade is so much larger than international trade, even between the US and Canada where many states and provinces are adjacent. Accepted rules are important because they embody national differences in behaviour, law, etc., but also because unforeseen contingencies associated with transactions and investments may be handled with facility that is not available across different jurisdictions. Such informal arrangements between firms encourage denser integrations within than among nations, because it reduces risks.

The conclusion of this Brookings study is that further economic integration will bring benefits as institutional differences are removed. At present, however, the effects of national borders remain significant and talk of globalization has far to go before it will be possible to refer to 'a single global market'. Helliwell concludes that the degree of openness existing among OECD economies is sufficient to permit the most advantageous trade to occur, and to allow free access to the best of foreign experiences and ideas. At the same time, he cautions that there is much more scope for national policies than is popularly thought, especially for institution building to support balanced and sustainable growth.

The neglected conclusion from the Brookings' study, that developing countries offer opportunities for the largest economic gains from policy liberalization and integration, is evident not only from Helliwell's measurements, but also from the records of the Asian 'Tigers'. These economies have been open to international trade since the 1960s; somewhat later for capital flows. This gave economic feedback to policy-makers and advanced institutional change in the direction of economic freedom. Future trade gains for developing countries could come from changed attitudes in OECD governments, which could remove protection from agriculture and textiles and clothing, both areas in which developing countries are competitive. Progress in these areas will continue to be slow because of domestic politics. Tightening conditions for access to contingency protection (so-called trade remedies) and reducing trade discrimination according to RTAs and rules of origin would help developing countries to increase their exports, but this would require a reversal of present trends in trade policies.

Some OECD governments are not signalling good intentions on any of these options. The EU and the US authorities demanded that China take steps to restrict clothing exports, even before OECD commitments to eliminate import quotas on 1 January 2005. High tariffs on TCF that remain in place in both these markets were not thought to give adequate protection. China responded by agreeing to new import quotas under the safeguards clause in the China/WTO accession agreement. While OECD countries preach the merits of liberal trade strategies, they show no guilt at turning their backs on this key Uruguay Round agreement to liberalize in favour of developing countries. (Technically, China was not a signatory of the Uruguay Round Final Act, but the EU and US retractions do not show good faith.) The US and EU producers now have three more years of import quotas, under safeguard rules, unless consumer and retailer interests can win a battle with domestic high cost manufacturers. Now anti-dumping action against China's exports of shoes is contemplated.

The competitiveness of Chinese producers also presents problems to smaller developing countries' exporters, which previously had guaranteed quotas in major OECD markets. One consequence of the EU and US resort to safeguard measures against China's competitive TCF exports will be that Chinese producers will move some of their production to developing countries not subject to import quotas, and the whole 'MFA' structure will begin to rebuild. Watching the European Commission trying to reconcile the protection demanded by EU textile, clothing and shoe manufacturers with the interests of fashion houses, retailers and consumers should convince observers that protectionism is not only futile, it is expensive for everyone.

Another concern about EU and US trade policies is their interest to link trade to social issues, such as the environment and labour standards. Justifiably, developing countries regard these proposals either as disguised protection or an intrusion into their economic sovereignty. These 'link' issues were removed from the Doha agenda in the closing stages of the Cancun ministerial meeting, but they are still in the background. The EU Commission has proposed that new economic partnership agreements should be negotiated with regional groups of ACP countries, at present covered by the Cotonou Agreement. The Commission wants rules included to cover investment, competition and government procurement to promote economic development, which would revive these 'Singapore issues'. This 'back-door' approach could represent another sign of EU duplicity. On the other hand, the Commission is proposing to revise 'rules of origin' used in its generalized system of preferences to increase access for ACP countries' exporters.

The EU conditionality being written into new trade arrangements for ACP developing countries is different from the liberalization granted in the 1950s and 1960s. In the earlier period, the non-discrimination principle meant all tariff reductions by OECD countries were provided to developing countries without demanding reciprocity. Now the EU is providing preferences for ACP countries on certain conditions: namely, labour and environmental standards, tough rules of origin (local content), etc. Because the EU is not promoting freedom of labour or allocations of property rights, the economic development of these poor countries is not being promoted. Rather, their export sectors are becoming adjuncts to the EU industrial complex.

The uncertainties that surround OECD countries' trade policies, where actions are more relevant than official advice and promises, suggest that developing countries should seek their own opportunities to benefit from comparative advantage. One untapped option for developing countries is expansion of 'South–South' trade, either by establishing intra-developing country preferences or by creating RTAs. Recent examples are SADC (South African Development Community), MERCOSUR and ASEAN. This would be more effective than most proposals coming from development NGOs. Development grants and debt forgiveness have been tried before. However, without basic commitment to develop and enforce free institutions, such as private property rights, the rule of law and social infrastructures, these financial gestures will come to nothing. Past experience in Africa and Latin America shows that aid and debt forgiveness alone being little reward. The first step must be to establish effective free domestic institutions.

DEVELOPMENT BEGINS AT HOME

Aid flows and trade preferences do not stimulate economic development unless accompanied by improvements in social infrastructures and new opportunities for people in developing countries. Unless private business activity is set free, whatever new trade opportunities are opened from abroad will bring little benefit. Above all, more efficiency gains from trade come from unilateral trade liberalization than from new preferences offered by OECD governments. Other countries' trade barriers are usually less of a problem than a developing country's own import barriers. Such liberalizing strategies must be adopted within the adjustment capacity of the economy, but without such liberal strategies development will not occur.

Public and private infrastructures should be priority targets for new aid flows to provide necessary support for industries to develop. Expenditure on health, education and social services will depend on establishing proper infrastructures to be effective. NGOs' focus on improving health and overcoming poverty are admirable goals, but making any progress will depend on a framework for delivery, which requires trained medical staff, distribution systems, medical centres, training schools, etc. All these take time to provide, and the cooperation and support of national governments and local authorities. These are rare in most SSA countries, yet it is neglected in most of the ambitious programmes advanced to assist development.

Too often, charitable agencies and NGOs have narrow interests and they carry their own prejudices. They provide finance on specific conditions that may limit its real value (e.g., health funding with bans on contraceptives, or agricultural services that deny use of fertilizers believed to damage the African environment). Aid funds should be directed to development and the needs of the recipient country, without prejudice, if the financial aid is to be productive. The first requirement is to provide freedom for the people to pursue opportunities.

Much of the policy debate around NGOs that are leading the present attack on poverty focusses on what the OECD economies or international agencies should do to help SSA countries to develop. This is an easy target for NGOs because they can blame OECD governments for being ungenerous, uncaring and niggardly, which gets NGOs wide media coverage. Yet, trade preferences or opening new trade opportunities is of little value to developing countries' producers unable to get to markets because merchants, transport and marketable quantities are not available. Similarly, advancing aid moneys will be counter-productive if projects have not been planned or prepared properly, and many governments insist on controlling use of aid funds. Indeed, it could encourage corruption to have money waiting in the bank.

Experts on the spot, such as Shikwati, Sowell and Bhalla (see comments in Chapter 7) argue that most aid is not only wasted but it does real harm by distracting indigenous human capital from productive enterprises. The highest return is to be found in bureaucratic corruption. Emergency aid (such as the tsunami assistance early in 2005) is necessary to overcome crises, but continuous food aid discourages local farmers and merchants, encourages corruption and one way or another finances violence and civil unrest. The sympathy and self-satisfaction generated by charities and churches in OECD countries is not evaluated in terms of the interests of the receiving country.

WHITHER GLOBALIZATION?

Economic integration has been underway since humankind began. These contacts led to transfers of information and exchanges of goods and services. This process accelerated as means of transport and communication improved, transport costs fell and trade became more profitable. The term 'globalization' has come into use since the economic upswing early in the 1990s turned into something more enduring. This was enhanced by new optimism after the collapse of the communist empire, the liberalization of capital markets, the establishing of the EU 'single market', the ICT revolution and the re-entry of China into world commerce. This triumph was the outcome of 50 years of increasing economic integration under the rules of the Bretton Woods system implemented at the conclusion of World War II, and in spite of the Cold War that divided the globe for 40 years.

Globalization comprises increasing economic integration and development of product and factor markets across political frontiers, provided by reducing impediments at frontiers, aided by the spread of liberal market strategies and new technologies. The consequence is 'a phenomenon by which economic agents in any given part of the world are much more affected by events elsewhere in the world' (Krueger, 2000). Liberalization of trade and capital markets, and the activities of multinational enterprises have integrated markets, not only for consumer goods and services but also for components, raw materials, labour of all kinds, technical information, production methods, etc. In addition, advances in transport and communications have reduced distances and made national frontiers less relevant. Travel has expanded the lives and the minds of ordinary people by giving them opportunities to enjoy new cultures, observe successes elsewhere and expand their horizons.

Paradoxically, globalization has come into common usage because it serves the interests of its opponents. It provides a convenient catchword around which to build crusades against social forces that are perceived to be threatening damage to the environment, workers' rights, social welfare programmes, human rights, the poor in developing countries, national cultures, animal rights, etc. The advantage from forming an 'anti-globalization coalition' (AGC) is that its constituent NGOs, with their many different and often conflicting interests, combine against a fabricated common enemy. They are united by their common disenchantment with economic liberalism. Yet, their organization and effectiveness depends on one of the major innovations behind globalization, namely, the internet: 'The AGC is the world's most successful internet-enabled service industry' (Martin Wolf, 2004).

The AGC collaboration is based on specific causes, not doctrines. Labour unions focus on workers' rights, which means protecting jobs in high-wage economies against competition from lower cost labour in developing countries. Development NGOs argue for trade liberalization or trade preferences from OECD governments to enable increased imports from – and therefore job creation in – developing countries. 'Green' NGOs want to slow economic growth, to reduce pollution, to protect species or to ameliorate climate change; international trade is seen as evil because it generates economic growth and requires transport, which both increase emissions. Cultural protectionists oppose development because it threatens previously sheltered national arts, crafts and entertainment, yet these same people are eager to travel to other countries to exhibit their cultural products.

As noted above, formal international liberalization (integration from above) has ground to a halt in the past decade, though informal links through travel and internet communications have emphasized other global links (integration from below). Little progress has been made towards further liberalizing trade in goods and services, and complaints are increasing about injustices in trade and investment flows. There is a strong case for further globalization, to facilitate economic development and to spread economic benefits to those living in poverty everywhere, to increase living standards and to shore up democracy. Globalization is driven by technical change and market liberalization. The former continues to advance but governments have become reluctant to review economic policies that might antagonize NGOs. Yet, if economic liberalization slows, market globalization will falter, and with it economic growth.

If national governments relinquish their powers to threats from nefarious NGOs and supporters of global governance, economic and social progress will be frustrated. Political opportunists could overwhelm the prospering world economy, as happened in the early twentieth century. Free-market internationalists have to mobilize to sustain economic progress by persuading national governments to meet their democratic responsibilities and to confront the NGO pretenders, domestically and internationally.

The economic case for more liberalization has a long pedigree, but recent success seems to have weakened the commitment. This has allowed political forces to promote interventionism for 'social/political ends', without respecting 'economic means'.

Everybody wants to see poverty in developing countries removed, disease and pollution overcome, the global environment guarded, etc. Just declaring these 'ends', however, will not see them achieved. The 'means' inevitably have economic content, which political activists ignore at their peril.

REFERENCES

Bhagwati, J.D. (2004), *In Defence of Globalization*, Oxford: Oxford University Press, Ch. 13.

Bhalla, S.S. (2002), *Imagine There's No Country: Poverty, Inequality and Growth in the Era of Globalization*, Washington, DC: IIE.

Diamond, J. (2005), *Collapse: How Societies Choose to Fail or Succeed*, London: Allen Lane.

Fonte, J. (2004), 'Democracy's Trojan Horse', *IPA Review*, **56**(4).

Helliwell, J.F. (1998), *How Much Do National Borders Matter?*, Washington, DC: Brookings Institution Press.

International Labour Organization (ILO) (2004), *A Fair Globalization: Creating Opportunities for All*, Geneva: World Commission on the Social Dimension of Globalization.

Kitson, M. and J. Michie (eds) (2000), *The Political Economy of Competitiveness*, New York: Routledge.

Krueger, A.O. (2000), 'Trading phobias: governments, NGOs and the multilateral system', John Bonython Lecture, presented to the CIS, Melbourne.

Meadows, D.H. and D.L. et al. (1972), *The Limits to Growth*, London: Earth Island.

Michie, J. (ed.) (2003), *The Handbook of Globalisation*, Cheltenham, UK and Northampton, MA, USA: Edward Elgar.

Monbiot, G. (2003), *The Age of Consent*, London: Harper Perennial.

OECD (2001), *The New Economy: Beyond the Hype*, Paris: OECD Secretariat.

Pettifor, A. (ed.) (2003), *Real World Economic Outlook*, New Economics Foundation, Basingstoke: Pelgrave-Macmillan.

Rogoff, K. (2003), 'The Fund bites back', *The Economist*, 6 July, Economic Focus.

Santayana, G. (1905), *The Life of Reason*, London: Constable.

Stiglitz, J.E. (2001), 'Capital market liberalization, economic growth and instability', *World Development*, June.

Tumlir, J. et al. (1977), *Trade Liberalization, Protectionism and Interdependence*, Geneva: GATT Studies in International Trade.

UNDP (1999), annual report.

Wolf, M. (2004), *Why Globalization Works*, New Haven, CT: Yale University Press.

Yeutter, C. and W. Maruyama (2003), 'Place the rule of law at the heart of trade', *Financial Times*, 17 February.

Index